QUEER INCLUSION IN TEACHER EDUCATION

"Innovative and thought provoking, this book's three-fold approach is particularly novel and useful. It engages with the material and with readers at multiple levels, which makes it all the more useful to a variety of audiences with diverse needs."
—**Luca Maurer, Program Director, Center for LGBT Education, Outreach & Services, Ithaca College, USA**

Queer Inclusion in Teacher Education explores the challenges and promises of building queer-inclusive pedagogy and curriculum into teacher education. Weaving together theory, research findings, and practical "how-to" strategies and materials, it fills an important gap by offering a clear road map and resources for influencing the knowledge, beliefs, and actions of faculty working with pre-service teachers. While the book has implications for policy change, most immediately readers will feel empowered with ideas for faculty development they can implement in their own teacher education programs. Looking at both the politics and practices of teacher education and the ways in which queer issues manifest in schools, it is hopeful in suggesting that if teachers and pre-service teachers can critically reflect on homophobia and heteronormativity, they can begin to think about and relate to queer youth in a different, more positive and inclusive way. A Companion Website (http://queerinclusion.com) with additional activities and materials for teacher educators and faculty development and a practical guide enhances the usefulness of the book.

Olivia J. Murray is Assistant Professor in the Curriculum and Instruction Department at Portland State University, USA.

QUEER INCLUSION IN TEACHER EDUCATION

Bridging Theory, Research, and Practice

Olivia J. Murray

NEW YORK AND LONDON

First published 2015 by Routledge
711 Third Avenue, New York, NY 10017

and by Routledge
2 Park Square, Milton Park, Abingdon, Oxon OX14 4RN

Routledge is an imprint of the Taylor & Francis Group, an informa business

© 2015 Taylor & Francis

The right of Olivia Murray to be identified as author of this work has been asserted by her in accordance with sections 77 and 78 of the Copyright, Designs and Patents Act 1988.

All rights reserved. No part of this book may be reprinted or reproduced or utilized in any form or by any electronic, mechanical, or other means, now known or hereafter invented, including photocopying and recording, or in any information storage or retrieval system, without permission in writing from the publishers.

Trademark notice: Product or corporate names may be trademarks or registered trademarks, and are used only for identification and explanation without intent to infringe.

Library of Congress Cataloging-in-Publication Data

Murray, Olivia Jo.
Queer inclusion in teacher education : bridging theory, research, and practice / Olivia J. Murray.
    pages cm
  Includes bibliographical references and index.
  1. Teachers—Training of—United States. 2. Homosexuality and education—United States. 3. Inclusive education—United States. I. Title.
  LB1715.M776   2014
  370.71'1—dc23
  2013050191

ISBN: 978-0-415-71185-2 (hbk)
ISBN: 978-0-415-71186-9 (pbk)
ISBN: 978-1-305-88430-1 (ebk)

Typeset in Bembo
by Apex CoVantage, LLC

Printed and bound in the United States of America by Publishers Graphics, LLC on sustainably sourced paper.

This book is dedicated to my wife, Bethany, whose unconditional love and support brings me sustained strength and happiness.

CONTENTS

Preface	ix
How to Use This Book	ix
Key Concepts of the Chapters	x
Terms and Definitions	xii

PART I
The Challenges and Promise of Queering Teacher Education — 1

1	Framing the Issue	3
2	Reading the Field	21
3	Theory and Queer Inclusion in Education Framework	43

PART II
Field Research and Visibility — 55

4	Teaching With Integrity	57
5	Teacher Candidates Engage With Queer Phenomena	67
6	Teacher Educators Queer Their Practice	109

PART III
A Toolkit for Queering Practice — 153

7 Activities and Materials for Faculty Development — 155

8 Activities and Materials for Teacher Educators — 174

9 A Call to Action — 206

Appendices — *213*
   Appendix A: Gender and Sexual Orientation Diversity Continuum — 213
   Appendix B: Queer Inclusion in Education Framework — 215
   Appendix C: LGBTQ Advocacy in K–12 Classrooms Outline and Schedule — 217
   Appendix D: Values Statement Questionnaire — 221
   Appendix E: Curriculum Analysis: A Tool for Interrogating Messages About Sexual Orientation and Gender — 223

Index — *227*

PREFACE

More than four million lesbian, gay, bisexual, transgender, and queer (LGBTQ) K–12 students currently receive an education in the United States. Far greater numbers of children and adolescents question their sexual orientation and present their gender in creative, fluid, and nonnormative ways. In light of these realities, it is tragic that most K–12 teachers are not adequately prepared to combat heterosexist and cissexist (the belief that cis, or non-transgender, is superior to all other gender identities) practices in education. This book argues that teacher education is the place to address this tension. It explores the promise of increased awareness about and use of queer-inclusive pedagogy and curriculum in teacher education by:

- Providing a rationale and original framework for queer inclusion in teacher education discourse and practice;
- Reporting findings from my current extensive qualitative research: how teacher candidates engage with queer phenomena in the field and how teacher educators queer their practice;
- Offering a how-to guide with curriculum entry points and resources for faculty development and for teacher educators to use in the classroom.

How to Use This Book

Although many avenues exist within education for increasing awareness of queer issues, this book focuses on teacher education. It is for all academics and practitioners who believe teachers, present and future, can change their school culture and provide a positive educational experience for queer students and their allies. It will appeal to readers holding leadership positions in colleges of education and K–12 school districts who seek to understand the knowledge, skills, and dispositions of teachers as they are being shaped by professional preparation programs. *Queer Inclusion in Teacher Education* can be used as a textbook/reader for a myriad of courses in teacher education to facilitate vital dialogue and provide tangible resources for social justice action. In addition, this book provides a conceptual framework and a series of activities for department leaders to guide their faculty toward gaining a queer perspective and becoming more inclusive.

Regardless of current knowledge and experience with queer issues in teacher education, individuals can read this book cover to cover to gain deeper understanding and acquire resources to queer their practice. If the reader is already familiar with current trends in education as they relate to gender and sexual orientation, they can benefit from beginning at Chapter 3. If the reader is solely interested in obtaining a collection of lessons and activities for immediate use, they may wish to move directly to Chapter 7.

Key Concepts of the Chapters

Part I, The Challenges and Promise of Queering Teacher Education, offers a new molding of literature that combines queer identity and K–12 school climate with current trends in teacher education. It includes a theoretical framework that can guide teachers toward queer-inclusive practices.

- **Chapter 1, Framing the Issue**, explains key terms such as *queer, cisgender, transgender, heteronormativity, cissexism, teacher education*, and *field experience*. It briefly describes the complex processes of sexual and gender identity development among queer youth in order to support the reader's understanding of the coming-out process. It also identifies the ways and extent to which schools serve as hetero- and cisnormative institutions. I discuss implications for queer youth and staff as well as straight allies, and I synthesize published research and expose some of the prevailing conditions in K–12 schools as they relate to risk factors for queer youth, the impact of teacher influence, and curriculum and pedagogy.
- **Chapter 2, Reading the Field**, situates trends in the K–12 school climate alongside aspects of teacher education, namely curriculum and instruction, the development of teacher dispositions, and reflective practice, while traversing queer content and pedagogy. Addressing the near silence surrounding queer inclusion in teacher education leads to an overview of why addressing queer issues in teacher education is vitally important and long overdue.
- **Chapter 3, Theory and Queer Inclusion in Education Framework**, explores critical social theory and queer theory as means for discussing democratic forms of schooling, social justice, and ethical educational practices. The section concludes with a Queer Inclusion in Education Framework,

a conceptual tool that not only serves as a road map for this book, driving chapter sequence and content, but also offers direction for interrupting hetero- and cissexist practices in schools across the nation.

Part II, Field Research and Visibility, presents my personal story of self-negotiation as a queer in the classroom as well as two recent research studies that explore the intersections of queer, identity, and visibility in education.

- **Chapter 4, Teaching With Integrity**, makes a personal case for providing significant space for the person in the profession in the process of teaching and learning to teach. I explore my vocation and describe a disturbing encounter as a K–12 teacher that led to my transformation into a queer researcher, activist, and educator.
- **Chapter 5, Teacher Candidates Engage With Queer Phenomena**, centers around five assertions generated from research findings from a seven-month study examining how pre-service teacher candidates encounter, make sense of, and respond to sexual and gender diversity in the classroom. Factual stories from participant experiences are provided as evidence to support these assertions and to candidly reveal how teacher candidates experience queer phenomena in K–8 public schooling.
- **Chapter 6, Teacher Educators Queer Their Practice**, tells the story of a large urban teacher education faculty that developed an LGBTQ task force to lead an organized effort to implement program policy change and transformational practices. This chapter equips readers with the knowledge and dispositions to lead colleagues in teacher preparation programs to better prepare teacher candidates to address LGBTQ issues in K–12 school communities.

Part III, A Toolkit for Queering Practice, is accompanied by a comprehensive **Companion Website** that provides a consolidation of ready-to-use materials that challenge readers to think critically about if, when, and how to infuse queer content and pedagogy into their teaching.

- **Chapter 7, Activities and Materials for Faculty Development**, provides department leaders and/or queer task force members with tangible activities for engaging teacher educators in initial conversations centered on gender and sexual orientation. It offers tools to assess school climate, analyze current policies, evaluate teacher candidate supports, and develop ongoing faculty development. Accompanied by a comprehensive Companion Website, the hope is that departments or schools of education will adapt the content and methods presented in this chapter to fit the unique needs of their institution.

- **Chapter 8, Activities and Materials for Teacher Educators**, explores multileveled curricular entry points for teacher educators to merge queer content and pedagogy. In addition to options for *where* to address queerness in teacher education, it gives instructors ideas for *what* this curriculum can entail. Lesson plans, exercise descriptions, and resources are included (and provided on the Companion Website) to support rich class discussions, critical assignments, and other vital learning opportunities around interrupting hetero- and cisnormativity.
- **Chapter 9, A Call to Action**, offers reflections and suggestions to further the argument that teacher education resides at the forefront of queer liberation. It provides one final narrative to illuminate the experience of queer youth and deconstruct the -isms and phobias present in schools.

Chapters 1 through 8 each end with a unique set of **Reflection Questions**, **Recommended Resources**, and **References**. These are intended to guide critical reflection, centralize valuable resources, and increase the likelihood of commitment and action.

Terms and Definitions

To be *queer* is to have a sexual orientation, gender identity, and/or gender expression different from that acceptable in mainstream society. Appendix A represents a simplified visual of gender and sexual orientation diversity. Throughout this book, *queer* will refer to lesbian, gay, and bisexual (LGB) orientations. By *queer orientation*, I mean a same-sex pattern of emotional, romantic, and/or sexual attraction. Queer also refers to a myriad of gender identities and ways of expressing or "performing" one's gender. When someone's assigned sex at birth matches his or her gender identity, he or she is considered *cisgender*, whereas those who are *transgender* identify in a way that falls outside the cultural norms for people of their assigned sex (TransActive, 2010). Prince coined the term *transgender* in the 1980s, describing it as someone who changes gender by changing his or her presentation of self through clothing and behavior rather than by changing his or her body (Stryker & Whittle, 2006). In this book, the term *queer* is inclusive of individuals who are transgender as well as significantly *gender nonconforming*, or *genderqueer*. Many cisgender people do not conform to the social or cultural stereotypes that are expected of them. Such gender-nonconforming individuals are identified because of the kind or color of their clothes, the way they speak or what they say, their occupations or hobbies, or their gestures; 10% of children are identified as gender nonconforming (Roberts, Rosario, Corliss, Koenen, & Austin, 2012).

I use the term *queer* because it is inclusive of several sexual and gender identities and it holds cultural and political significance (Pinar, 1998). Once used by straight society against homosexuals, the word was reappropriated by the LGBT community in the 1990s to revitalize the spirit of gay activism (Haggerty, 2000). When possible, I intentionally avoid the terms *homosexual* and *sexual minority* because these clinical terms reference behaviors (often reducing queer individuals to purely sexual beings) rather than multidimensional aspects of identity. There are, however, some places I use the word *homosexual(ity)* to refer to scholarly literature that espouses this term. In these cases, homosexuality describes the sexual orientation, behavior, and/or identity of persons inclined to be physically and emotionally attracted, committed to, or interested in persons of their same gender (Campos, 2005). Throughout this book, I use *queerness* as a synonym for both nondominant sexual orientations (gay, lesbian, bisexual) *and* nonnormative gender identities and performances (transgender and gender nonconforming). I sometimes refer to *queer issues* when describing if, and to what extent, schools are inclusive of queerness, by which I mean points of interest surrounding the claimed identities, experienced oppression, and resistances enacted by queer people and straight allies.

The term *heterosexism* indicates a form of oppression that assumes everyone is or should be heterosexual (Friend, 1993). It refers to acts, beliefs, or values that are maintained by power arrangements that ignore the experiences of gay, lesbian, and bisexual individuals. *Heteronormativity* describes the concept of an entire culture or community that institutionalizes heterosexuality as the only accepted and reproduced lifestyle. Thus, individual acts of heterosexism reinforce heteronormative values within a culture or community, and, likewise, heteronormative values enable heterosexist practices. For example, teacher educators often exclude queer topics because the issues are beyond their consciousness, they are unsure of whether and how to approach such subject matter, and/or because of personal homophobic beliefs (Lipkin, 2002; Sears, 1992). Intentional or not, omission of queer issues in education is a heterosexist behavior that reinforces heteronormative values and practices. Sumara and Davis (1999) wrote:

> "Normal" and "heterosexual" are understood as synonymous. This means that all social relations and all forms of thinking that exist with these relations are heteronormative. To put it crudely, heteronormativity creates a language that is "straight." Living within heteronormative culture means learning to "see" straight, to "read" straight, to "think" straight.
>
> *(p. 202)*

Transgender oppression (sometimes referred to as *cissexism, cisgender privilege*, or *genderism*) is closely related to sexism and heterosexism, yet there are notable differences (Catalano & Shlasko, 2013). *Cissexism* refers to the system privileges afforded to cisgender (i.e., non-transgender) people. It is a form of oppression that ignores and stigmatizes transgender identities. Institutionalized cissexism is referred to as *cisnormativity*, which assumes that having a cisgender life experience (having either XX or XY chromosomes, being assigned male or female, and identifying as male or female) is the "correct" life experience, superior to all others. Individual acts of cisgender privilege reinforce the assumption that everyone's assigned sex at birth should and does match their individual gender identities. These oppressive structures are supported by *transphobia*, the fear or hatred of individuals who transgress the gender binary.

Homophobia, on the other hand, is the fear and hatred of nonheterosexual orientations in oneself or others (Weinberg, 1972) and often emerges as a result of heterosexism and heteronormativity. Homophobia is often considered *institutionalized* because of social and cultural arrangements in society. Laws, cultural rules, social expectations, and religious beliefs reward people who are (or appear to be) heterosexual. They also often punish (or withdraw privileges from) those who appear to be queer (Campos, 2005). Homophobia not only affects individuals who represent minority subject positions; as Sumara (2007) explained, homophobia and heterosexism limit possibilities for everyone.

> Homophobia helps create the conditions for violence among men. Homophobia and heterosexism participate in the continued subjugation of women. Just as all of us need to be interested in seeking equal rights for women by learning about the way patriarchy continues to organize men's and women's experiences, all of us need to be interested in seeking equal rights for non-heterosexuals by learning about and interrupting heteronormativity.
>
> (p. 52)

In this book, *teacher education* refers to the process of equipping pre-service teachers, or *teacher candidates*, with the knowledge, skills, and dispositions required to become a classroom teacher. By *knowledge* I mean the process commonly understood in education whereby teachers lead students to know what they did not know before—for example, principles of learning theories, classroom management techniques, and essential components of a lesson plan. Acquiring *skills* embodies the facilitation of how to do things, such as writing and implementing a lesson plan that showcases elements of constructivism and sound classroom management. In this context, *dispositions* refer to the development of attitudes and behaviors a teacher takes on—for example, a disposition toward recognizing and acknowledging the different realities created by the multicultural diversity in a contemporary classroom. Pre-service teacher education generally consists of two central components: university coursework and field experience. Sometimes referred to as student teaching, *field experience* offers teacher candidates opportunities to observe and work in actual K–12 classrooms with a mentor or *cooperating teacher*.

References

Campos, D. (2005). *Understanding gay and lesbian youth: Lessons for straight school teachers, counselors, and administrators.* Lanham, MD: Rowman & Littlefield.

Catalano, C., & Shlasko, D. (2013). Introduction. In M. Adams, W. J. Blumenfeld, C. Castañeda, H.W. Hackman, M.L. Peters, & X. Zúñiga (Eds.), *Readings for diversity and social justice* (3rd ed., pp. 425–431). New York: Routledge.

Friend, R.A. (1993). Choices, not closets: Heterosexism and homophobia in schools. In L. Weis, & M. Fine (Eds.), *Beyond silenced voices: Class, race, and gender in United States schools* (pp. 209–235). Albany: State University of New York Press.

Haggerty, G.E. (2000). *Gay histories and cultures: An encyclopedia.* New York: Taylor & Francis.

Lipkin, A. (2002). The challenges of gay topics in teacher education: Politics, content, and pedagogy. In R.M. Kissen (Ed.), *Getting ready for Benjamin: Preparing teachers for sexual diversity in the classroom* (pp. 13–27). Lanham, MD: Rowman & Littlefield.

Pinar, W.F. (1998). *Queer theory in education.* Mahwah, NJ: Erlbaum.

Roberts, A.L., Rosario, M., Corliss, H.L., Koenen, K.C., & Austin, B. (2012). Childhood gender nonconformity: A risk indicator for childhood abuse and posttraumatic stress in youth. *Pediatrics, 129*(3), 410–417.

Sears, J. (1992). Educators, homosexuality, and homosexual students: Are personal feelings related to professional beliefs? In K. Harbeck (Ed.), *Coming out of the classroom closet: Gay and lesbian students, teachers and curriculum* (pp. 29–79). New York: Haworth Press.

Stryker, S., & Whittle, S. (Eds.). (2006). *The transgender studies reader.* New York: Routledge.

Sumara, D., & Davis, B. (1999). Interrupting heteronormativity: Toward a queer curriculum theory. *Curriculum Inquiry, 29*(2), 191–208.

Sumara, D.J. (2007). Small differences matter: Interrupting certainty about identity in teacher education. *Journal of Gay and Lesbian Issues in Education, 4*(4), 39–58.

TransActive. (2010). *TransActive: Supporting children and youth of all genders.* Retrieved from www.transactiveonline.org

Weinberg, G. (1972). *Society and the healthy homosexual.* New York: Anchor.

PART I
The Challenges and Promise of Queering Teacher Education

1
FRAMING THE ISSUE

In This Chapter

- Key terms and the processes of sexual and gender identity development among queer youth.
- Ways and extent to which schools serve as hetero- and cisnormative institutions.
- K–12 school climate including risk factors for queer youth, the impact of teacher influence, and how curriculum and pedagogy influence education.

Facing the Epidemic

Over the past 40 years, equal rights and antidiscrimination legislation have extended the umbrella of protection to many disenfranchised groups, but efforts have failed to adequately cover the health and safety of queer youth. This is, in part, because such policies are debated within a complex social and cultural history in this country. Philosophically, the U.S. Declaration of Independence and the Constitution emphasize the supremacy of individuality and equality. But when the philosophy is shaped into educational policy, the heterosexual and cisgender biases of many Americans leave no room for queer students or their issues. Thus, the hetero- and cissexist policies that countenance homophobia send painful and tragic messages to our youth, which can have fatal consequences.

Carl Walker-Hoover was an 11-year-old in Springfield, Illinois. Carl went home after school on April 6, 2009. The sixth grader grabbed an extension cord, walked up the stairs to his bedroom, and wove the cord through his closet rafters before slipping the plastic noose around his neck. Carl committed suicide because students at his school called him "faggot" and verbally threatened him. Classmates shouted homophobic remarks in the hallways and taunted him daily about being gay (Gay, Lesbian and Straight Education Network [GLSEN], 2009). The New Leadership Charter School that Carl attended offered grief counseling to students and staff and collected donations for Carl's family in response to the community's loss of a child. What the school failed to do, however, was to address the problem before it was too late. According to Carl's mother, Sirdeaner Walker, she had phoned the school every week since September 2008 to complain about children bullying her son. More than 20 phone calls from a concerned parent failed to persuade school officials to intercede on Carl's behalf.

Stories similar to Carl's are far too common in contemporary society. The Federal Bureau of Investigation (FBI; 2007) reported that hate crimes—violent, intentional attacks on people because of their actual or perceived race, ethnicity, religion, or national origin—occur nearly 10,000 times per year. The National Coalition of Anti-Violence Programs (NCAVP; 2005) reported that between 1990 and 1999, hate crimes in the United States increased each year, with crimes perpetrated against queer individuals increasing 328%. In 2007–2008 the number of hate crimes against LGBTQ youth, age 15–18, rose by 118% (NCAVP, 2010). A more recent study conducted by the NCAVP (2013) revealed that LGBTQ youth between the age of 14 and 18 represented 7.2% of overall hate violence survivors and victims in 2012.

Perhaps these trends are responsible for the return of federal hate crime legislation (18 U.S.C. § 245) to the Senate floor for revision in July 2007, nine years after the brutal torture and murder of 21-year-old Matthew Shepard near Laramie, Wyoming. However, the amendment was dropped by the Democratic leadership because of opposition, including a threatened veto from President George W. Bush. Resurfacing in April 2009, the act, designated H.R. 1913, passed the House Judiciary Committee and the Senate. President Barack Obama signed it into law on October 22, 2009, extending the 1969 federal hate-crime law to include crimes motivated by a victim's actual or perceived gender, sexual orientation, and/or gender identity. Many social conservatives remain opposed to the law, arguing that it will effectively prevent people of faith from expressing their moral and biblical concerns about homosexuality.

As this political saga dragged on, many more youth were targeted. On May 16, 2007, 20-year-old Sean Kennedy was pulled from his car by an 18-year-old who called him "faggot" as he administered a blow to Sean's face. Sean immediately collapsed to the asphalt, which cracked his head open and killed him. His murderer served only 12 months in prison. Equally tragic was the killing of 15-year-old Lawrence King on February 12, 2008. Lawrence, who like Sean was openly gay, was shot in the back of the head by a fellow student, 14-year-old Brandon McInerney. The district attorney's filings stated that Brandon sat behind Lawrence in class on that tragic day for 20 minutes before he fired one shot into the back of Lawrence's head. After Lawrence collapsed, Brandon stood up and fired a second shot before storming out of the classroom. Brandon had publicly stated that he was going to shoot Lawrence the day before the murder. He told one of Lawrence's friends, "Say goodbye to your friend Larry because you're never going to see him again" (Saillant, 2009, p. 3). After eight weeks of testimony and more than 15 hours of deliberation, a mistrial was declared because the jury was unable to reach a verdict. Prosecutors decided to seek a second trial but dropped the hate-crime charge. On November 21, 2011, Brandon pleaded guilty to second-degree murder, voluntary manslaughter, and use of a gun and was sentenced to 21 years imprisonment. Meanwhile those who could have prevented the destruction of these two boys' lives, the administrators and teachers who were directly involved, were transferred to other schools (Sammon, 2011). A week after the mistrial, 14-year-old Jamey Rodemeyer committed suicide. Jamey had uploaded an *It Gets Better* video a few months prior to taking his own life. In the video he talked about being bullied for publicly questioning his sexual orientation.

While the brutal murders and tragic suicides of Matthew Sheppard, Carl Walker-Hoover, Lawrence King, Jamey Rodemeyer, and other queer youth sometimes do receive minimal media attention, several untold stories are equally tragic and far more recurrent. This book acknowledges the lives that have been lost and honors the resilient queer youth currently surviving and thriving. Savage (2010) created the *It Gets Better Project* to show young queer people the levels of happiness, potential, and positivity their lives will reach—if they can just get through their adolescent years. This book offers an alternative reality, one where children are not asked to wish away their early experiences in life, a reality that requires stakeholders in education to *make it better*.

Prevalence and Significance

More than four million lesbian, gay, bisexual, and transgender (LGBT) school-age youth currently live in the United States (Bochenek, Brown, & Human Rights Watch, 2001). What's more, LGBT youth are becoming aware of, identifying, and disclosing their sexual and gender identities at younger ages (Grossman et al., 2009; Savin-Williams & Berndt, 1990). When we include LGBT parents and siblings, as many as 9 out of 30 students—nearly one-third of a classroom—are significantly affected by sexual orientation and gender variance (Fontaine, 1998). Despite this shift in youth culture and the diversification of student and family populations, teacher preparation programs rarely acknowledge queer aspects of multiculturalism (Letts, 2002). As a result, a majority of K–12 educators enter the field of teaching unprepared and/or unwilling to discuss queer issues as they relate to students and families, curriculum, and instruction.

In fact, several studies reveal that teachers have little knowledge about homosexuality and transgender identity, accepting the myths and avoiding the topics as much as possible (Sears, 1989, 1992). This culture of silence around queer issues is important for all of us to acknowledge and grapple with, regardless of our social and ideological perspectives. As a matter of social justice, based on the concepts of human rights and equality, it is important to consider how homophobia and transphobia, as well as hetero- and cisnormative practices, benefit some people in society while causing others to suffer.

Beyond striving for justice on a social scale, the significance of queer inclusion in the classroom lies in the fact that queer people exist and have always existed. Queer figures and events help shape history and compose our current reality. Education does not occur in a vacuum, and prospective teachers should be prepared to encounter and deal with the complex ways gender and sexuality influence the social and academic schooling experience. In addition, compared to their straight and gender-conforming peers, queer youth experience increased physical, emotional, and psychological risks as a result of real or perceived orientation and identity (Bochenek et al., 2001; Unks, 1995). Finally, all educational stakeholders, regardless of sexual orientation and gender identification, can benefit from learning about and discussing issues around sexual and gender diversity because doing so can lead to deepened understanding, increased empathy, and social action that reaches beyond one minority group and touches us all.

In order to explore the experience of queer youth and discuss the -isms and phobias present in schools, it is important to first frame the notion of sexual and gender identities. Savin-Williams and Berndt (1990) described sexual identity as a constant, enduring sense of one's own sexuality and of recurring sexual feelings, thoughts, and/or behaviors. Sumara (2007) believed the following:

> The experience of sexuality and the ways humans have learned to construct boundaries around different sexual expressions and experiences is part of this complex, ecological process. To understand human sexuality, then, it is necessary to think about the intricate intertwinings of the biological, the experiential, the historical, and the cultural.
>
> *(p. 42)*

In other words, sexual identity is made up of a person's sexual characteristics, which are based on biology as well as sexual orientation, which is socially, culturally, and historically constructed. At various ages, youth begin to conceptualize themselves and be conceptualized by others as sexual beings with particular desires and orientations (Mission, 2005). This stage in life can be difficult for all youth, but it poses specific challenges for queer youth, who must negotiate constant decisions regarding whether, how, and to whom to "come out." This figure of speech refers to queer people disclosing their sexual orientation and gender identity.

Individual gender identity is developed much earlier than sexual identity. According to the American Academy of Pediatrics, gender identity is securely established by age four. This includes children who do not experience their gender in a way that corresponds with their assigned sex at birth. Gender identity is established independently of sexual orientation. While some gender-nonconforming youth may eventually identify as something other than heterosexual, the vast majority (85%) will identify as heterosexual (Kosciw, Greytak, Bartkiewicz, Boesen, & Palmer, 2012). Negotiating gender identity is an internal process whereby we self-recognize as masculine, feminine, androgynous, non-gender, or a unique blend of all these.

School is where students acquire academic knowledge and ability. It is also where they develop personal and social skills that persist throughout life (Hansley & Pratt, 2005; Merrell & Gimpel, 1998). The product of social interactions among students and with teachers, which is influenced by educational and social values, is often referred to as the *school climate* (Emmons, Comer, & Haynes, 1996; Moos, 1979). How students perceive that school climate can greatly affect their academic achievement (Battistich, Solomon, Kim, Watson, & Schaps, 1995; Griffith, 1999), behavior (Battistich et al., 1995; Wilson, 2004), and attitude (Battistich et al., 1995).

The United States has experienced some positive changes in school climate for queer students, teachers, and staff over the past three decades. Research, scholarship, and legislation have contributed to alternative practices that are beginning to recognize queer issues in education with increasing depth and frequency. However, despite a steady growth in awareness, increased attention must be paid to the K–12 school climate because, as a growing volume of empirical research indicates, U.S. schools are imbued with the institutionalization of heterosexuality and cisgender dominance (Epstein & Johnson, 1998; Letts & Sears, 1999; Thorne, 1993). Changing that is what this book is about.

Risk Factors for Queer Youth

Although the topic of queer youth in the context of education has emerged only in the last four decades, recent research investigated school climate for this population. Studies of queer students show them to be at high risk for experiencing a negative school climate (Bochenek et al., 2001; Kosciw, Diaz, & Greytak, 2008; Kosciw, Greytak, Diaz, & Bartkiewicz, 2010; Payne & Smith, 2010). The Gay, Lesbian and Straight Education Network (GLSEN) has commissioned a National School Climate Survey every two years for the past decade. The 2011 school climate survey (Kosciw et al., 2012) examined the experiences of queer students in connection with indicators of negative school climate, such as pejorative and homophobic language, harassment, and violence as a result of actual or perceived sexual orientation. The sample included 8,584 LGBT students age 13 to 20. Survey responses indicated that nearly 82% of students reported verbal harassment and 38% of students had been physically harassed. These data are congruent with the Massachusetts 2005 Youth Risk Behavior Survey (Massachusetts Department of

Education, 2006), which identified that queer high school students are more likely than their heterosexual peers to experience bullying (44% vs. 23%), threats or injuries with a weapon (14% vs. 5%), and sexual contact against their will (34% vs. 9%).

Additional research has produced similar findings. In a study of 528 lesbian, gay, and bisexual youth, D'Augelli, Grossman, and Starks (2008) found that 78% reported experiencing verbal abuse, and 11% said they suffered physical abuse because of their sexual orientation. A study by Kimmel and Mahler (2003) situated homophobic brutality within the broader epidemic of school violence. The authors performed an extensive analysis of 28 random school shootings in American middle and high schools from 1982 to 2001. Based on their coding of adolescent masculinity, homophobia, and violence in schools, they contended that all of the 28 incidences involved some type of gay baiting or bullying resulting from gender expression and perceived sexual orientation. The sanctioning and institutionalizing of gender conformity in schools begins early and often has lasting effects. Children who do not conform to expected gender stereotypes are at significantly greater risk for physical, sexual, and psychological abuse during childhood and symptoms of posttraumatic stress disorder in young adulthood (Roberts, Rosario, Corliss, Koenen, & Austin, 2012).

Grossman et al. (2009) conducted a qualitative study aimed at "understanding what LGBT youth found as oppressive and destructive social conditions in their schools" (p. 27). Divided among five separate focus groups, the research team provided queer youth opportunities to talk about their past and current experiences of school violence. Data were recorded, transcribed, and then analyzed using grounded theory techniques (see Strauss & Corbin, 1990). Core themes focused on lack of community and empowerment leading to youth not having a sense of human agency in school. Negative attention themes were indicative of the vulnerability that the youth felt at school.

The harassment and violence queer youth experience can contribute to increased truancy and dropout rates as well as lowered academic achievement and educational aspirations (Grossman et al., 2009; Kosciw et al., 2008, 2010, 2012). In these cases, life outside school is also impacted. Tharinger and Wells (2000) researched the developmental challenges for gay and lesbian youth using attachment theory as a theoretical base to understand the impact that rejection of relationship connections can have on the development of queer youth. The authors argued that as queer youth become aware of their sexuality and attempt to integrate this knowledge into their identity, the potential for parental and societal rejection occurs or increases. Indeed, research has documented this disapproval rate. Ryan, Russell, Huebner, Diaz, and Sanchez (2010) found that 30% of families reject their child when they learn of the child's nonnormative orientation status. D'Augelli's (2006) research uncovered that many queer youth were verbally abused by their mothers (13%) or were afraid of being verbally abused by their parents (30%) because of their sexual orientation. Research has also suggested that family rejection and abuse is even higher for transgender youth (Roberts et al., 2012). One study found that 61% of the violence reported by queer youth happened in the home (Hunter, 1990). In another study, more than one-third of the youth surveyed had been verbally abused in the home, and 10% were physically assaulted by a family member because of their sexual orientation (Pilkington & D'Augelli, 1995).

In addition to alienation from friends, family, and religious institutions, studies indicate that when compared to heterosexual and cisgender peers, queer youth are also at a greater risk of suffering from social identity issues, depression, suicidal tendencies, drug and alcohol abuse, homelessness, and sexual harassment (Bochenek et al., 2001; Jennings, 1994; Kosciw et al., 2008, 2010, 2012; Unks, 1995; Walling, 1996). Several researchers have compared the patterns of alcohol and drug use among queer and non-queer youth. Congruent with other studies, Orenstein (2001) found substance abuse to be consistently higher for gay and lesbian youth with the gap widening as the substance became more dangerous. The urgency to examine, and eradicate, queer risk factors is intensified by the rate of suicide in the Western world, where an estimated 30% of youths who commit suicide struggle with issues of (homo)sexuality (Mac an Ghaill, 1994). Tragically, individuals who defy stereotypical gender performance expectations find themselves at an even greater risk. In a survey of more than 7,000 trans-identified people of diverse ages, 41% reported having attempted suicide (National Center for Transgender Equality/National Gay & Lesbian Task Force, 2010). The exact number of homeless queer youth is difficult to quantify, but based on his review of the literature, Campos (2005) estimated that about 1.2 million gay and lesbian youth run away from home each year. The National Coalition for the Homeless (2009) cited that 20% of homeless youth are LGBT. A large amount of the literature that investigates and reports on these tragic realities for queer youth turn toward teacher influence as a possible means for improving school climate and student experience.

Teacher Influence

Given that this book focuses on education, the most disheartening finding in the 2011 National School Climate Survey is the report's indictment of administrators and teachers. According to the study, the majority of queer students who experienced harassment or assault in school chose not to report it, believing little to no action would be taken. In fact, more than a third of the students who did report an occurrence said that school staff did nothing in response (Kosciw et al., 2012). Similar data are evidenced in studies performed by Holmes and Cahill (2005), Grossman et al. (2009), and Bochenek et al. (2001), which found queer youth to be aware that teachers and school staff are often silent and do nothing in response to reports of homo- and transphobic harassment. A study of 289 teachers and

52 principals from nine urban, suburban, and rural Connecticut high schools indicated that teachers are unwilling to discuss homosexuality with students (Woog, 1995). Of those polled, 65% of the teachers, 70% of the principals, and 100% of the teachers who self-identified as gay or lesbian believed that teachers were not open to the discussion of homosexuality with gay or nongay students (Woog, 1995). Reis (1999) verified this non-reporting of the victimization of queer students: Only one in four cases of queer youth victimization witnessed by adults was reported to the Washington State Safe Schools Coalition.

Russell, Seif, and Truong (2001) used data from more than 11,000 participants to examine the role of four different domains related to negative attitudes about school held by queer youth: family, teacher, social, and peer. As a means of increasing participant privacy and thus maximizing high levels of self-disclosure, queer youth and parents of queer youth listened to questions through earphones, and their responses were recorded on a laptop computer. Results indicated that teachers play the largest role in predicting school success or failure for queer youth. Among the sample population, youth with positive feelings about their teachers were significantly less likely than their peers to experience the broad range of school troubles. According to the study, teachers largely determine whether queer students pay attention, complete homework, and get along with other students. At the conclusion of their article, the authors claimed the following:

> Perhaps the most important implication for schools in the U.S. is the finding that relationships with teachers play a leading role in explaining the school troubles experienced by sexual minority adolescents. Supportive teachers can help prevent school troubles of sexual minority youth; teachers need the awareness and training to help them be supportive of their sexuality minority students.
>
> *(p. 124)*

At the same time that a body of research has documented educators' failure to intervene with bullying and harassment, several studies have indicated that queer youth who are able to identify at least one supportive school staff member are more likely to attend school, experience academic success, develop educational aspirations, and maintain a sense of belonging (Kosciw et al., 2008; Owens, 1998). Human Rights Watch, a national organization that reports on the experiences of queer youth, published a report called *Hatred in the Hallways* in 2001 stating that teachers play a vital role in the schooling experience of queer youth (Bochenek et al., 2001). "In virtually every case where lesbian, gay, bisexual, and transgender youth reported that their school experience has been positive, they attributed that fact to the presence of supportive teachers" (p. 79). The report went on to say, however, that most students do not receive such encouragement from teachers and administrators. A lack of training, fear of controversy, and homophobia are some reasons why educational professionals frequently neglect queer issues and fail to adequately support queer youth (Bochenek et al., 2001; Letts & Sears, 1999; Woog, 1995). Dave Buckel, a staff attorney with the Lambda Legal Defense and Education Fund, worked on the report and summarized a typical response he heard from administrators: "If you're going to be gay, you have to expect this kind of abuse, because you'll face it for the rest of your life" (Bochenek et al., 2001, p. 79). This widespread attitude among school leadership and educators' tendency to avoid queer issues combines with extant curricula and pedagogy to condone homo- and transphobic harassment in schools.

Curricula and Pedagogy

For queer youth and adolescents, the language and symbols at school serve as daily reminders of their marginalization. Heterosexist and gender-specific ideologies surface in kindergarten when students learn the standardized equation for what constitutes a family and when they survey social and gender norms from daily curricula and pedagogy (DePalma & Atkinson, 2009; Sears, 1999). Delamont (1990) suggested that the gender role beliefs of early childhood educators are predictive of their instructional strategies and curricula choices, which, in turn, are likely to shape children's gender role perceptions and behaviors. In other words, while not openly intending to do so, teachers often transmit norms, values, and beliefs about gender roles and expectations that directly affect children's identity development and behavior. Cahill and Adams's (1997) findings suggested that when teachers have limiting gender role beliefs (i.e., separate and traditional notions of the ways in which boys and girls should think, act, feel, and behave), homophobia ensues. These discoveries are significant because it has been repeatedly shown that early childhood educators play a vital role in the early socialization of young children, how children learn the values and behaviors accepted in society (e.g., Ashiabi, 2000; Kemple & Hartle, 1997; Mussen & Eisenberg, 1977; Piker & Rex, 2008). Thus, teachers may discourage cross-gender play and reinforce heteronormativity at a critical time when learners are forming identity and negotiating their place in an increasingly diverse world.

Often individual educators do not intend to perpetuate hetero- and cisnormativity. Cognizant of this, a number of researchers have investigated how schools as a whole function to value hegemonic sexual orientations and gender identities and presentations. Silin (1995) joined a long list of scholars (e.g., hooks, 1994; McLaren, 2003; Sears & Williams, 1997; Sedgwick, 1990) who have examined the ways in which dominant gender norms and heteronormativity manifest in school curricula and classroom instruction. He wrote, "We attempt to regulate sexuality and desire, the reproduction of heterosexual norms, through covert communication about appropriate feminine and masculine behaviors and aptitudes and through the overt products of popular culture" (p. 159). Silin linked his assertion to a narrative study in which Walkerdine (1990) examined how young girls are taught to conceptualize the ideology of romantic love and are prepared for entering heterosexual practices through children's literature. Regardless of teachers' intent, students such as those described in Walkerdine's study receive messages about what is deemed normal and accepted in society (e.g., submissive princess falls for strong, masculine prince) through classroom content and experience.

The 2011 National School Climate Survey reported that only a small percentage of students (16.8%) were taught positive representations about queer people and history. Less than half reported access to queer-inclusive materials in the school library, and even fewer were able to retrieve LGBT-related information on school computers (Kosciw et al., 2012). Studies have cited many reasons for excluding queer curricula and discouraging classroom dialogue on sexual and gender diversity. Owens (1998), in a survey of 89 school districts, found that fewer than 25% of the districts used queer adults and organizations as classroom resources or consultants. The districts cited these reasons for not using these resources: that outside aid is unnecessary and that use might raise vocal opposition in the community. In addition to political and ideological motives for withholding queer issues in education, researchers have demonstrated that school personnel and educators lack the awareness, sensitivity, knowledge, and skills appropriate for meeting the needs of queer youth. Fricke (1981) showcased his school's lack of understanding in his book *Reflections of a Rock Lobster: A Story About Growing up Gay*. Fricke's ethnographic research tells the story of his desire to take a male date to his high school prom and details the ignorant and traumatic reactions he received from the school.

An inclusive curriculum containing positive images and stories of queer individuals, history, and events can promote social justice and improve queer students' school experiences. Schools with an inclusive curriculum have lower reports of homophobic slurs and anti-transgender epithets than those without such a curriculum (Kosciw et al., 2012). Additionally, queer students who attend schools that recognize LGBTQ identity and issues in their curriculum report higher levels of acceptance among classmates (Kosciw et al., 2012).

Queering Elementary Education

Introducing young children to sexual orientation is contentious (DePalma & Atkinson, 2006; Epstein, 1997; Letts & Sears, 1999; Renold, 1999; Weems, 1999), mostly due to the rhetoric of the innocent and nonsexual child as created through the belief that children need to be protected from unwanted sexual advances and desires. This gives rise to a discourse of protection, which in turn makes talking about sexuality, and particularly homosexuality, in elementary school risky and unsafe (Bickmore, 1999). However, as Bickmore argued, it is not innocence but rather young children's relative lack of power and knowledge that forms the basis of children's vulnerability. This lack, she contended, negates children's rights to self-determination in their pursuit of full citizenship.

Although most of the research from the 1980s and 1990s focused on problematizing the issue of queer inclusion in education (e.g., Kochheiser, 1975; Liebert, 1971), there has been an increase in literature over the past decade that offers a way forward. Pioneering investigations into queering early childhood education, DePalma and Atkinson (2009) as well as Sears (1999) contribute alternative pedagogies that challenge traditional views of childhood, gender, and sexuality. "Those who teach queerly," Sears attested, "refuse to participate in the great sexual sorting machine called schooling wherein GI Joes and Barbies become star quarterbacks and prom queens, while the Linuses and Tinky Winkys become wallflowers or human doormats" (p. 5).

The research and scholarship contributed by Sears (1992, 1999, 2002) urged educators to reexamine the way they perceive childhood and schooling. He envisioned queer elementary classrooms as those that challenge categorical thinking, promote interpersonal intelligence, and foster critical consciousness. This pedagogy demands that we explore assumptions about diversity, identities, childhood, and prejudice. Toward this end, Sears (1999) offered five propositions for elementary classrooms that, he argued, force educators to reconceptualize who, what, and how they teach.

1. *Diversity is a human hallmark.* When it comes to sexuality and gender, he argued, educators tend to mold children into "curriculum cookie cutter identities" (p. 12) whereas a cornerstone to teaching queerly is to deconstruct sexual and gender binaries.
2. *(Homo)sexualities are constructed essences*, meaning sexual identity is structured and restructured within a social and cultural context. When it comes to supporting queer youth, rather than focusing on what causes homosexuality, Sears challenged educators to consider the factors that contribute to homophobia and heterosexism.
3. *Homophobia and heterosexism are acquired.* In other words, hatred and fear of those who love the same gender are acquired early in life. Sears posited that queering elementary education requires educators to confront personal prejudices indoctrinated through decades of heterosocialization.
4. *Childhood innocence is a fictive absolute.* All too often adults seem to mask their fear of discomfort by underestimating children's capacity for critical thinking and deep understanding.
5. *Families are first*, by which Sears acknowledged the ways in which concepts, such as family and parenthood, have become "unhinged" (p. 10). He proposed that educators identify and teach reality (e.g., some families have two mommies or two daddies who love each other and are committed to their families).

In recent years, DePalma and Atkinson (2009) have adopted their own conclusions about "putting queer into practice" (p. 1). Borrowing existing theory from researchers like Sears, the team of British scholars created the *No Outsiders Project*. Designed according to the participatory action research model, which links practice and systematic reflection, DePalma and Atkinson recruited a team of educators to examine gender normalization and heteronormativity inherent in their own practice. In order to explore alternative pedagogies, descriptive data were collected from September 2006 to December 2008 and published in their book, *Interrogating Heteronormativity in Primary Schools*. Through the vivid use of vignettes and personal narrative, the researchers espoused possibilities of including queer content and conversation in the elementary classroom and revealed the transformative power of disrupting heterosexism in schools. Of particular interest is the authors' salient critique on tolerance training around homophobic bullying and harassment. They argued that a "don't ask, don't tell" approach silences real dialogue and can perpetuate stereotypes and propagate assumptions that all people fit neatly and permanently into existing categories. Rather, they asserted:

> Primary teachers must go beyond an anti-bullying discourse of tolerance in the form of quiet acceptance . . . teachers need to reach beyond passive and disingenuous tolerance of 'those LGBT people' to proactively incorporate discussions of sexuality and gender into their curriculum.
>
> *(pp. 3–4)*

Middle and High School Curricula and Practice

A failure to acknowledge queer issues and to interrupt heterosexism and cisgender dominance in early grades can perpetuate the homophobia and transphobia in middle and high school. Phrases like "no homo" and "that's so gay" run rampant in classrooms and hallways. In fact, the average queer youth hears antigay slurs such as "homo," "faggot," and "dyke" about 26 times a day, or once every 14 minutes of an average school day (Kosciw et al., 2008). In the 2011 National School Climate Survey, nearly three-quarters (71.3%) of LGBTQ students reported hearing students make derogatory remarks often or frequently in school (Kosciw et al., 2012). More than half (56.9%) reported hearing homophobic remarks from their teachers or other school staff.

Middle and high school are also marked by a "hidden curriculum" that emphasizes the perspective of the dominant group (Nieto, 2000; Sleeter & Grant, 1999). For example, a lesson that recognizes poet and writer Langston Hughes as an African American but fails to acknowledge and discuss his queer identity or a curriculum that honors and teaches Martin Luther King Jr. while exploring the civil rights movement but ignores the influence of Harvey Milk, Anne Kronenberg, and the Stonewall Riots on the American political landscape during the 1960s and 1970s.

Temple (2005) used content analysis to examine 20 high school textbooks for content related to sexuality and relationships. She found that 95% of the 610 pages she coded made no reference to queerness: 133 pages explicitly defined sexuality as heterosexuality, and only 33 pages made reference to homosexual relationships. Interestingly, where homosexuality was mentioned, it was "in negative contexts almost 80% of the time" (p. 281).

Conclusion

This description of current trends in K–12 school climate helps position recent advances in practices that acknowledge queer issues within a larger framework. Although we have witnessed great strides in queer "tolerance" over the past few decades in social, political, and educational arenas, our schools remain relatively unchanged. Current mainstream curricula appear to be void, for all good intents and purposes, of any mention of queer history, people, and events. Although several organizations such as Welcoming Schools and Groundspark have created resources to assist educators (e.g., lesson modules, videos, and books), these are not widely publicized. Beyond a lack of awareness, many educators don't even know if they are allowed to discuss queer topics in their schools. This, in addition to the fear of being fired or labeled queer themselves, often deters educators from the topic altogether. The fact that teacher preparation programs rarely address these issues only exacerbates fearful unknowns and perpetuates risk factors for queer youth.

Reflection Questions

1. Think back to your earliest memory of gender difference. What was going on in that moment? Who was present? What values were attached to what you learned?
2. What messages did you receive as a child and young student about homosexuality? Looking back, can you identity a hidden curriculum (i.e., unspoken and unofficial norms, beliefs, and values you learned from teachers, family, and/or friends)?
3. How do you rate yourself and your institution on students' experiences of hearing biased language, on experiences of harassment and assault, on discriminatory school policies and practices, and on the availability and impact of supportive school resources?
4. How, if at all, do Sears's five propositions for elementary classrooms challenge you to reconceptualize who, what, and how you teach?

Recommended Resources

Books on K–12 School Climate and Queer Youth

Campos, D. (2005). *Understanding gay and lesbian youth: Lessons for straight school teachers, counselors, and administrators*. Lanham, MD: Rowman & Littlefield.

DePalma, R., & Atkinson, E. (2006). The sound of silence: Talking about sexual orientation and schooling. *Sex Education, 6*, 333–349.

DePalma, R., & Atkinson, E. (Eds.). (2009). *Interrogating heteronormativity in primary schools: The No Outsiders Project*. Oakhill, VA: Trentham.

DeWitt, P.M. (2012). *Dignity for all: Safeguarding LGBT students*. Thousand Oaks, CA: Corwin.

Letts, W.J., & Sears, J.T. (Eds.). (1999). *Queering elementary education: Advancing the dialogue about sexualities and schooling*. Lanham, MD: Rowman & Littlefield.

Owens, R.E. (1998). *Queer kids: The challenges and promise for lesbian, gay, and bisexual youth*. New York: Haworth Press.

Sears, J.T. (Ed.). (2011). *Gay, lesbian, and transgender issues in education: Programs, policies, and practices*. New York: Routledge.

Unks, G. (1995). *The gay teen: Educational practice and theory for lesbian, gay, and bisexual adolescents*. New York: Routledge.

Walling, D.R. (Ed.). (1996). *Open lives, safe schools: Addressing gay and lesbian issues in education*. Bloomington, IN: Phi Kappa Educational Foundation.

Books on Gender Complexity and Gender Fluidity

Bornstein, K. (1994). *Gender outlaw: On men, women, and the rest of us*. New York: Vintage.

Feinberg, L. (1996). *Transgender warriors: Making history from Joan of Arc to Dennis Rodman*. Boston, MA: Beacon.

Feinberg, L. (1998). *Transgender liberation: Beyond pink or blue*. Boston: Beacon.

Munoz, J.E. (1999). *Disidentifications: Queers of color and the performance of politics*. Minneapolis: University of Minnesota Press.

Styrker, S., & Aizura, A. (2013). *The transgender studies reader 2*. New York: Routledge.

Wilchins, R. (1997). *Read my lips: Sexual subversion and the end of gender*. Ithaca, NY: Firebrand.

Wilchins, R. (2004). *Queer theory, gender theory*. Los Angeles, CA: Alyson.

National Research Reports on School Climate and Queer Youth

Bochenek, M., Brown, A.W., & Human Rights Watch. (2001). *Hatred in the hallways: Violence and discrimination against lesbian, gay, bisexual, and transgender students in U.S. schools*. New York: Human Rights Watch. Retrieved from www.hrw.org/sites/default/files/reports/usalbg01.pdf

Gay, Lesbian and Straight Education Network. *GLSEN and the National School Climate Survey*. Retrieved from www.glsen.org/nscs

Kosciw, J.G., Greytak, E.A., Bartkiewicz, M.J., Boesen, M.J., & Palmer, N.A. (2012). *The 2011 National School Climate Survey: The experiences of lesbian, gay, bisexual and transgender youth in our nation's schools*. New York: GLSEN.

References

Ashiabi, G. (2000). Promoting the emotional development of preschoolers. *Early Childhood Education Journal, 28*(2), 79–84.

Battistich, V., Solomon, D., Kim, D., Watson, M., & Schaps, E. (1995). Schools as communities, poverty levels of student populations, and students' attitudes, motives, and performance: A multilevel analysis. *American Educational Research Journal, 32*, 627–658.

Bickmore, K. (1999). Why discuss sexuality in elementary school? In W.J. Letts & J.T. Sears (Eds.), *Queering elementary education: Advancing the dialogue about sexualities and schooling* (pp. 15–25). Lanham, MD: Rowman & Littlefield.

Bochenek, M., Brown, A.W., & Human Rights Watch. (2001). *Hatred in the hallways: Violence and discrimination against lesbian, gay, bisexual, and transgender students in U.S. schools*. New York: Human Rights Watch. Retrieved from www.hrw.org/sites/default/files/reports/usalbg01.pdf

Cahill, B., & Adams, E. (1997). An exploratory study of early childhood teachers' attitudes toward gender roles. *Sex Roles, 36*(7/8), 517–529.

Campos, D. (2005). *Understanding gay and lesbian youth: Lessons for straight school teachers, counselors, and administrators*. Lanham, MD: Rowman & Littlefield.

D'Augelli, A.R. (2006). Developmental and contextual factors and mental health among lesbian, gay, and bisexual youths. In A.M. Omoto & H.S. Kurtzman (Eds.), *Sexual orientation and mental health: Examining identity and development in lesbian, gay, and bisexual people* (pp. 37–53). Washington, DC: American Psychological Association.

D'Augelli, A.R., Grossman, A.H., & Starks, M.T. (2008). Gender atypicality and sexual orientation development among lesbian, gay, and bisexual youth: Prevalence, sex differences, and parental responses. *Journal of Gay & Lesbian Mental Health, 12*(1/2), 121–143.

Delamont, S. (1990). *Sex roles and the school*. New York: Routledge.

DePalma, R., & Atkinson, E. (2006). The sound of silence: Talking about sexual orientation and schooling. *Sex Education, 6*, 333–349.

DePalma, R., & Atkinson, E. (Eds.). (2009). *Interrogating heteronormativity in primary schools: The No Outsiders Project*. Oakhill, VA: Trentham.

Emmons, C.L., Comer, J.P., & Haynes, N.M. (1996). Translating theory into practice: Comer's theory of school reform. In J.P. Comer, N.M. Haynes, E. Joyner, & M. Ben-Avie (Eds.), *Rallying the whole village* (pp. 27–41). New York: Teachers College Press.

Epstein, D. (1997). Cultures of schooling/cultures of sexuality. *International Journal of Inclusive Education, 1*, 37–53.

Epstein, D., & Johnson, R. (1998). *Schooling sexualities*. Buckingham, UK: Open University Press.

Federal Bureau of Investigation (FBI). (2007). *Uniform crime reports: Hate crime statistics*. Retrieved from www.fbi.gov/ucr/hc2007/index.html

Fontaine, J.H. (1998). Evidencing a need: School counselors' experiences with gay and lesbian students. *Professional School Counseling, 1*(3), 8–14.

Fricke, A. (1981). *Reflections of a rock lobster: A story about growing up gay*. Boston: Alyson.

Gay, Lesbian and Straight Education Network (GLSEN). (2009, April 9). *11-year-old hangs himself after enduring daily anti-gay bullying*. Message posted to www.glsen.org/cgi-bin/iowa/all/news/record/2400.html

Griffith, J. (1999). School climate as "social order" and "social action": A multi-level analysis of public elementary school student perceptions. *School Psychology of Education, 2*, 339–369.

Grossman, A.H., Haney, A.P., Edwards, P., Alessi, E.J., Ardon, M., & Howell, T.J. (2009). Lesbian, gay, bisexual and transgender youth talk about experiencing and coping with school violence: A qualitative study. *Journal of LGBT Youth, 6*, 24–46.

Hansley, M., & Pratt, D. (2005). *Tools for teaching social skills in school*. Boys Town, NJ: Boys Town Press.

Holmes, S.E., & Cahill, S. (2005). School experiences of gay, lesbian, bisexual and transgender youth. In J.T. Sears (Ed.), *Gay, lesbian, and transgender issues in education: Programs, policies and practices* (pp. 63–76). New York: Harrington Park Press.

hooks, b. (1994). *Teaching to transgress: Education as the practice of freedom*. New York: Routledge.

Hunter, J. (1990). Violence against lesbian and gay male youths. *Journal of Interpersonal Violence, 5*, 295–300.

Jennings, K. (1994). *Becoming visible: A reader in gay and lesbian history for high school and college students.* Los Angeles, CA: Alyson.

Kemple, K.M., & Hartle, L. (1997). Getting along: How teachers can support children's peer relationships. *Early Childhood Education Journal, 24*(3), 139–146.

Kimmel, M.S., & Mahler, M. (2003). Adolescent masculinity, homophobia, and violence: Random school shootings, 1982–2001. *American Behavioral Scientist, 46*(10), 1439–1458.

Kochheiser, C. (1975). What happened when a speaker for gay liberation addressed high school students? *Social Education, 39*(4), 219–221.

Kosciw, J.G., Diaz, E.M., & Greytak, E.A. (2008). *2007 National School Climate Survey: The experiences of lesbian, gay, bisexual and transgender youth in our nation's schools.* New York: GLSEN.

Kosciw, J.G., Greytak, E.A., Bartkiewicz, M.J., Boesen, M.J., & Palmer, N.A. (2012). *The 2011 National School Climate Survey: The experiences of lesbian, gay, bisexual and transgender youth in our nation's schools.* New York: GLSEN.

Kosciw, J.G., Greytak, E.A., Diaz, E.M., & Bartkiewicz, M.J. (2010). *The 2009 National School Climate Survey: The experiences of lesbian, gay, bisexual and transgender youth in our nation's schools.* New York: GLSEN.

Letts, W.J. (2002). Revisioning multiculturalism in teacher education: Isn't it queer? In R.M. Kissen (Ed.), *Getting ready for Benjamin: Preparing teachers for sexual diversity in the classroom* (pp. 119–131). Lanham, MD: Rowman & Littlefield.

Letts, W.J., & Sears, J.T. (Eds.). (1999). *Queering elementary education: Advancing the dialogue about sexualities and schooling.* Lanham, MD: Rowman & Littlefield.

Liebert, R. (1971). The "gay" student: A psychopolitical view. *Change, 3*(6), 38–44.

Mac an Ghaill, M. (1994). *The making of men: Masculinities, sexualities and schooling.* Buckingham, UK: Open University Press.

Massachusetts Department of Education. (2006). *2005 Massachusetts youth risk behavior survey results.* Malden, MA: Author.

McLaren, P. (2003). *Life in schools: An introduction to critical pedagogy in the foundations of education* (4th ed.). New York: Allyn and Bacon.

Merrell, K.W., & Gimpel, G.A. (1998). *Social skills of children and adolescents: Conceptualization, assessment, treatment.* Mahwah, NJ: Lawrence Erlbaum.

Mission, R. (2005). Sexual identity. In J. Sears (Ed.), *Youth, education, and sexualities: An international encyclopedia, Vol. 2* (pp. 778–781). Westport, CT: Greenwood Press.

Moos, R.H. (1979). *Evaluating educational environments: Procedures, measures, findings, and policy implications.* San Francisco, CA: Jossey-Bass.

Mussen, P., & Eisenberg, N. (1977). *Roots of caring, sharing, and helping: The development of prosocial behavior in children.* San Francisco, CA: Freeman.

National Center for Transgender Equality/National Gay & Lesbian Task Force. (2010). *National transgender discrimination survey: Report on health and health care.* Retrieved from www.thetaskforce.org/reports_and_research

National Coalition for the Homeless. (2009). *LGBT homeless.* Retrieved from www.nationalhomeless.org/factsheets/lgbtq.html

National Coalition of Anti-Violence Programs (NCAVP). (2005). *National publications: Anti-LGBT violence in 2004.* Retrieved from www.ncavp.org/common/document_files/Reports/2004NationalHV%20Report.pdf

National Coalition of Anti-Violence Programs (NCAVP). (2010). *2009 report on lesbian, gay, bisexual, transgender, queer, and HIV-affected hate violence.* Retrieved from http://avp.org/storage/documents/Reports/2009_NCAVP_HV_Report.pdf

National Coalition of Anti-Violence Programs (NCAVP). (2013). *Lesbian, gay, bisexual, transgender, queer and HIV-affected hate violence in 2012*. Retrieved from www.avp.org/storage/documents/ncavp_2012_hvreport_final.pdf

Nieto, S. (2000). *Affirming diversity: The sociopolitical context of multicultural education* (3rd ed.). New York: Longman.

Orenstein, A. (2001). Substance use among gay and lesbian adolescents. *Journal of Homosexuality*, *41*(2), 1–15.

Owens, R.E. (1998). *Queer kids: The challenges and promise for lesbian, gay, and bisexual youth*. New York: Haworth Press.

Payne, E., & Smith, M. (2010). Reduction of stigma in schools: An evaluation of the first three years. *Issues in Teacher Education*, *19*(2), 11–36.

Piker, R.A., & Rex, L.A. (2008). Influences of teacher-child social interactions on English language development in a Head Start classroom. *Early Childhood Education Journal*, *36*, 187–193.

Pilkington, N.W., & D'Augelli, A.R. (1995). Victimization of lesbian, gay, and bisexual youth in community settings. *Journal of Community Psychology*, *23*, 33–56.

Reis, B. (1999). *They don't even know me! Understanding anti-gay harassment and violence in schools*. Seattle, WA: Safe Schools Coalition.

Renold, E. (1999). *Presumed innocence: An ethnographic exploration into the construction of sexual and gender identities in the primary school*. Unpublished dissertation, University of Wales, Cardiff.

Roberts, A.L., Rosario, M., Corliss, H.L., Koenen, K.C., & Austin, B. (2012). Childhood gender nonconformity: A risk indicator for childhood abuse and posttraumatic stress in youth. *Pediatrics*, *129*(3), 410–417.

Russell, S.T., Seif, H., & Truong, N.L. (2001). School outcomes of sexual minority youth in the United States: Evidence from a national study. *Journal of Adolescence*, *24*, 111–127.

Ryan, C., Russell, S.T., Huebner, D., Diaz, R., & Sanchez, J. (2010). Family acceptance in adolescence and the health of LGBT young adults. *Journal of Child and Adolescent Psychiatric Nursing*, *23*(4), 205–213.

Saillant, C. (2009, February 12). Details in gay student's slaying revealed. *Los Angeles Times*, 3.

Sammon, P. (2011, August 5). McInerney trial. *Ventura County Star*. Retrieved from www.vcstar.com/news/2011/aug/05/mcinerney-trial

Savage, D. (2010). *It Gets Better Project*. Retrieved from www.itgetsbetter.org

Savin-Williams, R.C., & Berndt, T.J. (1990). Friendships and peer relations. In S.S. Feldman & G.R. Elliott (Eds.), *At the threshold: The developing adolescent* (pp. 277–307). Cambridge, MA: Harvard University Press.

Sears, J.T. (1989). *Personal feelings and professional attitudes of prospective teachers toward homosexuality and homosexual students: Research findings and curriculum recommendations*. Paper presented at American Educational Research Association, San Francisco. (ERIC Document Reproduction Service No. ED 312222)

Sears, J. (1992). Educators, homosexuality, and homosexual students: Are personal feelings related to professional beliefs? In K. Harbeck (Ed.), *Coming out of the classroom closet: Gay and lesbian students, teachers and curriculum* (pp. 29–79). New York: Haworth Press.

Sears, J.T. (1999). Teaching queerly: Some elementary propositions. In W.J. Letts & J.T. Sears (Eds.), *Queering elementary education: Advancing the dialogue about sexualities and schooling* (pp. 3–14). Lanham, MD: Rowman & Littlefield.

Sears, J.T. (2002). The institutional climate for lesbian, gay and bisexual education faculty: What is the pivotal frame of reference? *Journal of Homosexuality*, *43*(1), 11–37.

Sears, J.T., & Williams, W.L. (1997). *Overcoming heterosexism and homophobia*. New York: Columbia University Press.

Sedgwick, E.K. (1990). *Epistemology of the closet*. Berkeley: University of California Press.

Silin, J. (1995). *Sex, death, and the education of children: Our passion for ignorance in the age of AIDS*. New York: Teachers College Press.

Sleeter, C.E., & Grant, C.A. (1999). *Making choices for multicultural education: Five approaches to race, class, and gender* (3rd ed.). Upper Saddle River, NJ: Merrill.

Strauss, A., & Corbin, J. (1990). *Basics of qualitative research: Grounded theory procedures and techniques*. Newbury Park, CA: Sage.

Sumara, D.J. (2007). Small differences matter: Interrupting certainty about identity in teacher education. *Journal of Gay and Lesbian Issues in Education, 4*(4), 39–58.

Temple, J.R. (2005). People who are different from you: Heterosexism in Quebec high school textbooks. *Canadian Journal of Education, 28*(3), 271–294.

Tharinger, D., & Wells, G. (2000). An attachment perspective on the developmental challenges of gay and lesbian adolescents: The need for continuity of caregiving from family and schools. *School Psychology Review, 29*(2), 158–172.

Thorne, B. (1993). *Gender play: Boys and girls in school*. Buckingham, UK: Open University Press.

Unks, G. (1995). *The gay teen: Educational practice and theory for lesbian, gay, and bisexual adolescents*. New York: Routledge.

Walkerdine, V. (1990). *School girl fictions*. London, UK: Verso.

Walling, D.R. (Ed.). (1996). *Open lives, safe schools: Addressing gay and lesbian issues in education*. Bloomington, IN: Phi Kappa Educational Foundation.

Weems, L. (1999). Pestalozzi, perversity, and the pedagogy of love. In W.J. Letts & J.T. Sears (Eds.), *Queering elementary education: Advancing the dialogue about sexualities and schooling* (pp. 27–36). Lanham, MD: Rowman & Littlefield.

Wilson, D. (2004). The interface of school climate and school connectedness and relationships with aggression and victimization. *Journal of School Health, 74*, 293–299.

Woog, D. (1995). *School's out*. Boston: Alyson.

2
READING THE FIELD

In This Chapter

- Literature and trends in teacher education with a focus on curriculum and instruction, critical reflection, and the development of teacher dispositions.
- Promising emerging research surrounding queer inclusion in teacher education, which leads into a discussion of why addressing queer issues in teacher education is vitally important and long overdue.

Curriculum and Instruction

The marginalization of queerness not only threatens K–12 school environments but higher education institutions as well. Teacher education is particularly vulnerable to muted queer discourse as many educators are reluctant to confront homophobia and heterosexism in schools because it is saturated in controversy and conflict. Research shows that educational systems and teaching practices establish and disseminate discrimination toward queer individuals through the policing of hegemonic discourses of heterosexuality and gender (Britzman, 1997; McClean, 1996).

Multicultural education courses have long been a part of teacher education programs in the United States (King, Hollins, & Hayman, 1997; Ladson-Billings, 1995). Early approaches to acknowledging diversity and comprehending multiculturalism in teacher education stem from the melting pot theories of the 1950s and 1960s: Diversity was recognized and valued, but the ultimate goal was to create a homogeneous society within classrooms where all students were assumed to be equal. As the civil rights movement matured and the nation engaged in postmodern discourse, teacher education began to emphasize the importance of individual identity. Minority students were no longer viewed as interchangeable (Banks, 1997; Grant & Sleeter, 1989), and thus, prospective teachers needed to learn how to meet the needs of an increasingly diverse student population (Banks, 2006).

Current national and state standards, among other diversity and equity values, require teacher preparation programs to prepare candidates who are able to "teach from multicultural and global perspectives that draw on the histories, experiences, and diverse cultural backgrounds of all people" (National Council for Accreditation of Teacher Education [NCATE], 2008, p. 36). The National Council for Accreditation of Teacher Education includes sexual orientation among the forms of diversity that teacher preparation programs must address. Standard 4 states that programs must help candidates "to understand the potential impact of discrimination based on race, class, gender, disability, sexual orientation, and language on students and their learning" (NCATE, p. 37). The Interstate Teacher Assessment and Support Consortium (InTASC) is a group of education stakeholders dedicated to the reform of the preparation and professional development of teachers. InTASC Standard 2 states, "The teacher uses understanding of individual differences and diverse cultures and communities to ensure inclusive learning environments that enable each learner to meet high standards" (Council of Chief State School Officers, 2011, p. 8). Yet despite recent efforts to implement such standards, research reveals that many pre-service teachers enter classrooms with limited awareness of how marginalized youth experience school. Sleeter's 2001 literature review, which examined research on the preparation of teachers for diverse and underserved school settings, provides evidence of this phenomenon. Her work cited a study by Barry and Lechner (1995), who found that although teacher education students thought their coursework increased awareness of cultural diversity, a majority felt unprepared to teach a multicultural curriculum and to effectively interact with diverse students.

Schools across the nation are opening their doors to an increasingly diverse student population. Teacher preparation programs have responded by adding multicultural education curriculum and courses that address a usually narrow understanding of diversity issues (Villegas & Lucas, 2002). A major charge of teacher preparation programs is to develop in future teachers the knowledge, skills, and dispositions that will enable them to work more effectively with students from diverse social and cultural backgrounds; how this goal is achieved varies upon academic scholarship. Bennett (2003), Brown (2004), Gay (2000), and Pang (2001) all agreed that, to be effective, classroom teachers must possess multicultural knowledge, dispositions, and behaviors that respond to issues of student diversity and cross-cultural acceptance. Additional multicultural theorists espoused the idea that classroom teachers must be prepared to recognize biases and advocate for equity (Banks, 1995; Pai, 1990). Howard (2002) and Zeichner (1993) emphasized the importance for future educators to view multicultural education from a global perspective and to learn how to transfer ideas about social justice and equity to students. Advocating for a broader definition, Nieto (2003) contended that multicultural education should permeate all areas of schooling. She argued that it is for all students, encompassing "not only race, ethnicity, and language, but also gender, social class, sexual orientation, ability, and other differences" (p. 17).

According to Cochran-Smith (1995), teachers need to examine personal experiences and tacit assumptions surrounding teaching and learning in order to form their understanding of their roles as teachers. She stated the following:

> In order to learn to teach in a society that is increasingly culturally and linguistically diverse, prospective teachers ... need opportunities to examine much of what is usually unexamined in the tightly braided relationships of language, culture, and power in schools and schooling. This kind of examination inevitably begins with our own histories as human beings and as educators—our own cultural, racial, and linguistic backgrounds and our own experiences as raced, classed, and gendered children, parents, and teachers in the world. It also includes a close look at the tacit assumptions we make about the motivations and behaviors of other children, other parents, and other teachers and about the pedagogies we deem most appropriate for learners who are like us and who are not like us.
>
> (p. 500)

Cochran-Smith's (1995) point of view centered on "the personal" is particularly important when considering queerness because exploring aspects of queer experience requires us to question taken-for-granted assumptions about gender, expression, relationships, and sexual orientation. Her ideas in the quotation also illuminate the larger landscape of assumptions teachers make about children and families, beliefs that are often informed by, and perpetuated through, hetero- and cisnormative school culture.

The diverse perspectives outlined here directly inform approaches for implementing multicultural education in school practice. Based on my review of the literature, two bodies of thought consistently emerged. The first was offered by Sleeter and Grant (Grant & Sleeter, 1993; Sleeter & Grant, 1988), who examined the published literature on multicultural education to determine how researchers, teachers, and academic scholars conceptualized the field. Analysis led them to articulate five common approaches: (a) teaching culturally different students to fit into mainstream society; (b) a human relations approach, which emphasizes diverse individuals living together amicably; (c) the single group studies approach, which focuses on developing awareness, respect, and acceptance for diversity; (d) reducing prejudice and providing equal opportunities for all groups in society; and (e) education that is multicultural and social reconstructionist, which advocates for students to become critical thinkers and social reformers committed to equity. Banks (1995) also contributed to the ways we approach social justice in schools by offering five dimensions to multicultural education: (a) content integration, (b) knowledge construction process, (c) prejudice reduction, (d) equity pedagogy, and (e) empowering school culture and social structure. Banks argued that to implement multicultural education effectively, teachers and administrators must attend to all five approaches.

Given the wide range of literature on the purposes and approaches to multicultural education, it is not surprising that colleges and universities around the nation implement different methods. One common approach is to require teacher candidates to enroll in a stand-alone multicultural or diversity course. Although this forum provides an opportunity for teacher candidates to talk explicitly about issues of diversity, a growing number of teacher educators say that a single course is insufficient to bring about significant changes in future teachers' attitudes, understanding, and practice (Ahlquist, 1992; Brown, 2004; Weisman & Garza, 2002). Despite the variance in programmatic philosophies and methods, one common element does exist: Queer issues are frequently excluded from the multicultural education received by preparing teachers.

Although perspectives focused on inequities related to gender, class, race, ethnicity, and ability have drawn the increased attention of educators and researchers, when it comes to preparing teachers to work effectively with queer youth, there is near silence (Letts, 2002). The scarce research that does exist linking queer issues to teacher education has concentrated on the victimization of queer youth and the creation of safe schools (Epstein, 1994; Letts & Sears, 1999; Woog, 1995). Teacher education textbooks habitually exclude sexual orientation topics and often present queer individuals in ways that reinforce negative stereotypes (Jennings & Macgillivray, 2008). Alternatively put, there has been little focus on influencing the knowledge and beliefs of teacher candidates about queer issues (Blackburn & Donelson, 2004; Butler, 1999; Rofes, 1985; Szalacha, 2004).

In a dissertation, Baldwin (2002) described her examination of teacher candidates' perceptions of current equity practices related to queer issues in teacher preparation. Baldwin administered a 60-item survey to 250 pre-service teachers at three Northwest universities. All participants were completing their final two years of teacher education programs and were currently enrolled in either diversity or social foundations courses. One objective of Baldwin's research was to give teacher candidates an opportunity to assess if and how their program approached queer issues as they related to education. The quantitative data were analyzed by site using descriptive statistics, and written comments were analyzed using content analysis. Of the 208 surveys returned, 72% indicated that their instructors did not use activities that highlighted the importance of educating queer youth. Almost a third of the participants felt there would be resistance from the college if an instructor wanted to include queer issues in a teacher preparation course, and half expressed that students would probably be resistant. When asked if they thought instructors seemed comfortable addressing queer issues in classes, only 44% of the total population said yes. Overall, Baldwin found that current practices used to educate teacher candidates neglect discussions about the lives of LGBT people and fail to emphasize the importance of educating queer youth.

Shifting the focus from teacher candidate to teacher education faculty, Jennings and Sherwin (2008) collected data from 65 public university elementary teacher preparation programs across the nation to find that half (55.6%) addressed sexual orientation topics within official program curricula. This content, however, was largely restricted to foundation courses and rarely resurfaced as the teacher candidates approached practicum and professional practice. The authors concluded that elementary teacher preparation programs "work to sustain homophobic and heterosexist school cultures through the omission of sexual orientation topics, despite the apparent commitment of the field to prepare teachers for diverse schools and communities" (p. 261).

The limited, albeit growing, empirical research from this field of study supports Baldwin's (2002) findings and the claim of Jennings and Sherwin (2008): Relatively little has been done to integrate sexual and gender diversity into teacher education curriculum. Queer issues are seldom reflected in course syllabi (Lipkin, 2002) and rarely make their way into class discussions (Lipkin, 2002; Sears, 2002). Perhaps this is because the climate of higher education—specifically any given department of education—is reported to be rampant with homophobia and heterosexism (Dolan, 1998; Euben, 1999; Hunsicker & Freedley, 2000). Research suggests that queer people often experience negative attitudes, harassment, and violence on college campuses (Eddy & Forney, 2000). D'Augelli (1992) conducted a study to determine the school climate for queer youth on college campuses. He concluded that harassment is a predictable outcome for college students who openly identify as queer. "The many instances of abuse, mistreatment, and violence [on college campuses] provide ample evidence that gay/lesbian affectional status leads to repeat violations of personal dignity, personal choices, and freedom to pursue personal and professional goals" (p. 392).

If and how queerness is addressed in teacher education varies by geography, accreditation and program requirements, the values and knowledge of faculty, and school and community culture. Teacher educators who have attempted to introduce issues of gender and sexual identity into teacher preparation have used a variety of approaches. Lipkin (2002) produced a substantial amount of literature surrounding queer politics, content, and pedagogy in teacher education. He proposed that colleges and graduate courses prepare teacher candidates to do the following (p. 18):

- Understand the significance of LGBT issues in education;
- Teach more comprehensively about the human experience through the integration of LGBT subject matter into the core of learning in a variety of disciplines;
- Promote the psychological and physical health and intellectual development of all students;
- Reduce bigotry, self-hatred, and violence by increasing tolerance for sexual differences;
- Aid communication between LGBT youth and their families and schools;

- Facilitate the integration of LGBT families into the school community;
- Nurture the well-being of faculty, staff, and administrators of all sexual orientations;
- Collaborate with the greater community in achieving these ends.

Lipkin (2002) offered solid approaches to increasing visibility and support for queer youth; however, more concrete strategies are needed to guide comprehensive and long-term inclusion. Care also needs to be taken to adequately differentiate between sexual orientation and gender identity to ensure that both areas are covered accurately and thoroughly.

In the article "Visibility Matters: Policy Work as Activism in Teacher Education," Horn et al. (2010) also offered a synthesis of recommendations for teacher education programs. Their proffers are informed by an investigation centered on the extent to which 57 Illinois teacher education programs pay public (i.e., Internet) attention to LGBTQ issues. They recommended faculty in teacher education do the following (pp. 77–78):

- Make visible the practices in which faculty were already engaging that prepare educators to be knowledgeable about and advocate for LGBTQ youth and their families;
- Ensure that sexual orientation and gender identity are included in all program definitions of diversity;
- Infuse sexual orientation and gender identity topics into multicultural education and diversity courses, child and adolescent development courses, and specific content-area courses, such as English and history methods courses;
- Ensure that conceptual framework and disposition statements include sexual orientation and gender identity;
- Utilize statements from national organizations, such as the National Council for Teachers of English and the American Educational Research Association, to advocate for the inclusion of LGBTQ topics into the teacher preparation curriculum;
- Seek to codify ethical standards of practice, particularly within teacher disposition frameworks, to address conflicts between professional values, personal beliefs, and positions of faith;
- Find allies within the university, as well as within the surrounding community, to help advocate for changes within teacher preparation programs (e.g., students, families, and teachers from local schools; local and state LGBTQ organizations; local and state human rights organizations; teacher and faculty unions);
- Network with other educators and teacher preparation professionals.

As with Lipkin's (2002) list, Horn et al. (2010) envisioned queer inclusion in teacher education as something that permeates the program and includes increased visibility, knowledge, and safety.

A third collection of recommendations for teacher education programs to consider was offered by Petrovic and Rosiek (2007). Drawing from Lipkin (2002), Straut and Sapon-Shevin (2002), Kluth and Colleary (2002), and Kosciw and Diaz (2006), they argued that teachers must be taught to do the following (pp. 209–210):

- Understand the significance and language of LGBT issues in education;
- Teach more comprehensively about the human experience through the integration of LGBT subject matter into the core of learning in a variety of disciplines;
- Promote the psychological and physical health and intellectual development of all students;
- Reduce bigotry, self-hatred, and violence by increasing tolerance for sexuality differences;
- Aid communication between LGBT youth and their families and schools;
- Facilitate the integration of LGBT families into the school community;
- Nurture the well-being and acceptance of faculty, staff, administration, and students of all sexual orientations;
- Collaborate with the greater community in achieving these ends.

Again, as with Lipkin's ideas, Petrovic and Rosiek identified needs of LGBT teachers and students calling explicit attention to sexual orientation, but they failed to differentiate or address the unique needs of transgender and gender-nonconforming persons. However, the list does contribute to a growing record of what teacher education programs should do to increase the visibility and safety of LGB individuals and improve the overall knowledge and awareness of queer culture and identity.

In her article "Considering Transgender People in Education," Rands (2009) argued for a "gender-complex approach" (p. 426) in teacher education whereby teacher educators begin to think about gender in more complex ways, work with future and current teachers to think about gender in more complex ways, and finally, support teacher candidates to actually enact gender-complex education with students. Beginning with her first step, she observed the following:

> For teacher educators to support future teachers in enacting gender-complex education, teacher educators must interrogate their own thinking about gender. Most teacher educators have themselves experienced schooling that is gender stereotyped, gender blind, gender sensitive, or some combination of these. Settings outside of school also most often contribute to gender-stereotyped, gender-blind, and gender-sensitive ways of thinking about gender. Hence, most teacher educators do not think about gender in complex ways.
>
> (p. 427)

Although the body of literature exploring queer inclusion in teacher education is in its infancy, there is growing evidence for its efficacy in preparing teacher candidates to meet the needs of queer students and families. Swartz (2003) used the film *It's Elementary* (Chasoff, 1995) to teach prospective teachers in Appalachia about the ways heterosexuality is normalized. The film, which addresses homophobic prejudice by providing adults with practical lessons on how to talk with kids about queerness, enabled the students in Schwarz's course to "interrogate their prejudices and cultural constructions as well as to think critically about how to introduce such discussions" (p. 53). Her experience of using the film to generate discussion on queer issues among "Appalachians living in socio-economically depressed rural areas and small towns" (p. 52) is chronicled in her ethnographic research.

Athanases and Larrabee (2003) conducted a study of nearly 100 pre-service teachers enrolled in one of three *Cultural Diversity and Education* courses at a large California public state university. The purpose of the study was to examine the process and outcomes of providing prospective teachers with instruction on queer issues as they relate to education. Classroom activities included readings, a video, a guest speaker, discussion, and writings. Written responses of 97 students indicated a lack of knowledge of queer youth prior to instruction and a strong appreciation for new knowledge. Audiotaped interviews with course instructors revealed that students made many links to broader social justice issues.

Payne and Smith (2010, 2011, 2012) conducted research on the first three years of their Reduction of Stigma in Schools (RSIS) program—a professional development initiative that strives to empower educators, through a series of workshops, to create affirming environments for queer youth. In their most recent analysis of the program (2012), the researchers noted that after taking their workshops, teachers embraced a call to understand and protect queer students by engaging in one-time events (e.g., Day of Silence, World AIDS Day) to increase visibility. The authors argued that this superficial coverage falls short and ignores the ways in which schools contribute to the marginalization of queer youth. Based on their findings, Payne and Smith (2012) asserted:

> Teacher education programs need to integrate issues of gender and sexuality throughout their programs of study—with particular attention to how hegemonic gender norms manifest in the policies, practices, and curricula of K–12 education. These social norms are fundamental to how schools envision the "successful" student, reward achievement, practice classroom management, and execute countless other seemingly mundane institutional procedures.
>
> *(p. 283)*

Larrabee and Morehead (2010) wrote "Broadening Views of Social Justice and Teacher Leadership: Addressing LGB Issues in Teacher Education," which concerns teacher leaders attending to homophobia in classrooms as part of a social justice component in their teacher education programs. Their findings support those of Payne and Smith (2010, 2011, 2012) as well as of Athanases and Larrabee (2003): Teacher candidates want to learn more about queer issues and to acknowledge their lack of awareness of the insensitive remarks or actions of their own students in the classroom.

When considering how to achieve these objectives, faculty members of teacher education programs may want to think about the essential questions posed in the article, "The Invisible Minority: Preparing Teachers to Meet the Needs of Gay and Lesbian Youth." In this article, Mathison (1998) identified questions related to teacher educators' responsibility in preparing teacher candidates to work with queer youth. These questions included, "What teacher behaviors most alienate queer students? What negative messages does the school/classroom communicate? What messages does the curriculum send?" (p. 152). The questions, and the complex issues they raise, can challenge teacher educators not only to look at the underlying principles of their program, but also to wrestle with and make sense of the mystifying phenomena encountered in K–12 schools. As described here, the process by which teachers engage in thought and discourse models another common aim of teacher education, which is to engage teachers in the development of ongoing and meaningful reflection.

Critical Reflection

In addition to entertaining a variety of ideological definitions of multicultural education, teacher education also employs a vast conceptualization of teacher reflection. According to Dewey (1933, 1938), reflection is the process of stepping back and analyzing a puzzling situation or experience. He envisioned reflection used by educators in a holistic way that encourages teachers to think about and respond to everyday problems experienced in schools. Schön (1983) coined the term *reflective practice*, which involves an individual considering his or her own experiences in applying knowledge to practice while at the same time receiving guidance from professionals in the field. Schön also contributed the distinction between *reflection-on-action* and *reflection-in-action*. In teaching, reflection-on-action consists of the thought that leads to lesson design and instructional planning (i.e., theory) whereas reflection-in-action occurs as teachers respond to students and adjust instruction (i.e., practice). Both instances engage educators in a cycle of using knowledge and information from their setting to inform practice. Zeichner and Liston (1996) noted, however, that two essential components of reflection are omitted from Schön's conception. In their book, *Reflective Teaching: An Introduction*, Zeichner and Liston highlighted the important roles that communication and context play in the process of reflection, noting that dialogue with school stakeholders and expanding reflection beyond classroom walls can lead to deeper meaning and a broader understanding of teaching and learning.

A thorough review of literature prompted Grimmett, Erickson, Mackinnon, and Riecken (1990) to describe three distinct perspectives on reflection. The first, reflection as instrumental mediation of action, conceptualizes the use of knowledge to direct practice. The second, reflection as deliberating among competing views of teaching, emerged from a group of studies that highlighted the importance of context, deliberation, and choice among competing views of effective practice. Finally, according to their review of the literature, Grimmett et al. (1990) proposed reflection as reconstructing experience, which considers reflective action as the reconstruction of experience. Within this third perspective, perplexing experiences and subsequent reflection can lead to new or reconceptualized meaning found in situations or within teachers themselves. The metaphor of reflection as reconstruction includes "taken-for-granted assumptions about teaching" (p. 31), which the authors offered as a means by which critical theory can be practiced.

The critical approach to reflective practice views schools as cultural and political organizations that help reproduce a capitalistic society based on unjust social relations (Giroux & McLaren, 1986; Valli, 1990). Or as Beyer (1984) wrote:

> Rather than seeing the school as an essentially apolitical and meritocratic institution, which provides for social and economic mobility by giving students a fair chance at enjoying the wealth and advantages of our society, these critical investigations have sought to uncover the ideological dimensions of aspects of school life.
>
> *(p. 37)*

In their article on dealing with lesbian and gay issues in teacher education, Robinson and Ferfolja (2001) noted that through the process of critical reflection, students conceptualize, analyze, and theorize the construction of their own subjectivity including the bidirectional effects of discrimination in which we experience both benefits and burdens. "Exploring and understanding the construction of one's own subjectivity is, as Davies (1994) suggests, critical to teachers and students in order to see its effects on us and on the learning environments that we collaboratively produce" (p. 123).

Mezirow (1998, 2000) defined critical reflection by making an important distinction. He noted that reflection does not necessarily involve making an assessment of what is being reflected upon. Critical reflection, however, involves a learning process of "becoming critically aware of one's own tacit assumptions and expectations and those of others and assessing their relevance for making an interpretation" (p. 4). According to Mezirow (1998), this type of reflection can lead to psychological, convictional, and behavioral transformation.

Offering his contribution to the field of critical reflection, Brookfield (1988) identified four activities that he believed essential: assumption analysis, contextual awareness, imaginative speculation, and reflective skepticism. The first step in the critical reflection process, assumption analysis, involves thinking in a way that challenges personal beliefs, values, cultural practices, and social structures in order to assess their impact on daily life. Second, contextual awareness consists of realizing that assumptions are personally and socially constructed and embedded within historical and cultural context. The third activity, imaginative speculation, includes thinking about phenomena and imagining alternative or challenging ways of knowing. Finally, according to Brookfield, reflective skepticism is the act of suspending universal truths and constantly questioning the status quo.

Whether employing Brookfield's (1988) methodology or through other means, using a critical approach enables teachers to reflect upon and perhaps alter the circumstances of their schools that benefit some student populations (e.g., cisgender, gender-conforming, and straight students) while limiting experiences and opportunities for others (e.g., queer students). This link between reflection and practice was noted by Valli (1990), who observed, "The primary goal of teacher preparation is to assist prospective teachers in understanding ways in which schools might be contributing to an unjust society for the purpose of engaging in emancipatory action" (p. 46).

Moss (2001) conducted a study rooted in critical theory that examined student reflection in a graduate-level multicultural education course. The 15 participants were asked to engage in group activities that required them to take on different cultural viewpoints. The mixed-methods study used survey, interview, and personal narrative data to determine what kind of critical pedagogical development had occurred in the teacher candidates. Several patterns emerged.

> Most of the participants were critically impacted during one or more of the learning activities in a way that resulted in a broader perspective and critical self-reflection with regard to their teaching practices ... the changed practices reflect critical pedagogy because the practices are culturally sensitive and empower students and their families to have a greater participation in the educational process.
>
> *(Moss, 2001, p. 9)*

The findings illustrated that critical reflection can be used to raise cultural awareness and foster transformational learning (Mezirow, 1998) among teacher candidates. Representative of other literature in the field, Moss's study (2001) described how one course can provide space and structure for teachers to move beyond the acquisition of new knowledge into reflection that questions personal and societal assumptions, values, and perspectives. By restructuring the existing curriculum, the instructor provided opportunities for students to engage in meaningful activities and discourse. Support and guidance were provided to learners as they processed phenomena, and this, in part, was documented as having led students toward a more critical disposition.

Teacher Dispositions

Reflection and growth surrounding disposition is also apparent in teacher education. In fact, an essential aim of teacher preparation programs is to develop in teacher candidates the knowledge, skills, and dispositions necessary to meet the needs of diverse learners (NCATE, 2008). A large body of research has demonstrated that educators' beliefs and tendencies, indeed their dispositions, determine what is and what is not important in their practice (Charlesworth, Hart, Burts, & Hernandez, 1990; Clark, 1988; Cole, 1989; Dewey, 1933). *Disposition* here includes our personal beliefs as well as our "attitudes, values, interests, self-concept, and motivation" (Stiggins, 2001, p. 101). In other words, our disposition is composed of our core qualities, beliefs, and actions.

NCATE (2008) defined *dispositions* as the "professional attitudes, values, and beliefs demonstrated through both verbal and non-verbal behaviors as educators interact with students, families, colleagues, and communities" (pp. 89–90). Further, NCATE argued that "these positive behaviors support student learning and development" (p. 90) and that teacher preparation programs need to assess professional dispositions in educational settings.

The charge for teacher education programs to help develop and assess professional dispositions is particularly important around issues of social justice and specifically vital when it comes to queerness. Some educators maintain that personal dispositions and even societal values do not interfere with providing support and education to students. Yet it has been found that students' race, class, gender, and sexual orientation can have an impact on how they are perceived by peers and evaluated by teachers (Bochenek, Brown, & Human Rights Watch, 2001; Harbeck, 1992; Kosciw, Diaz, & Greytak, 2008). Classroom teachers, historically, often have negative attitudes toward queer individuals (Blackburn & Donelson, 2004; Butler & Byrne, 1992; Morgan, 2003; Roffman, 2000; Sears, 1992; Szalacha, 2004; Taylor, 2001). This aversion to queerness is particularly alarming given the powerful influence dispositions have on a teacher's performance. Nespor (1987) proposed that dispositions have a stronger affective and evaluative component than knowledge and that they often operate independently of cognition. Thus, regardless of teacher awareness or intent, personal dispositions can significantly influence classroom behavior and practice.

What's more, students are acutely aware of teachers' dispositions and stereotyped beliefs. A study by Rosenbloom and Way (2004) found that Latino and African American students perceived their teachers as racist or discriminatory. Interviews and participant observation revealed that students perceived teachers as uncaring and ineffective as a result of perceived low academic expectations and stereotypes about behavior problems relating to race. Petrovic and Rosiek (2007) examined the kind of practical knowledge needed by teachers to respond to the needs of queer students. Their analysis showed that this knowledge goes beyond knowing about their students. "It also requires teachers to have a critical knowledge of themselves—an understanding of their own thoughts, feelings, and values as the product of historical and cultural processes of which they may not be fully aware" (pp. 202–203).

Sears (1992) articulated further ways that educators' beliefs and behaviors influence classroom teaching and learning, specifically drawing attention to dispositions toward sexual diversity.

> It is an educator who chooses how to teach the prescribed sexuality curriculum; it is the educator who challenges or winks at homophobic comments or jokes among students; it is the educator who comforts or ignores a student suffering from heterosexist tirades of peers or doubts about their sexual identity; it is the educator who fosters dialogue among fellow professionals about the penalties all pay in a heterosexual mandated society.
>
> (p. 61)

Sears reminds us that teaching often comes down to the art of decision making. In the hearts and minds of queer youth, overt and subtle choices about if, when, and how to respond to homophobia and transphobia can have a profound impact on how students perceive their teacher, their school, and themselves.

It has been argued that teacher dispositions can be transparently communicated to students and influence classroom practice. It has also been demonstrated that NCATE and other professional organizations value the development and evaluation of teacher disposition in order to support teacher candidates and ensure effective learning. To increase the likelihood that educators have a positive impact on queer youth, scholars have examined how to assess educators' dispositions toward queerness.

Several of the instruments currently available to assess individuals' disposition toward queer people and culture were developed in the 1980s. Some scales use a very small number of items (e.g., Nyberg & Alston, 1976) while other instruments are longer (e.g., Leitner & Cado, 1982; Smith, 1971). Differences also occur in defining what types of questionnaire items measure attitudes toward queerness. Some researchers asked only questions concerning the sexual act itself or the individual's desire to participate in a homosexual act (e.g., Smith, Resick, & Kilpatrick, 1980; Young & Whertvine, 1982). Others have focused on whether homosexuality is morally wrong (e.g., Glenn & Weaver, 1979; Nyberg & Alston, 1976). Hudson and Ricketts (1980) measured only the desire to associate with queers.

The Internalized Homophobia (IHP) scale (Meyer, 1995) and the Attitudes Toward Lesbians and Gay Men (ATLG) scale (Herek, 1994) are prominent assessment instruments. Data collected from these instruments over the past few decades has suggested that heterosexual males consistently hold more negative attitudes toward queers and homosexuality than do heterosexual females (Clift, 1988; Herek, 1988); males' attitudes are more negative toward gay men than they are toward lesbians; and negative attitudes toward homosexuals correlate with traditional attitudes about gender and family roles, strong devotion to an orthodox religion, and past negative experiences with queer people (Clift, 1988; Herek, 1984, 1988; Nyberg & Alston, 1976).

A thorough review of the literature produced limited research that specifically examined teacher candidate dispositions toward queerness. Sears (1992) examined pre-service teachers' knowledge about, and disposition toward, homosexuality. He found that 80% of the prospective teachers surveyed held negative feelings toward queer people. Of this sample population, one-third was considered highly homophobic. Interestingly, Sears's research reported that the more knowledge teacher candidates had about homosexuality, the less the likely they were to harbor negative dispositions toward queerness.

Butler (1994) and Petrovic and Rosiek (2003) conducted separate studies to examine prospective teachers' attitudes toward homosexuality and their willingness to discuss the topic as future teachers. Both studies yielded similar results: Pre-service teachers demonstrated a lack of knowledge about homosexuality, slightly homophobic attitudes, and an unwillingness to include queer issues in their future classrooms. In response, Butler suggested that teacher candidates engage in cognitive activities to experience transformational knowledge (e.g., lecture, discussion, audiovisuals, and assigned readings) as well as affective pursuits that focus more on feelings, attitudes, and emotions (e.g., speaker panels, role-plays, simulations, small-group discussions, and case studies). Petrovic and Rosiek (2007) claimed that pre-service teachers need opportunities to rework their habits of subjectivity. They asserted that through a dialectical process involving authentic interaction, adult learners can transform homophobic attitudes.

> Only by engaging pre-service teachers in dialogue about LGB issues that address the malignant silences, as well as the explicitly espoused bigotry in their thinking about the issues, will we have teachers who can provide spaces for LGB youth and their families to flourish in schools.
>
> *(p. 168)*

Sadowski's (2010) article, "Core Values and the Identity-Supportive Classroom: Setting LGBTQ Issues Within Wider Frameworks for Preservice Educators," focuses on the core values that teacher candidates bring to teaching and then incorporates research about queer youth and school-related issues. His approach places queer issues within larger ideals that reflect generally agreed-upon beliefs about public schooling (e.g., all children have a right to learn, all students have the right to feel safe at school). Thus, he incorporates queer students and issues into the overall curriculum rather than focusing on them as separate from mainstream, heteronormative discourse. His inclusive approach is supported by Payne and Smith's (2010, 2011, 2012) research, described earlier, on the professional responsibility of teacher educators to deconstruct the hidden curriculum of heteronormativity.

Although a substantial absence exists in the literature on teacher candidates' beliefs about queer students and issues, the research that is available concludes that many prospective teachers hold homophobic and transphobic dispositions. Given the impact disposition can have on teaching and learning outcomes, further research is needed to determine how teacher candidates' dispositions, as well as those of experienced teachers, affect queer youth.

Conclusion

The three bodies of literature explored in this chapter are vast. For decades, scholars have examined and documented teacher preparation programs: if and how they infuse multicultural education, reflective practice, and the development of teacher dispositions. Although literature on queer youth in education, as we saw in Chapter 1, has a shorter history, the burgeoning evidence of risk factors for this population warrants further research. Yet there has been little effort to combine these multiple fields of study.

An essential aim of teacher education programs is to develop in teachers the knowledge, skills, and dispositions necessary to meet the needs of diverse learners. There is also ah historical trend within most teacher preparation programs to address issues around student diversity in a multicultural education course. Thus, it is logical to see how a course that intentionally provides opportunities for teacher candidates to gain accurate knowledge about queer issues and culture, for example, can help them understand, relate to, and support queer youth. But knowledge alone is not enough. Teacher preparation programs need to equip teacher education students with the skills needed to implement a queer-inclusive pedagogy and interact meaningfully with queer colleagues, students, and families.

In addition to knowledge and skills, teacher candidates need support in developing professional dispositions toward queerness. A self-awareness of their own disposition can help teacher candidates confront queer issues in school even in the presence of self-conflicting ideological beliefs. For instance, a teacher who opposes gay marriage yet is able to reflect upon this disposition as it relates to his or her professional work among same-sex families and queer youth may be more likely to interrupt homophobic name-calling at school even if the teacher internally tolerates the hateful language.

Lastly, teacher candidates must be taught how to engage in ongoing critical reflection. The Queer Inclusion in Education Framework described in the next chapter demonstrates that teacher educators should facilitate the process of learning to analyze, reconsider, and question experiences within a broad context of issues. I believe that teacher candidates able to critically reflect on knowledge, skills, and personal dispositions related to queerness will prompt social action to emancipate knowledge and affirm diverse ways of being. Engaging in this form of praxis (Freire, 1970) will prepare them to disrupt hetero- and cisnormativity as K–12 educators and provide increased support for queer youth.

Reflection Questions

1. Did your teacher preparation program include sexual orientation and gender identity in its curriculum?
2. What were your experiences with multicultural education as a teacher candidate? What were some of the highlights and shortcomings of the curriculum, instruction, and overall learning experience?
3. How would you describe your professional dispositions? In other words, what values, commitments, and ethics guide your work as an educator? What is your current disposition toward queerness as it relates to teaching and learning?
4. How do you see curriculum and instruction, reflection, and teacher dispositions interrelated? How might contemplating a response to this question help you in assessing your current effectiveness in working with queer youth?

Recommended Resources

Books and Articles About Multicultural Education

Banks, J. (2013). The construction and historical development of multicultural education, 1962–2012. *Theory into Practice, 52*(1), 73–82.

Banks, J.A., & McGee-Banks, C.A. (2012). *Multicultural education: Issues and perspectives.* Hoboken, NJ: Wiley.

Bennett, C.I., (2010). *Comprehensive multicultural education theory and practice.* Upper Saddle River, NJ: Pearson.

Grant, C.A., & Sleeter, C.E. (2010). *Doing multicultural education for achievement and equity.* New York: Routledge.

Ladson-Billings, G.J. (1995). But that's just good teaching! The case for culturally relevant pedagogy. *Theory into Practice, 34,* 159–165.

Sleeter, C.E. (1996). Multicultural education as a social movement. *Theory into Practice, 35,* 239–247.

Books and Articles About Critical Reflection

Grimmett, P.P., Erickson, G.L., Mackinnon, A.M., & Riecken, T.J. (1990). Reflective practice in teacher education. In R.T. Clift, W.R. Houston, & M.C. Pugach (Eds.), *Encouraging reflective practice in education: An analysis of issues and programs* (pp. 20–38). New York: Teachers College Press.

Mary, R. (2013). The pedagogical balancing act: Teaching reflection in higher education. *Teaching in Higher Education, 18*(2), 144–155.

Mezirow, J. (1998). On critical reflection. *Adult Education, 48*(3), 185–198.
Mezirow, J. (2000). *Learning as transformation: Critical perspectives on a theory in progress.* San Francisco, CA: Jossey-Bass.
Schön, D. (1983). *The reflective practitioner.* New York: Basic Books.
Zeichner, K.M., & Liston, D.P. (1996). *Reflective teaching: An introduction.* Mahwah, NJ: Lawrence Erlbaum.

Books and Articles About Dispositions

Blackburn, M.V., & Donelson, R. (2004). Sexual identities and schooling [Special issue]. *Theory into Practice, 43*(2), 99–101.
Diez, M.E., & Raths, J. (2007). *Dispositions in teacher education.* Charlotte, NC: Information Age.
Murrell, P.C., Jr., Diez, M., Feiman-Nemser, S., & Schussler, D.L. (2010). *Teaching as a moral practice: Defining, developing, and assessing professional dispositions in teacher education.* Cambridge, MA: Harvard Education Press.
Sadowski, M. (2010). Core values and the identity-supportive classroom: Setting LGBTQ issues within wider frameworks for preservice educators. *Issues in Teacher Education, 19*(2), 53–63.
Sears, J. (1992). Educators, homosexuality, and homosexual students: Are personal feelings related to professional beliefs? In K. Harbeck (Ed.), *Coming out of the classroom closet: Gay and lesbian students, teachers and curriculum* (pp. 29–79). New York: Haworth Press.

References

Ahlquist, R. (1992). Manifestations for inequity: Overcoming resistance in a multicultural foundations course. In C.A. Grant (Ed.), *Research & multicultural education: From the margins to the mainstream* (pp. 89–105). Bristol, PA: Taylor & Francis.
Athanases, S.Z., & Larrabee, T.G. (2003). Toward a consistent stance in teaching for equity: Learning to advocate for lesbian- and gay-identified youth. *Teaching and Teacher Education, 19,* 237–261.
Baldwin, E.S. (2002). *Lesbian, gay, bisexual, and transgender equity issues: A study of preservice teachers' perceptions of current practices in teacher education.* Unpublished doctoral dissertation, Washington State University, Pullman, WA.
Banks, J. (1995). Multicultural education: Historical development, dimensions, and practice. In J.A. Banks & C.A. McGee Banks (Eds.), *Handbook of research on multicultural education* (pp. 3–24). New York: Simon and Schuster Macmillan.
Banks, J. (1997). *Teaching strategies for ethnic studies* (6th ed.). Boston: Allyn & Bacon.
Banks, J. (2006). *Cultural diversity and education: Foundations, curriculum, and teaching* (5th ed.). Boston: Pearson Education.
Barry, N.H., & Lechner J.V. (1995). Preservice teachers' attitudes about and awareness of multicultural teaching and learning. *Teaching & Teacher Education, 11*(2), 149–161.
Bennett, C. (2003). *Comprehensive multicultural education: Theory and practice* (5th ed.). Needham Heights, MA: Allyn & Bacon.
Beyer, L.E. (1984). Field experience, ideology, and the development of critical reflectivity. *Journal of Teacher Education, 35*(3), 36–41.
Blackburn, M.V., & Donelson, R. (2004). Sexual identities and schooling [Special issue]. *Theory into Practice, 43*(2), 99–101.

Bochenek, M., Brown, A.W., & Human Rights Watch. (2001). *Hatred in the hallways: Violence and discrimination against lesbian, gay, bisexual, and transgender students in U.S. schools*. New York: Human Rights Watch.

Britzman, D.P. (1997). What is this thing called love? New discourses for understanding gay and lesbian youth. In S. de Castell & M. Bryson (Eds.), *Radical interventions: Identity, politics, and differences in educational praxis* (pp. 183–207). Albany: State University of New York Press.

Brookfield, S. (1988). Developing critically reflective practitioners: A rationale for training educators of adults. In S. Brookfield (Ed.), *Training educators of adults: The theory and practice of graduate adult education*. New York: Routledge.

Brown, E.L. (2004). Relationship of self-concepts to changes in cultural diversity awareness: Implications for teacher educators. *Urban Review, 36*(2), 119–145.

Butler, K.L. (1994). *Prospective teachers' knowledge, attitudes, and behavior regarding gay men and lesbians*. (ERIC Document Reproduction Service No. ED379251)

Butler, K.L. (1999). Preservice teachers' knowledge and attitudes regarding gay men and lesbians. *Journal of Health Education, 30*(2), 125–129.

Butler, K., & Byrne, T. (1992). Homophobia among pre-service elementary teachers. *Journal of Health Education, 23*(6), 355–359.

Charlesworth, R., Hart, C.H., Burts, D.C., & Hernandez, S. (1990, April). *Kindergarten teachers' beliefs and practices*. Paper presented at the annual meeting of the American Educational Research Association (AERA), Boston, MA.

Chasoff, D. (Producer/Director). (1995). *It's elementary: Talking about gay issues in school* [DVD]. New York: Women's Educational Media.

Clark, C.M. (1988). Asking the right questions about teacher preparation: Contributions of research on teaching thinking. *Educational Researcher, 17*(2), 5–12.

Clift, S.M. (1988). Lesbian and gay issues in education: A study of the attitudes of first-year students in a college of higher education. *British Educational Research Journal, 14*(1), 31–50.

Cochran-Smith, M. (1995). Color blindness and basket making are not the answers: Confronting the dilemmas of race, culture, and language diversity in teacher education. *American Educational Research Journal, 32*(3), 493–522.

Cole, A.L. (1989, April). *Making explicit implicit theories of teaching: Starting points in preservice programs*. Paper presented at the Annual Meeting of the American Educational Research Association (AERA), San Francisco, CA.

Council of Chief State School Officers. (2011, April). *Interstate Teacher Assessment and Support Consortium (InTASC) model core teaching standards: A resource for state dialogue*. Washington, DC: Author.

D'Augelli, A.R. (1992). Lesbian and gay male undergraduates' experiences of harassment and fear on campus. *Journal of Interpersonal Violence, 7*, 383–395.

Davies, B. (1994). *Poststructuralist theory and classroom practice*. Geelong, Australia: Deakin University Press.

Dewey, J. (1933). *How we think*. Lexington, MA: D.C. Health.

Dewey, J. (1938). *Logic: The theory of inquiry*. New York: Holt, Rinehart and Winston.

Dolan, J. (1998). Gay and lesbian professors out on campus. *Academe, 84*(5), 40–45.

Eddy, W., & Forney, D.S. (2000). Assessing campus environments for the lesbian, gay and bisexual population. In V.A. Wall & N.J. Evans (Eds.), *Toward acceptance: Sexual orientation issues on campus* (pp. 131–154). Lanham, MD: University Press of America.

Epstein, D. (1994). *Challenging lesbian and gay inequalities in education*. Buckingham, UK: Open University Press.

Euben, D. (1999). Domestic partnerships benefits for faculty. *Academe, 85*(2), 111.

Freire, P. (1970). *Pedagogy of the oppressed*. New York: Continuum.

Gay, G. (2000). *Culturally responsive teaching: Theory, research and practice*. New York: Teachers College Press.

Giroux, H., & McLaren, P. (1986). Teacher education and politics of engagement: The case for democratic schooling. *Harvard Educational Review, 56*(3), 213–238.

Glenn, N.D., & Weaver, C.N. (1979). Attitudes toward premarital, extramarital and homosexual relations in the U.S. in the 1970s. *Journal of Sex Research, 15*, 108–118.

Grant, C.A., & Sleeter, C. (1989). *Turning on learning: Five approaches for multicultural teaching plans for race, class, gender, and disability*. New York: Macmillan.

Grant, C.A., & Sleeter, C.E. (1993). Race, class, gender, exceptionality, and educational reform. In G.A. Banks and C.M. Banks (Eds.), *Multicultural education: Issues and perspectives* (2nd ed., pp. 48–68). Boston: Allyn & Bacon.

Grimmett, P.P., Erickson, G.L., Mackinnon, A.M., & Riecken, T.J. (1990). Reflective practice in teacher education. In R.T. Clift, W.R. Houston, & M.C. Pugach (Eds.), *Encouraging reflective practice in education: An analysis of issues and programs* (pp. 20–38). New York: Teachers College Press.

Harbeck, K.M. (1992). *Coming out of the classroom closet: Gay and lesbian students, teachers and curricula*. New York: Harrington Park Press.

Herek, G.M. (1984). Beyond "homophobia": A social psychological perspective on attitudes toward lesbians and gay men. *Journal of Homosexuality, 10*(1/2), 1–21.

Herek, G.M. (1988). Heterosexuals' attitudes toward lesbians and gay men: Correlates and gender differences. *Journal of Sex Research, 25*(4), 451–477.

Herek, G.M. (1994). Assessing heterosexuals' attitudes toward lesbians and gay men: A review of empirical research with the ATLG scale. In B. Greene & G.M. Herek (Eds.), *Lesbian and gay psychology: Theory, research, and clinical applications* (pp. 206–228). Thousand Oaks, CA: Sage.

Horn, S.S., Konkol, P., McInerney, K., Meiners, E.R., North, C., Nuñez, I., . . . Sullivan, S. (2010). Visibility matters: Policy work as activism in teacher education. *Issues in Teacher Education, 19*(2), 65–80.

Howard, J. (2002). Technology-enhanced project-based learning in teacher education: Addressing the goals of transfer. *Journal of Technology and Teacher Education, 10*(3), 343–364.

Hudson, W.W., & Ricketts, W.A. (1980). A strategy for the measurement of homophobia. *Journal of Homosexuality, 5*, 357–371.

Hunsicker, J., & Freedley, J. (2000). Significant labor and employment law issues in higher education during the past decade and what to look for now. *Journal of Law and Education, 29*(3), 343–351.

Jennings, T., & Macgillivray, I.K. (2008, March). *A content analysis of LGBT topics in multicultural education textbooks*. Paper presented at the Annual Meeting of the American Educational Research Association, New York.

Jennings, T., & Sherwin, G. (2008). Sexual orientation topics in elementary preparation programs in the USA. *Teaching Education, 19*(4), 261–278.

King, J.E., Hollins, E.R., & Hayman, W.C. (Eds.). (1997). *Preparing teachers for cultural diversity*. New York: Teachers College Press.

Kluth, P., & Colleary, K. (2002). Talking about inclusion like it's for everyone: Sexual diversity and the inclusive schooling movement. In R.M. Kissen (Ed.), *Getting ready for Benjamin: Preparing teachers for sexual diversity in the classroom* (pp. 105–118). Lanham, MD: Rowman & Littlefield.

Kosciw, J.G., & Diaz, E.M. (2006). *The 2005 National School Climate Survey: The experiences of lesbian, gay, bisexual and transgender youth in our nation's schools.* New York: GLSEN.

Kosciw, J.G., Diaz, E.M., & Greytak, E.A. (2008). *2007 National School Climate Survey: The experiences of lesbian, gay, bisexual and transgender youth in our nation's schools.* New York: GLSEN.

Ladson-Billings, G. (1995). Multicultural teacher education: Research, practice, and policy. In J. Banks & C. Banks (Eds.), *Handbook of research on multicultural education* (pp. 747–759). New York: Macmillan.

Larrabee, T.G., & Morehead, P. (2010). Broadening views of social justice and teacher leadership: Addressing LGB issues in teacher education. *Issues in Teacher Education, 19*(2), 37–53.

Leitner, L.M., & Cado. S. (1982). Personal constructs and homosexual stress. *Journal of Personality and Social Psychology, 43,* 869–872.

Letts, W.J. (2002). Revisioning multiculturalism in teacher education: Isn't it queer? In R.M. Kissen (Ed.), *Getting ready for Benjamin: Preparing teachers for sexual diversity in the classroom* (pp. 119–131). Lanham, MD: Rowman & Littlefield.

Letts, W.J., & Sears, J.T. (Eds.). (1999). *Queering elementary education: Advancing the dialogue about sexualities and schooling.* Lanham, MD: Rowman & Littlefield.

Lipkin, A. (2002). The challenges of gay topics in teacher education: Politics, content, and pedagogy. In R.M. Kissen (Ed.), *Getting ready for Benjamin: Preparing teachers for sexual diversity in the classroom* (pp. 13–27). Lanham, MD: Rowman & Littlefield.

Mathison, C. (1998). The invisible minority: Preparing teachers to meet the needs of gay and lesbian youth. *Journal of Teacher Education, 49*(2), 151–155.

McClean, C. (1996). Men, masculinity and heterosexuality. In L. Laskey & C. Beavis (Eds.), *Schooling and sexualities: Teaching for a positive sexuality.* Victoria, Australia: Deakin Centre for Education and Change.

Meyer, I.H. (1995). Minority stress and mental health in gay men. *Journal of Health and Social Behavior, 36,* 38–56.

Mezirow, J. (1998). On critical reflection. *Adult Education, 48*(3), 185–198.

Mezirow, J. (2000). *Learning as transformation: Critical perspectives on a theory in progress.* San Francisco, CA: Jossey-Bass.

Morgan, D. (2003). *Knowledge and attitudes of pre-service teachers towards students who are gay, lesbian, bisexual and transgendered.* Unpublished doctoral dissertation, University of North Texas, Denton, TX.

Moss, G. (2001). Critical pedagogy: Translation for education that is multicultural. *Multicultural Education, 9*(11), 2–11.

National Council for Accreditation of Teacher Education (NCATE). (2008). *Professional standards accreditation of teacher preparation institutions.* Retrieved from www.ncate.org/public/standards.asp

Nespor, J. (1987). The role of beliefs in the practice of teaching. *Journal of Curriculum Studies, 19,* 317–328.

Nieto, S. (2003). *What keeps teachers going?* New York: Teachers College Press.

Nyberg, K.L., & Alston, J.P. (1976). Analysis of public attitudes toward homosexual behavior. *Journal of Homosexuality, 2,* 99–107.

Pai, Y. (1990). *Cultural foundations of education.* New York: Merrill.

Pang, V.O. (2001). *Multicultural education: A caring-centered, reflective approach.* New York: McGraw-Hill.

Payne, E., & Smith, M. (2010). Reduction of stigma in schools: An evaluation of the first three years. *Issues in Teacher Education, 19*(2), 11–36.

Payne, E., & Smith, M. (2011). The reduction of stigma in schools: A new professional development model for empowering educators to support LGBTQ students. *Journal of LGBTQ Youth, 8*(2), 174–200.

Payne, E.C., & Smith, M.J. (2012). Safety, celebration, and risk: Educator responses to LGBTQ professional development. *Teaching Education, 23*(3), 265–285.

Petrovic, J. E., & Rosiek, J. (2003). Disrupting the heteronormative subjectivities of Christian pre-service teachers: A Dewyan prolegomenon. *Equity & Excellence in Education, 36*(2), 161–169.

Petrovic, J.E., & Rosiek, J. (2007). From teacher knowledge to queered teacher knowledge research: Escaping the epistemic straight jacket. In N.M. Rodriguez & W.F. Pinar (Eds.), *Queering straight teachers* (pp. 201–231). New York: Peter Lang.

Rands, K.E. (2009). Considering transgender people in education: A gender-complex approach. *Journal of Teacher Education, 60*(4), 419–431.

Robinson, K., & Ferfolja, T. (2001). "What are we doing this for?" Dealing with lesbian and gay issues in teacher education. *British Journal of Sociology of Education, 22*(1), 121–133.

Rofes, E. (1985). *Socrates, Plato and guys like me: Confessions for a gay schoolteacher.* Boston: Alyson.

Roffman, D.M. (2000). A model for helping schools address policy options regarding gay and lesbian youth. *Journal of Sex Education & Therapy, 25*(2/3), 130–136.

Rosenbloom, S.R., & Way, N. (2004). Experiences of discrimination among African American, Asian American, and Latino adolescents in an urban high school. *Youth and Society, 35,* 420–451.

Sadowski, M. (2010). Core values and the identity-supportive classroom: Setting LGBTQ issues within wider frameworks for preservice educators. *Issues in Teacher Education, 19*(2), 53–63.

Schön, D. (1983). *The reflective practitioner.* New York: Basic Books.

Sears, J. (1992). Educators, homosexuality, and homosexual students: Are personal feelings related to professional beliefs? In K. Harbeck (Ed.), *Coming out of the classroom closet: Gay and lesbian students, teachers and curriculum* (pp. 29–79). New York: Haworth Press.

Sears, J.T. (2002). The institutional climate for lesbian, gay and bisexual education faculty: What is the pivotal frame of reference? *Journal of Homosexuality, 43*(1), 11–37.

Sleeter, C.E. (2001). Preparing teachers for culturally diverse schools: Research and the overwhelming presence of whiteness. *Journal of Teacher Education, 52*(2), 94–106.

Sleeter, C.E., & Grant, C.A. (1988). *Making choices for multicultural education: Five approaches to race, class, and gender.* Columbus, OH: Merrill.

Smith, A.D., Resick, P.A., & Kilpatrick, D.G. (1980). Relationships among gender, sex-role attitudes, sexual attitudes, thoughts and behavior. *Psychological Reports, 46,* 359–367.

Smith, K. (1971). Homophobia: A tentative personality profile. *Psychological Reports, 29,* 1091–1094.

Stiggins, R. (2001). *Student-involved classroom assessment* (3rd ed.). Upper Saddle River, NJ: Merrill Prentice-Hall.

Straut, D., & Sapon-Shevin, M. (2002). But no one in the class is gay: Countering invisibility and creating allies in teacher education programs. In R.M. Kissen (Ed.), *Getting ready for Benjamin: Preparing teachers for sexual diversity in the classroom* (pp. 29–41). Lanham, MD: Rowman & Littlefield.

Swartz, P.C. (2003). It's elementary in Appalachia: Helping prospective teachers and their students understand sexuality and gender. *Journal of Gay & Lesbian Issues in Education, 1*(1), 51–71.

Szalacha, L. (2004). Educating teachers on LGBTQ issues: A review of research and program evaluations. *Journal of Gay and Lesbian Issues in Education, 1*(4), 67–79.

Taylor, P. (2001, April). *Good news and bad news: A comparison of teacher educators' and preservice teachers' beliefs about diversity issues.* Paper presented at the Annual Meeting of the American Educational Research Association, Seattle, WA. (ERIC Document Reproduction Service No. ED454216)

Valli, L. (1990). Moral approaches to reflective practice. In R.T. Clift, W.R. Houston, & M.C. Pugach (Eds.), *Encouraging reflective practice in education: An analysis of issues and programs* (pp. 39–56). New York: Teachers College Press.

Villegas, A.M., & Lucas, T. (2002). *Educating culturally responsive teachers: A coherent approach.* Albany, NY: SUNY.

Weisman, E.M., & Garza, A. (2002). Preservice teacher attitudes toward diversity: Can one class make a difference? *Equity & Excellence in Education, 35*(1), 28–34.

Woog, D. (1995). *School's out.* Boston: Alyson.

Young, N.L., & Whertvine, J. (1982). Attitudes of heterosexual students toward homosexual behavior. *Psychological Reports, 51,* 673–674.

Zeichner, K. (1993). Connecting genuine teacher development to the struggle for social justice. *Journal of Education for Teaching, 19*(1), 5–20.

Zeichner, K.M., & Liston, D.P. (1996). *Reflective teaching: An introduction.* Mahwah, NJ: Lawrence Erlbaum.

3
THEORY AND QUEER INCLUSION IN EDUCATION FRAMEWORK

In This Chapter

- The importance of theory and how it can be used to make deeper sense of phenomona.
- The interconnection between critical social theory and queer theory as both are lenses for interpreting and understanding the research described in Chapters 5 and 6.
- A Queer Inclusion in Education Framework proposing an intentional and explicit presence of queer content and pedagogy in education by equipping teachers with the knowledge, skills, and dispositions necessary for implementing inclusive practices that interrupt hetero- and cisnormative discourses.

Critical Social Theory

At its broadest, theory is a strand of principles and ideas used to explain something. For educators and researchers, theory provides a reference point to transmit underlying assumptions, values, and beliefs about nature, knowledge, and reality. In other words, theory offers a framework for discussing phenomena and making sense of the world. From a critical standpoint, theory creates the conditions necessary for marginalized groups to engage in debate and to voice and construct a transformed reality.

This research is informed by investigations into the extent to which current education is inclusive of queer issues. How much do educational institutions develop, implement, and respond to curricula, instruction, discourse, and policies that reflect an intentional recognition and inclusion of queer identity and culture? In the current literature, three major categories surface that describe educational approaches to queer issues of safety (e.g., verbal and physical harassment against queer students, anti-bullying policies), issues of equity (e.g., gay-straight alliance clubs, gender-neutral bathrooms), and critical social theory (Szalacha, 2004).

As a theoretical framework, critical social theory offers a way to analyze "the social" as a construction that is molded and influenced by context, beliefs, and the power maintained within dominant groups (Grace, 2005). McLaren and Giarelli (1995), in their introduction to *Critical Theory and Educational Research*, observed:

> Critical theory is, at its center, an effort to join empirical investigation, the task of interpretation, and a critique of this reality. Its purpose is to reassert the basic aim of the Enlightenment ideal of inquiry; to improve human existence by viewing knowledge for its emancipatory or repressive potential.
>
> *(p. 2)*

In education, critical social theory provides a lens for discussing democratic forms of schooling, social justice, and ethical educational practices. It also encourages educators to critique practices that normalize stereotypical gender roles, cisgenderism, and heterosexuality. Allman (1999) argued that critical social theory helps us consider how education can play a pivotal role in transforming a society through political and cultural action. By building students' knowledge and understanding of why and how queer individuals have been marginalized, schools can begin to question and perhaps transform their practices to reflect a more critical pedagogy. In other words, theory can aid us in understanding our own and students' understanding of homophobia and the prevailing rigid gender binary and help them question and alter contemporary contexts. Thus, critical social theory provides a lens to investigate how education, a societal institution influenced by social and political ideology, legitimates particular ways of being (McLaren, 2003).

Although it would be appropriate to recognize Dewey (see Sirotnik & Oakes, 1986) as an early influence on the development of critical social theory in education, the enormous influence of Brazilian educator Paulo Freire cannot be overstated. Freire drew from a wide variety of thinkers including Fanon, Memmi, Fromm, Gramsci, Dewey, and Althusser (Austin, 1999; Mayo, 1999); however, he was clearly a man of his time and context.

Critical social theory holds basic assumptions about the distribution of power and privilege in society and seeks to expose bias to change the world (Kincheloe & McLaren, 1994). On the surface, critical social theory can be described as possessing three core components: criticism, dialogical engagement, and transformative action. Within a classroom, critical social theory is marked by a critical discourse in which students are encouraged to question and challenge institutional conditions, particularly those deemed oppressive. Leonardo (2004) noted:

> Critical social theory is an intellectual form that puts criticism at the center of its knowledge production. Theory criticism, [critical social theory] pushes ideas and frameworks to their limits, usually by highlighting their

contradictions. In quality education, criticism functions to cultivate students' ability to question, deconstruct, and then reconstruct knowledge in the interest of emancipation.

(p. 12)

In "Critical Social Theory and Transformative Knowledge," Leonardo (2004) cautioned readers to view criticism as a vehicle for intellectual engagement rather than "a form of refutation or an exercise in rejection" (p. 12). Thus, criticism should invite conversation and engage thinking rather than be passively dismissed or unquestionably accepted. In the context of education, conflict leads to creativity when students are provided opportunities to learn important skills centered on posing and responding to critical questions about the world and when they have access to knowledge and discourses on social inequalities and oppression.

As understood by critical theorists, it is fundamental that individuals understand that knowledge is not neutral; rather it is constructed in relation to power and social dimensions. Critical educators internalize this by acknowledging their responsibility to teach students to encounter and interpret text, images, and dialogue critically, with an awareness of cultural codes and social messaging.

A second component of critical social theory is dialogic engagement. Freire (1970) proposed a dialogic view of the creation of knowledge, that learning is a conversation among individuals. In between these people is the cognizable object, the thing known. As they engage in dialogue about this thing, it becomes clearer. In his words, "Dialogue is the encounter between [people], mediated by the world, in order to name the world" (p. 88).

In contrast with a "banking" model whereby students are perceived as passive learners whom teachers deposit knowledge into, critical dialogic engagement is composed of a richer, student-centered dialogue to promote deliberation. Through the process of long and careful discussion, students do a self-inventory and critique ways of thinking. Dialogic theorists (e.g., Giroux, Bourdieu, and Freire) emphasize the importance of language as a theoretical and political practice. Participating in exchanges that highlight multiple viewpoints enables students to understand diverse frames of reference. The assumptions and interpretations of *all* participants are reviewed and can be openly challenged. Within such a learning community, students relate to others and are transformed but without necessarily sacrificing their individuality. Oppositional paradigms create new languages that can be used to challenge unjust and oppressive systems and provoke action toward emancipation.

Critical dialogic engagement opens doors for transformative action, the third component of critical social theory; however, people cannot change social reality through dialogue alone. Simply surfacing alternative narratives will not guarantee social change. As Feldman (2000) offered, "Stories alone are not enough, for effective stories need 'already willing listeners' . . . [they rely] upon a willingness on the part of the audience to participate, to be changed, or at least to acquiesce to the telling" (p. 559). Still, critical social theory adjures a language of transcendence and possibility. By this I mean that operating under a critical social perspective requires us to dream up alternative ways of being in this world. A critical social theory stance in education illuminates the social struggles of some to examine oppression and must also reimagine circumstances to alleviate oppression and create a more socially just and equitable society.

For example, teacher educators initiate dialogue among teacher candidates that places the ways in which gender is policed and taught in the K–5 classroom in the center of the conversation. The candidates (who already universally acknowledge that individuals are informed by their unique sets of knowledge, beliefs, values, and experiences) engage in critical discourse to illustrate their independent realities. The teacher educators are there to offer literature, images, and other support that reflect social and cultural ideology. They also provide anti-oppressive frameworks and sociohistorical context that helps the teacher candidates understand the issue. Open and honest dialogue, as well as meaningful critique, is encouraged. Concrete action is translated directly out of this personal reflection and collective discourse; teacher candidates articulate three things they will do in their field placement classroom as a result of their conversation, or the cohort works together to determine a larger, more universal project they could implement to attain gender equality and gender fluidity in K–5 classrooms. The cycle of critique and action described here is praxis, which, combined with queer theory, is capable of shifting belief systems about reality and the nature of disrupting power.

Queer Theory

Critical social theory has greatly influenced queer theory, and the two share many of the same concerns: oppression, domination, power, resistance, and social change (Sears, 2005). Although they are considered two distinct theories, both focus on challenging unethical public practices and dismantling social hierarchies.

Many complex and nuanced definitions of queer theory exist. Plummer (2005) argued that defining *queer theory* is problematic because individuals interpret the word *queer* various ways. To demonstrate his point, he cited six different interpretations of *queer* suggested by Doty (2000), all of which have different implications for the construction of queer theory.

> Sometimes it is used simply as a synonym for lesbian, gay, bisexual, and transgender (LGBT). Sometimes it is an "umbrella term" that puts together a range of so-called "non-straight positions." Sometimes it simply describes non-normative expression of gender (which could include straight). Sometimes it is used to describe "non-straight things" not clearly signposted as lesbian, gay, bisexual, and transgender but that bring with them a possibility for such reading, even if incoherently. Sometimes it locates the

"non-straight" work, positions, pleasures, and readings of people who don't share the same sexual orientation as the text they are producing or responding to. Taking it further, Doty suggests that 'queer' may be a particular form of cultural readership and textual coding that creates spaces not contained within conventional categories such as gay, straight, bisexual, and transgendered. Interestingly, what all his meanings have in common is that they are in some way descriptive of texts and they are in some way linked to (usually transgressing) categories of gender and sexuality.

(Plummer, 2005, p. 365)

While these six variations promote important discussion around ways that queer individuals are defined, understood, and represented, other theorists have provided alternative perspectives on queer and queer theory. Pinar (1998) defined queer as separate and distinct from labels such as *gay* or *lesbian*. Queer is a fluid term that is used to disrupt assumptions and deconstruct how named sexualities are internalized and perceived. For Pinar, queer is a term that complicates the binary between gay and straight and reconfigures assumptions of identity through reclaiming the word *queer*, which once was pejorative. Queer theory, according to Pinar, "challenges the reproduction of sameness, of indifference, of patriarchy" (p. 13). Within the classroom, queer theory is a framework that allows educators to see individual students rather than categories. Applying queer theory, "we work overtime to teach tolerance, to teach the truth, to try to find ways to decenter, destabilize, and deconstruct the heterosexist normalizations that so essentialize many of the students we teach" (Pinar, 1998, p. 44).

Other theorists (Morris, 1998; Shlasko, 2005) argued that *queer* transcends language and should be defined by the subject position, politic, and aesthetic of an individual or group. Capturing this perspective on queer theory in his dissertation research, Rummell (2013) noted:

> The subject position involves one's location in reference to the norms of society. Individuals that identify as queer have undergone a tension between what is considered normal within dominant societal standards and have become part of the *Other*, usually as a result of their sexuality or gender identity. This identification shapes and defines their subjective location and understanding of the norms of society. As a politic, queer challenges the very idea of normal and promotes an assertion that disrupts the constructed norms which have marginalized and oppressed. These assertions may seek to break down socially constructed barriers that protect and police the boundaries between normal and *Other*. The third part of this definition, the aesthetic, refers to the seeking of "subversive content in cultural texts of any media, from academic research papers to television advertisements to graffiti" (Shlasko, [2005], p. 124). Through these three components, queer moves

> beyond the umbrella term for individuals that identify as either gay, lesbian, bisexual, transgender, intersex, or same-gender loving and into a collective group that asserts, challenges, and redefines what it means to be normal or different through seeking to visibly represent their presence, ultimately subverting the assumed norms of society (Shlasko, [2005]).
>
> *(p. 82)*

Applying this understanding of *queer*, queer theory offers a comprehensive lens for examining the tension between normal and *Other*, an analysis of and from the viewpoint of people who are marginalized or *Othered* based on gender and sexual orientation.

A majority of queer theorists use critical social theory and feminism as scaffolding to create structures that transgress postmodern discourse. For example, Butler's seminal text *Gender Trouble* (1990) and Sedgwick's (1990) *Epistemology of the Closet* position gender as a social construct. In their unique ways, both authors drew necessary lines between gender and desire by highlighting the regulatory function of gender that privileges heterosexuals. From an asset perspective, Butler and Sedgwick contributed discourse on how the deconstruction of normative images of gender can ultimately affirm queerness. Sullivan (2003) observed that queer theory, "as a deconstructive strategy, aims to denaturalize heteronormative understandings of sex, gender, sexuality, sociality, and the relations between them" (p. 81). Indeed, queer theory calls into question the hegemonic forces that restrict and mandate sex, gender, and desire. It falsifies the notion of any "normal" or "natural" sexuality or gender performance and reframes binaries that have structured contemporary culture into heterosexual and nonheterosexual, male and female. Public schools, as a microcosm of larger society, can use such notions of queer theory to reexamine hetero- and cisnormative practices. Schools can also look toward other frameworks for challenging oppression in schools.

In his book *Troubling Education*, prominent queer theorist Kumashiro (2002) offered four approaches to challenging oppression in schools: "education for the *Other*, education about the *Other*, education that is critical of privileging and *Othering*, and education that changes students and society" (p. 31). As these words imply, the first approach focuses on bettering the school experience for the *Other*, such as creating a safe space for queer students. Yet Kumashiro was quick to point out that this approach fails to address the destructive hold that oppression has on privileged students (i.e., students who identify or pass as gender conforming and heterosexual). So while queer students might have access to a safe environment, this approach falls short in dealing head-on with students who are (consciously or not) actively participating in the oppression of others. The second approach, education about the *Other*, runs the risk of perpetuating stereotypes and myths about the *Other*. The third approach, education that is critical of privileging and *Othering*, recognizes that schools are not socially and politically neutral; rather, they privilege specific groups and identities in society while disenfranchising others. Although this third approach encourages the critique and transformation of oppression, Kumashiro acknowledged that oppression is a broad construct and cannot be defined universally. He also admitted that this particular approach has the potential to harm students who are traditionally marginalized in society.

Kumashiro (2002) advocated for the final approach to challenge oppression in schools: education that changes students and society. Here, his poststructuralist conceptualization of oppression recognizes that oppression is produced by particular repeated discourse that privileges one group and marginalizes the *Other*. Power resides in the utterance of such language, often manifested in stereotypes, but also in the history of how the language has been used within particular contexts and communities. Kumashiro pointed to the need to rectify curricula that embodies oppressive knowledge and to "include differences in ways that change the underlying story and the implications of the story for thinking, identifying, and acting in oppressive and/or anti-oppressive ways" (p. 59). Finally, referencing Britzman's (1998) work, Kumashiro cited the need to have students work through crisis and rethink who they are by seeing the *Other* as an equal.

Kumashiro's (2002) anti-oppressive approaches invite educators to examine multiple pedagogical practices and to imagine teaching critical content involving both critique and transformation. It is an application of queer and critical social theories that further articulates a world in which queer identities are validated in the classroom and queer oppression is emancipated. It is also a model with theoretical underpinnings that informed the framework here for queer inclusion in education.

Kumashiro (2002) observed, "Researchers and scholars have argued that understanding oppression requires examining more than one's dispositions toward, treatment of, and knowledge about the *Other*" (p. 44). He mentioned the need for educators and students to consider how some groups and identities are *Othered* and some groups are privileged in society. In recognizing this duality, Kumashiro stressed that we must acknowledge the social structures and competing ideologies at play. Citing Stambach (1999), he noted, "Schools, after all, are part of society, and understanding oppression in schools requires examining the relationship between schools and other social institutions and cultural ideas" (p. 44).

The intersection of critical social theory and queer theory as applied to the research studies described in Chapters 5 and 6 informs a classroom-based discourse capable of cultivating our ability as teachers to critique hetero- and cisnormativity. Extending beyond discourse, these theories promote a language of transcendence and social action that can lead to transforming the ways in which educational institutions (pre-K–21) categorize and teach sex, gender, and sexual orientation.

It is critical to understand how teacher candidates experience the phenomena of sexual diversity and nonconforming gender identification and expression in the field. Chapter 5 describes a research study that I conducted to reveal teacher candidates' encounters and sense-making with such phenomena. This led to a three-year participatory action research study (described in Chapter 6) focused on working with faculty to improve a teacher preparation program to better meet the needs of queer teacher candidates and K–12 youth. However, it is important to first describe my Queer Inclusion in Education Framework.

Queer Inclusion in Education Framework

The Queer Inclusion in Education Framework (see Appendix B) begins with an acknowledgement of the overarching structures (i.e., politics, culture, and ideology) that influence education. Participants in the two studies mentioned earlier (teacher candidates and teacher educators, respectively) constantly negotiated and reflected on the politics (e.g., norms, operations, interrelations) of the university as well as the K–12 schools where the candidates conducted their student teaching. As a (queer) researcher and newly appointed faculty member, I was also deeply entangled in the political structure, negotiating my observations and experience. I maintained a heightened awareness of teacher educators and K–12 administrators and staff who were supportive of me examining how gender and sexual orientation surfaced in their institutions, and I kept an even closer eye on those who were unconcerned with or skeptical of my investigation.

Roles within the teacher preparation program (and interpretations of the two studies themselves) are also influenced by culture. Chapter 5 describes some teacher candidates' fear to embrace their true identities in the field because they perceive the school culture as homophobic, unsupportive, or even threatening. These individuals withhold and safeguard personal information—for example, avoiding the pronoun *we* when describing weekend plans with colleagues to avoid questions about partnership.

Ideology, a set of ideas that constitutes goals, expectations, and actions, comes into play in Chapter 6 when teacher educators voice a desire for professional development on queer issues; this request is often immediately overshadowed by a hesitancy upon considering the university's commitment to fostering K–12 school partnerships (i.e., K–12 schools that partner with the university to explore ways to improve professional preparation and development of teachers and often host teacher candidates in the field). In other words, faculty wanted to learn ways to become more inclusive of queerness in the college classroom, but they feared this would clash with K–12 school value systems and jeopardize existing and potential partnerships. As one faculty member put it:

> This is so complex! It raises issues about relationships across institutions: [Graduate School of Education], school districts, schools, and families. I feel like it is risky for us to advocate for LGBTQ students because we are still establishing partnerships. This leaves us a bit voiceless on this stuff.
>
> (Estella, personal communication, May 10, 2010)

Understanding and challenging the marginalization of queer students requires looking not only at phobias and normative language and behaviors, but also at institutional authority and curricular ideologies that favor straight and cisgender identities. It is important to acknowledge the presence and influence of an overarching political, cultural, and ideological landscape, which motivates and persuades educational stakeholders. The Queer Inclusion in Education Framework suggests that recognition of these, however, is not enough. Critical social theorists would argue a need to penetrate the outer ring of influence to consider what individual programs can, and should, do to equip teacher educators and teacher candidates with the knowledge, dispositions, and skills necessary to implement queer-inclusive practices. The studies presented in Part 2 found that K–12 students indeed experience sexual and gender diversity (and at times, oppression) that is seldom addressed in their schools. Thus, it is logical to propose a course, or several courses, within a professional teacher education program that intentionally provides opportunities for teacher candidates to gain accurate knowledge, skills, and dispositions around queer issues, identity, history, and culture. As illustrated in Appendix B, a precursor to offering these learning experiences to teacher candidates is to facilitate teacher educators in working toward queer inclusion by means of curriculum and instruction. Chapter 6 disseminates research about a faculty that experienced this undertaking to develop the necessary knowledge, skills, and dispositions (with built-in opportunities for critical reflection and identity negotiation) to support queer teacher candidates and include queer content and pedagogy in their instruction.

Transforming hetero- and cisnormative practices in teacher education can lead to teacher candidates working toward queer inclusion. As illustrated in the framework, reproducing learning experiences that teacher educators incur for teacher candidates can help prospective teachers acquire the necessary knowledge (e.g., queer-inclusive terms, laws and policies, available resources) to adopt a queer-inclusive pedagogy. However, as illustrated in the framework and confirmed by the literature, knowledge alone is not enough (Bennett, 2003; Brown, 2004; Gay, 2000; Pang, 2001). Because the topic of sexual and gender diversity can be contentious in education, particularly elementary education (DePalma & Atkinson, 2009; Sears, 1999), it is important for teacher educators to develop professional dispositions toward queerness in candidates. A self-awareness of dispositions can help teachers confront queer dilemmas in education.

Teacher educators need to provide opportunities for queer exposure and reflection, such as in-class panel discussions, reflective writing, and case studies. Increased knowledge and deeply developed dispositions will cause teachers to yearn for practical skills (e.g., using inclusive language, increased ability to recognize and interrupt hetero- and cissexist practices as well as homo- and transphobic language and behaviors) so that they may interact with queer colleagues, students, and families in an authentic way.

Finally, the Queer Inclusion in Education Framework implies that all stakeholders must be taught how to engage in ongoing critical reflection as they develop knowledge, skills, and dispositions centered on queerness. Consequently, teacher educators need to facilitate the process of learning to analyze, reconsider, and question their own knowledge and experiences with heterosexism, homophobia, cissexism, and transphobia. This process undoubtedly influences self-awareness and further negotiates individual identity. As the upcoming research findings reveal, teachers who critically reflect on knowledge, skills, and personal dispositions related to queerness are prompted toward social action to liberate knowledge and validate diverse ways of being. All stakeholders engaged in this form of praxis articulated a sense of preparedness, willingness, and desire to disrupt hetero- and cisnormativity as educators and to provide increased support for queer students.

Reflection Questions

1. What does it look and feel like to teach from a critical social theorist's perspective?
2. How can teachers use queer theory to create inclusive and accepting learning environments for all students and families?
3. Compare critical social theory and queer theory. Where do the two schools of thought intersect, and where do they disjoin?
4. What is your interpretation of the Queer Inclusion in Education Framework (see Appendix B)? Which element, or pathway, do you feel most comfortable implementing? Which do you feel least comfortable implementing and why?

Recommended Resources

Books and Articles on Critical Social Theory

Freire, P. (1970). *Pedagogy of the oppressed*. New York: Continuum.
Kincheloe, J.L. (2008). *Critical pedagogy*. New York: Peter Lang.
McLaren, P.L., & Giarelli, J.M. (1995). *Critical theory and educational research*. Albany: State University of New York Press.
Szalacha, L.A. (2004). Educating teachers on LGBTQ issues: A review of research and program evaluations. *Journal of Gay & Lesbian Issues in Education*, 1(4), 67–79.

Books and Articles on Queer Theory

Britzman, D.P. (1998). *Lost subjects, contested objects: Toward a psychoanalytic inquiry of learning*. Albany: State University of New York Press.
Butler, J. (1990). *Gender trouble: Feminism and the subversion of identity*. New York: Routledge.
Jagose, A. (1997). *Queer theory: An introduction*. New York: New York University Press.
Kumashiro, K. (2002). *Troubling education: Queer activism and antioppressive pedagogy*. New York: Routledge.
Pinar, W.F. (1998). *Queer theory in education*. Mahwah, NJ: Erlbaum.
Sedgwick, E.K. (1990). *Epistemology of the closet*. Berkeley: University of California Press.

References

Allman, P. (1999). *Revolutionary social transformation: Democratic hopes, political possibilities and critical education.* Westport, CT: Bergin and Garvey.

Austin, R. (1999). Popular history and popular education: El consejo de educación de adultos de America Latina (The advisory board for adult education of Latin America). *Latin American Perspectives, 26*(4), 39–68.

Bennett, C. (2003). *Comprehensive multicultural education: Theory and practice* (5th ed.). Needham Heights, MA: Allyn & Bacon.

Britzman, D.P. (1998). *Lost subjects, contested objects: Toward a psychoanalytic inquiry of learning.* Albany: State University of New York Press.

Brown, E.L. (2004). Relationship of self-concepts to changes in cultural diversity awareness: Implications for teacher educators. *Urban Review, 36*(2), 119–145.

Butler, J. (1990). *Gender trouble: Feminism and the subversion of identity.* New York: Routledge.

DePalma, R., & Atkinson, E. (Eds.). (2009). *Interrogating heteronormativity in primary schools: The No Outsiders Project.* Oakhill, VA: Trentham.

Doty, A. (2000). *Flaming classics: Queering the film canon.* London, UK: Routledge.

Feldman, A. (2000). Othering knowledge and unknowing law: Oppositional narratives in the struggle for American Indian religious freedom. *Social & Legal Studies, 9*(4), 557–582.

Freire, P. (1970). *Pedagogy of the oppressed.* New York: Continuum.

Gay, G. (2000). *Culturally responsive teaching: Theory, research and practice.* New York: Teachers College Press.

Grace, A.P. (2005). Critical social theory. In J. Sears (Ed.), *Youth, education, and sexualities: An international encyclopedia, Vol. 1* (pp. 218–222). Westport, CT: Greenwood Press.

Kincheloe, J.L., & McLaren, P.L. (1994). Rethinking critical theory and qualitative research. In N. Denzin & Y.S. Lincoln (Eds.). *The handbook of qualitative research* (pp. 138–157). Thousand Oaks, CA: Sage.

Kumashiro, K. (2002). *Troubling education: Queer activism and anti-oppressive pedagogy.* New York: Routledge.

Leonardo, Z. (2004). Critical social theory and transformative knowledge: The functions of criticism in quality education. *Educational Researcher, 33*(6), 11–18.

Mayo, P. (1999). *Gramsci, Freire, and adult education.* London, UK: Zed Books.

McLaren, P. (2003). *Life in schools: An introduction to critical pedagogy in the foundations of education* (4th ed.). New York: Allyn and Bacon.

McLaren, P.L., & Giarelli, J.M. (1995). *Critical theory and educational research.* Albany: State University of New York Press.

Morris, M. (1998). Understanding the curriculum: Queer projects, queer imaginings. In W.F. Pinar (Ed.), *Queer theory in education.* Mahwah, NJ: Erlbaum.

Pang, V.O. (2001). *Multicultural education: A caring-centered, reflective approach.* New York: McGraw-Hill.

Pinar, W.F. (1998). *Queer theory in education.* Mahwah, NJ: Lawrence Erlbaum.

Plummer, K. (2005). Critical humanism and queer theory: Living with tensions. In N.K. Denzin & Y.S. Lincoln (Eds.), *The handbook of qualitative research.* Thousand Oaks, CA: Sage.

Rummell, C. (2013). *A unique support for sexual-minority identity development: An interpretative phenomenological analysis of a long-term formal mentoring relationship between an adult and a youth from the gay community.* Unpublished doctoral dissertation, Portland State University, Portland, OR.

Sears, J. (2005). *Youth, education, and sexualities: An international encyclopedia.* Westport, CT: Greenwood.

Sears, J.T. (1999). Teaching queerly: Some elementary propositions. In W.J. Letts & J.T. Sears (Eds.), *Queering elementary education: Advancing the dialogue about sexualities and schooling* (pp. 3–14). Lanham, MD: Rowman & Littlefield.

Sedgwick, E.K. (1990). *Epistemology of the closet*. Berkeley: University of California Press.

Shlasko, G.D. (2005). Queer (v.) pedagogy. *Equity and Excellence in Education, 38*, 123–134.

Sirotnik, K., & Oakes, J. (1986). Critical inquiry for school renewal: Liberating theory and practice. In K. Sirotnik & J. Oakes (Eds.), *Critical perspectives on the organization and improvement of schooling* (pp. 3–93). Boston: Kluwer-Nijhoff.

Stambach, A. (1999). Gender-bending anthropological studies of education. *Anthropology and Education Quarterly, 30*(4), 441–445.

Sullivan, N. (2003). *A critical introduction to queer theory*. Edinburgh, UK: Edinburgh University Press.

Szalacha, L.A. (2004). Educating teachers on LGBTQ issues: A review of research and program evaluations. *Journal of Gay & Lesbian Issues in Education, 1*(4), 67–79.

PART II
Field Research and Visibility

4
TEACHING WITH INTEGRITY

In This Chapter
- My story of self-negotiation and claiming a queer identity in academia.
- A broader commentary about vocation and honoring the "person in the profession" (Intrator & Kunzman, 2006, p. 16) in the process of teaching and learning to teach.

My Story

The subsequent two chapters illuminate my arrival as a queer researcher, activist, and educator. My journey in acquiring these roles, however, began much earlier and includes turbulent life events that have shaped who I am. I often wonder what my life would be like if I were in a different profession or if I were straight. How does my identity as a queer woman shape my performance as an educator and my interactions and relationships with students? What would it feel like to be forced back into the closet? What is it like for current educators who want to share core aspects of themselves (including queerness) with their students but don't out of fear?

I am a white woman in my early 30s. I was raised in a rural, agricultural town in western Oregon and had a happy childhood. I thrived in high school, serving as yearbook and newspaper editors and student body activities manager. I also competed in varsity tennis and volleyball, founded a club called S.T.O.P. (Students Together Opposing Prejudice), and, ironically, was crowned prom queen my senior year. I had a consistent boyfriend throughout high school and into college, a man who remains my dear friend today. After a few more flings with other men, I dated my first woman, Jen. I wasn't expecting it and truthfully had never actively questioned my sexual orientation. Growing up, sexuality was not talked about; I, and everyone else, was assumed to be heterosexual, and I did not even know what a lesbian was until I was 11 and my parents told me my aunt was one. I remember feeling confused and automatically thinking she was a different person. These feelings subsided as my thinking matured; still, I never sensed the innate desire to be with a woman . . . at least not at that point.

Then I met Jen. I was a full-time college student and also worked as a salon receptionist. As clichéd as it may be, my best friend, a gay hair stylist, convinced me to accompany him to a gay bar. He ushered Jen over after noticing that she was "giving me the eye," and she bought me a drink as we began to flirt. Over the course of the next two months, while I dated Jen, I began searching for words to describe the shift. I examined my childhood experiences and tendencies to see if there were inclinations of queerness; I deconstructed past relationships to ascertain symptoms of unhappiness and fraudulence. Today I find solace in understanding my sexual identity as a complex and ever-evolving relationship between the biological and the phenomenological. Or as Sumara and Davis (1999) described it:

> One's sexuality is always structured by the various narratives and experiences of gender, race, ethnicity, access to resources, physical capacities, and so on. At the same time, one's experienced sexuality, in part, functions to restructure those things that participate in its own creation. Experiencing same-sex attraction or opposite-sex attraction—or both—or neither—is both informed by and informs one's perceptions, identification and representation practices, and interpretations.
>
> *(p. 196)*

Despite having liberal and loving parents, I fell short of finding the right words and opportunity to tell them. I was terrified of coming out to my sister and wondered if she would have the same reaction we had shared a decade earlier when we learned our aunt was gay. When I finally surrendered the words "I think I might be a lesbian," my family responded with curiosity, support, and unconditional love. I am very fortunate.

Like any lousy movie or book plot, my relationship with Jen was underdeveloped and anticlimactic. Two months into it, I came to the realization that we were incompatible, and because I fall within the category of people who are psychologically terrified of breaking up with others, I applauded my past-tense self for applying to the Peace Corps a year prior. Thus, two weeks after graduating from my teacher preparation program (and breaking up with Jen), I boarded a plane to South Africa. From 2003–2005, I lived with a host family and worked in the village of Mutwatwasi as a community resource and education volunteer in the Limpopo province.

I discovered South Africa to be an extremely complex place. It is a nation of surreal contradiction, between urban and rural, wealth and poverty, between the beauty of racial and tribal diversity and wholesale prejudice against entire classes of race and gender. Race permeated everything. I discovered strong feelings about racial inequality as I experienced the discomfort of owning white privilege in a nation that still transparently and violently oppresses black Africans. I took advantage of every opportunity to be social and meet people, to interact with others and to assimilate. In private I was also processing my sexual identity. *Matipa* or "gay people" in the local language, Northern Sotho, were invisible in my village. Because I was the only white person who had ever lived in my village, I resided in a fish bowl and was not about to outwardly question my sexual orientation or embrace the lesbian identity I was so close to owning.

When I returned to the United States, I landed my first job teaching in a K–5 public school. My position was split between being an English language development (ELD) specialist and a mainstream kindergarten teacher. During my first year, my grade-level team decided they wanted to launch a family unit. Dissatisfied with the lack of family diversity represented in children's literature at the time, I created my own "big book" that provided illustrations and narrative on all types of families (e.g., same-sex parents, single-parent families, families who adopt). When I read this story to my five- and six-year-olds, they were mesmerized by the idea that a child could have two moms. They asked open and honest questions. I had anticipated some of these questions and had prepared age-appropriate responses that I felt were just and necessary. Bianca asked, "So a mom and a mom can love each other?" "Yes," I said, "there are many same-sex parents all over the world." Danny pointed to the family portrait of two women standing behind their three children and in broken English he said, "Teacher, you mean they kiss each other, the two moms?" "Well, what do you think?" I asked. Bianca, who had grown increasingly vocal, responded, "Yeah probably, they love each other just like my mom and dad . . . and they kiss." I concluded the lesson confident that I had presented a counter-narrative that is necessary in today's heteronormative society. I facilitated dialogue that hopefully expanded students' perception of this world and helped them redefine *family* in a way that more accurately reflects the world we live in. I remember thinking: This is what it feels like to confront critical content.

The next day Bianca's angry mother stormed into my classroom. "I raise my children as good Christians, and in our house we do not talk about homosexuality. Bianca told me you talked about gays yesterday, and that is not okay with me!" I listened to her and fought the urge to be or appear defensive. I tried to provide Bianca's mom with more context and explain my job as a public school educator as one that requires I teach children about the world they live in. I often recount this experience when queer and straight ally teacher candidates approach me asking for assistance in navigating these murky waters. I am the first to admit I don't have all the answers, but I always engage in the conversation.

Two years after my encounter with Bianca's mom, I hit another crossroads in my teaching career. As I mentioned, in addition to teaching kindergarten I served as an ELD specialist. During my third year at the school, I returned from spring break with an engagement ring on my finger. My students noticed right away and bombarded me with questions ("What is his name? What does he do? How did you meet him?"). Now, some people might argue that these questions are too personal and that responding to them at all is inappropriate, but heterosexuals do it all the time, void of inner dialogue questioning job security, parent/community backlash, humiliation, and rejection. I wanted to share the truth with my students. I wanted to say, "Her name is Bethany, she is an ER nurse, and we met at a coffee shop." For me, sharing these things communicated to my students that I was a real person who trusted them and wanted to share my life with them in hopes that they would invest time and effort in sharing their lives with me. For years I witnessed straight colleagues do this ostensibly with ease to the point where it naturalized their ways of being and situated mine as divergent. The unchallenged prevalence of heterosexuality—the sheer lack of openness about other sexualities—made me feel different and excluded.

I negotiated this public/private polarity as many queer educators do. Despite an overwhelming desire to tell students my truth, I held my tongue. I dodged their questions as long as I could, and after weeks of redirection (children are persistent), I walked into my principal's office and asked if I could tell my fifth graders the truth, that I was engaged to an incredible woman. I sensed in her voice and facial expression that it pained her to resign herself to the two-letter word. She explained that such a move would require her to tend to the phones for a week straight dealing with outraged and concerned parents. "I'm very happy for you and your engagement, but I want to protect you from what might happen if you tell your students," she said. I left her office ashamed I had even asked. Emotional pain is not static, but our memory of it is. Once I memorized the sensation of shame and restriction—its location and the meaning I gave it—I began responding to its "history" rather than what it *was* in the moment. I hated my principal and my job. I began to resent my students. That shame turned to anger, and that anger turned to action. I finished out the academic year and then enrolled full-time in the doctoral program at Portland State University (PSU). I immediately started researching queer issues in education that led me to defend my dissertation in 2011. I simultaneously began teaching as a fixed-term faculty member in the Graduate School of Education and juggling the invigorating and crucial work of the Curriculum and Instruction (CI) LGBTQ Task Force.

As traces of my story convey, I have taught from the closet, which forced me to hide a core aspect of my being. In contrast, under different circumstances at PSU, I was awakened by the opportunity to teach in an environment that recognized and embraced my queer identity. I was, for the first time in a professional setting, openly and unapologetically queer, and I believe it is this authenticity that currently sustains me in my vocation.

Identity, Integrity, and the Sense of Vocation

Hansen (1995) described *vocation* as the crossroads of public obligation and lasting personal fulfillment. This means that a sense of vocation can be achieved through work that is personally meaningful and of value to society. The Latin root of vocation, *vocare*, means "to call," denoting an individual being summoned into service. Although the term is frequently affiliated with religious commitments, a growing number of scholars (Danielowicz, 2001; Hansen, 1995; Huebner, 1999; Palmer, 1998, 2007) have considered the process of learning to teach as identity development and described this journey as acquiring a sense of vocation.

But how does identity influence our sense of vocation? To explore this connection, we must first look at the construct of identity. In *The Courage to Teach*, Palmer (1998) defined *identity* thus:

> An evolving nexus where all the forces that constitute my life converge in the mystery of self: My genetic makeup, the nature of the man and woman who gave me life, the culture in which I was raised, people who have sustained me and people who have done me harm, the good and ill I have done to others and to myself, the experience of love and suffering—and much, much more. In the midst of that complex field, identity is a moving intersection of the inner and outer forces that make me who I am, converging in the irreducible mystery of being human.
>
> *(p. 13)*

Identity, then, is fluid and constantly negotiated. My sense of self does not exist in a vacuum; rather, it is shaped and reshaped in relation to others. When my principal denied my request to share my inner truth with my students, I felt ashamed and began to disassociate with my queer identity. The degrees of my outness hinged upon my perceptions of safety and job security, and I felt that to remain a teacher, I had to simultaneously endure the closet. Historical and social significances influencing this situation further shaped my identity. Institutional heterosexist practices have combined with homophobia to create a school culture with historical social roles—a distinct understanding of what it means to be *teacher, student, heterosexual,* and *queer*. In other words to be a *teacher* at this school (and many others) meant being a *straight teacher*.

In *Negotiating the Self*, Evans (2002) wrote of identity, sexuality, and emotion in learning to teach. She asserted that we negotiate our identities in relation to our experiences as individuals (*the local*) and larger concepts (*the global*). "By using 'local' and 'global,' I am attempting to denaturalize the individual/society dichotomy. Local and global are in complex interaction" (p. 4). Evans expanded by saying what could be interpreted as an individual choice may be impacted by global sociohistorical matters. For instance, school faculty aware that I was a lesbian might have assumed I preferred not to be out to my students, or they might have (subconsciously) believed it would be inappropriate to discuss my private life with students, blind to their own heterosexual privilege. This version of tolerance (e.g., "I'm fine with gay people. What they do in their bedrooms is their own business, I just don't want to see it in public.") reduces queer people to behaviors, denying us the right to be fully human.

Indeed, something destructive was brewing inside me. During my final year at the elementary school, I built a divide between my public/work life and my personal/home life. I began to employ a performative sense of self at work. Feeling trapped, robbed of the choice to teach as a queer educator, I took on a straight identity. I removed the photo of my "best friend" (as students knew her) that was previously propped on my desk. I stopped asking colleagues about their weekend out of fear that they would return the question and force me to reveal pieces of myself that were not acceptable. Anger took me over. I became isolated and viewed every professional action and decision around me as unfair and unjust. I tried not to let my emotions interfere with my positive interactions with students, but I imagine they sometimes fell victim to my circumstance. I grew short and irritable with my principal and colleagues. In retrospect, I sense that I wanted them to feel the pain and torture that I experienced every day when I entered the building. But when I arrived at home each afternoon, I was greeted by my fiancée, and the anger and pain subsided. Centered in my true self, I felt whole.

The tension I experienced as a result of the incongruence of my personal and public life is not uncommon. Indeed, the presence of this divide happens more often than one might think, particularly among queer individuals. Palmer (1998) noted, "Unlike many professions, teaching is always done at the dangerous intersection of personal and public life" (p. 17). By this he meant "as we [teachers] try to connect ourselves and our subjects with our students, we make ourselves, as well as our subjects, vulnerable to indifference, judgment, ridicule" (p. 17). Palmer suggested that a teacher decreases vulnerability by creating distance from students, from subjects, and even from himself or herself, creating a wall between "inner truth and outer performance" (p. 17). Perhaps the tendency to self-protect in this way is best known to queer students and educators, who, like me, are forced to navigate institutionalized homophobia that manifests in schools in the form of queer-as-danger-to-children and queer-as-deviant discourses. "Workplaces will often protect LGBTQ people's right to be gay but not overt expressions of 'gayness,' such as photos of partners or perceived overly feminine or masculine behaviors" (Horn et al., 2010). In these cases, a failure to weave a central strand of our identity into our vocation can lead to what Palmer (1998) called a *divided self*.

"The self is not infinitely elastic—it has potentials and it has limits. If the work we do lacks integrity for us, then we, the work, and the people we do it with will suffer" (p. 16). By *integrity*, Palmer meant the wholeness an individual is able to find through understanding and negotiating personal identity.

In essence, being forced to hide my queer identity in the teaching profession required me to sacrifice my integrity, which in turn jeopardized my vocation. I no longer felt a sense of self, of personal identity in the classroom. Outwardly, I was going through the motions of being a teacher, but inwardly I felt like a fraud, and over time the work I once loved became unfulfilling as I lost my sense of agency. Upon realizing this extreme dividedness, and it took six months, I decided to live "divided no more."

Identity Shifts and Visibility

During my shift from the K–5 classroom to a public university, I held the tension of being both nervous and relieved. I was anxious about leaving my paid position as a teacher to once again take up the role of a student. I was also unsure if and how my queer identity would be embraced within academia. But as described earlier, I was fortunate to find an inclusive and open-minded home at PSU. I found a new center to my life, a wholeness rooted in my newfound integrity. My identity as a queer educator, researcher, and scholar was acknowledged and valued, which brought me back to my vocation and my joy for teaching. I sensed what Palmer (1998) described as the undivided self:

> Every major thread of one's life experience is honored, creating a weave of such coherence and strength that it can hold students and subject as well as self. Such a self, inwardly integrated, is able to make the outward connections on which good teaching depends.
>
> *(p. 15)*

I am not trying to oversimplify my transition, which did require an adjustment period. When I was hired as a fixed-term faculty member during my third year as a doctoral student, I continued to monitor my outness in ways that guaranteed job security. I constantly negotiated my identity in relation to others and specific contexts. As I worked with a new cohort of teacher candidates or classroom of students, I deliberately refrained from answering personal questions for fear of surfacing my sexual orientation in conversation before I was ready. On a less conscious level, I surveyed students to decipher if anyone "looked" queer and observed how others in the group responded to this perceived queerness. But, over time, with the existence of the CI LGBTQ Task Force, support from my colleagues, and strength and inspiration from my research, I integrated my life in seamless harmony.

In *Lesbians in Academia: Degrees of Freedom*, Mintz and Rothblum (1997) gathered 32 essays from lesbians in higher education and concluded the following based on the collection of texts:

> Lesbians in academia continue to occupy an intermediate position between the straight and non-straight world. With some significant exceptions, the experiences of lesbians are more positive than ever before in history and the comfort levels higher. And yet, these many years later, our locker room conversation still turns to questions of difference as we experience the world around us.
>
> *(p. 10)*

In her submission to the volume, Stuck (1997) did a further analysis of the 32 essays and wrote, "For many, if not most, of these authors, teaching and classroom interactions, while difficult at times, are also some of the most rewarding of their experiences and often provide the most suitable contexts for coming out" (p. 216). The conclusions these authors drew capture my experience with vivid detail—the tension, the questions of difference and ongoing sense-making, the reward of vocation and an integrated life.

Currently in my role as a teacher educator, especially as the CI LGBTQ Task Force has "gone public" and gained visibility, I am approached by pre-service and in-service teachers who identify as queer. Some want to tell me their stories while others elicit advice regarding specific questions or concerns about the program or field. Whether they yearn for contact/community, validation, or answers, it is clear that all negotiate the tension of teacher *and* queer. This conflict is not likely to vanish in the next decade or two so the question becomes this: How can teacher education be transformed to honor the declaration of queer identity and a claiming of the possibility of wholeness?

Conclusion

As an American, Caucasian, cisgender female raised in rural Oregon, I did not encounter much adversity until I began questioning my sexual orientation. Growing up, I had an identity that was congruent with societal expectations. I did not live between cultures, and I was afforded daily privileges based solely on visible characteristics of a "normal" life. As I evolved into a feminist and queer activist, and I tangled these roles into my identity as a teacher, life got far more complicated. I grew up realizing my dream of becoming a teacher, and I, like many individuals, have experienced how it feels to live a divided life and lose my sense of self in my profession. Yet I also know the joy of demanding and realizing more. The fulfillment that comes from embracing my identity and living with integrity is overpowering at times. It has reinvigorated my passion for teaching and propelled me to honor my queer self within my vocation. It brings me closer to my students and to the subjects I teach. It allows me to live with no regret.

I opened the chapter with a variety of questions, some of which I still seek answers to. When it comes to others, I think I have a pretty solid grasp on things. How does my identity as a queer woman shape my performance as an educator and my interactions and relationships with students? My queer identity is an asset that allows me to empathize with students and gain their empathy in return. Sharing my queer identity with students helps us connect and invites critical discourse capable of enriching the way we see our students, the world. And what would it feel like to be forced back into the closet? Well, I'll just have to make it my life's work to never find out.

Reflection Questions

1. What aspects of your identity do you openly share with students and colleagues? What aspects of your identity do you hide and why?
2. What are the challenges of negotiating "the self" in schools?
3. How and why does academic culture discourage individuals from living connected lives?
4. How does education encourage teachers to distance themselves from their students?
5. What steps can you take to live an "undivided life"?

Recommended Resources

Books and Articles About Identity and Queer Visibility in Education

Butler, J. (1990). *Gender trouble: Feminism and the subversion of identity.* New York: Routledge.
Evans, K. (2002). *Negotiating the self: Identity, sexuality, and emotion in learning to teach.* New York: Routledge.
Hansen, D.T. (1995). *The call to teach.* New York: Teachers College Press.
Horvitz, L. (2010). *Queer girls in class.* New York: Peter Lang.
Palmer, P.J. (1998). *The courage to teach: Exploring the inner landscape of a teacher's life.* San Francisco, CA: Jossey-Bass.

References

Danielowicz, J. (2001). *Teaching selves: Identity, pedagogy, and teacher education.* Albany: State University of New York Press.
Evans, K. (2002). *Negotiating the self: Identity, sexuality, and emotion in learning to teach.* New York: Routledge.
Hansen, D.T. (1995). *The call to teach.* New York: Teachers College Press.
Horn, S.S., Konkol, P., McInerney, K., Meiners, E.R., North, C., Nuñez, I., ... Sullivan, S. (2010). Visibility matters: Policy work as activism in teacher education. *Issues in Teacher Education, 19*(2), 65–80.

Huebner, D. (1999). Teaching as vocation. In V. Hillis (Ed.), *The lure of the transcendent: Collected essays by Dwayne E. Huebner.* Mahwah, NJ: Lawrence Erlbaum.

Intrator, S.M., & Kunzman, R. (2006). The person in the profession: Renewing teacher vitality through professional development. *Educational Forum, 71*(1), 16–32.

Mintz, B., & Rothblum, E.D. (Eds.). (1997). *Lesbians in academia: Degrees of freedom.* New York: Routledge.

Palmer, P.J. (1998). *The courage to teach: Exploring the inner landscape of a teacher's life.* San Francisco, CA: Jossey-Bass.

Palmer, P.J. (2007). *The courage to teach: Exploring the inner landscape of a teacher's life. 10th anniversary edition.* San Francisco, CA: Jossey-Bass.

Stuck, M.F. (1997). The lesbian experience: An analysis. In B. Mintz & E.D. Rothblum (Eds.), *Lesbians in academia: Degrees of freedom* (pp. 210–220). New York: Routledge.

Sumara, D., & Davis, B. (1999). Interrupting heteronormativity: Toward a queer curriculum theory. *Curriculum Inquiry, 29*(2), 191–208.

5
TEACHER CANDIDATES ENGAGE WITH QUEER PHENOMENA

In This Chapter

- Methodology and findings from a study that examined how teacher candidates encountered, made sense of, and responded to sexual and gender diversity in their elementary and middle school classrooms.
- Five assertions that were generated from research findings.
- Factual stories from participant experiences to candidly reveal how teacher candidates experience queer phenomena in K–8 public schooling.

Valentine's Day, 2012

Students in Mrs. Woodruff's second-grade class are consumed with an assortment of heart-themed activities. Purple, red, and pink worksheets are scattered about the room. Mrs. Woodruff interrupts independent work time to launch one more task, "A Valentine's Day Math Challenge." She presents a worksheet filled with story problems. Students need to complete a minimum of five. They can work with a partner and choose which items they want to compute. Mrs. Woodruff reads aloud a few using the document camera at the front of the classroom. One question, item 10 of 10, requires students to "match the couples" and provides clues, or criteria, for the task (Figure 5.1).

As Mrs. Woodruff disperses the worksheets, students immediately grab a partner and get to work. I am surprised to see that 100% of the students start working on item number 10. A few minutes into independent work time, Mrs. Woodruff approaches me and whispers that a particular pair of learners just matched two boy couples and two girl couples. The simple acknowledgement, in addition to her voice inflection and tone, tell me that she is uneasy with these queer pairings.

> **Try to match the couples:**
> Randy has blue eyes.
> Sam is 17 and has green eyes.
> Rhonda has green eyes.
> Sabrina is 16 and has hazel eyes.
> Matt is 16 and has brown eyes.
> Chris has hazel eyes.
> Megan is 17 and has blue eyes.
> Carla has brown eyes.
>
> **Clues:**
> No one goes with someone whose name begins with the same letter.
> No one goes with someone with the same color eyes.
> No one goes with someone the same age.

FIGURE 5.1. *A Valentine's Day Math Challenge.* A math problem presented to students in Mrs. Woodruff's second-grade class whereby they were challenged to "match the couples."

The look she gives me transcends surprise and borders on fear. *Fear of what?* I think. Is it the fear of not knowing if and how to say something to affirm or challenge student answers, student concepts of what constitutes a couple, a legitimate loving partnership? Is it fear of having her morals, her value system, challenged... by a couple of seven-year-olds? I cannot say for sure, but I imagine it might be a little bit of all these things. Chances are Mrs. Woodruff hasn't unpacked the dilemma herself. And why should she? The students are wrong... they are the outliers, the ones who are defying a heteronormative culture embedded within the larger institutional educational norms.

After our brief encounter in which Mrs. Woodruff has said so much without saying much at all, I continue to circulate the room, listening to the students' problem solving. I came to one small group of three boys working on item 10 together. One said, "I've got it... they just go across." He made short, uncomplicated, parallel lines connecting Randy with Matt, Sam with Chris, Rhonda with Megan, and Sabrina with Carla. The boy next to him says, "That means they're all gay." "So?" the boy asks, placing his pencil down onto his desk. "Well, like a guy and a guy, that means they're gay." "So?" the boy asks again... this time adding, "It doesn't matter. I'd still want to play with them and be their friend." Can it be true that a seven-year-old understands what so many adults do not: That gay people exist and deserve love?

Before I left the room, I whispered in this boy's ear: "I really like the way you think about things." He might not have known what I meant, and it doesn't matter. My words are meaningless compared to his. This boy is courageous. This boy gives me hope, hope that if either of the two other boys grow up to discover they are gay, that they will meet this realization with at least one memory of acceptance and affirmation. Or, if the boy, the courageous boy, knows or grows to learn that he is gay, he will have already acted with integrity in defending a core aspect of his identity.

Research Goals and Paradigm

Although I began with an account of my own vivid experience in the field, the purpose of this chapter is to share methodology and findings from a study that asked the question: How do teacher candidates encounter, make sense of, and respond to issues of sexual and gender diversity in their field placements?

Encounter here is defined as how teacher candidates came to know or recognize an event, situation, and/or experience involving gender and/or sexual diversity and how they processed such a meeting. In other words I wanted to consider how teacher candidates *make sense of* what they encountered. Upon encounters, I asked teacher candidates to articulate events or situations for which sexual and gender diversity could be talked into existence and more clearly understood. Finally, I collected data on how pre-service teachers *respond to* queer issues in the field.

In this study, I used commonly referenced descriptions of sexual and gender classifications (Bridge 13 Program, 2006; Sears, 2005) that recognize their complex yet fluid nature (e.g., man, woman, genderqueer; masculine, feminine, androgynous). *Sexual diversity* encompasses a range of emotional, erotic, and/or physical attractions toward others. Labels to describe these orientations include *heterosexual* (i.e., emotional, erotic, and/or physical attractions toward people of the "opposite" gender) and *homosexual* (i.e., attractions toward people of the "same" gender). Sexual diversity also includes people who identify as *bisexual* (a person who is attracted, but not necessarily equally attracted, to males and females), *asexual* (a person who is not interested in or does not desire sexual activity), and *pansexual* (a person who is attracted to some individuals of any gender identity).

Contrary to popular belief, millions of Americans (including children) currently reside outside the gender binary. By opening up the dichotomy of male/female, we are able to see the rich gender diversity and creativity in the world. Embedded within *gender diversity* is our *gender identity*, *gender expression*, and *perceived gender expression*. The first refers to how we experience and conceptualize our own gender (how we feel inside as man, woman, somewhere in-between, and/or, neither, regardless of biological sex). *Gender expression* is the way we manipulate our appearance and/or behavior to express our gender whether it's feminine, masculine, or androgynous. In addition to how we self-identify and express our gender, we also carry with us a perceived gender expression. This includes the way others (society) perceive our gender identity based on our gender expression (appearance/mannerisms).

My decision to examine both sexuality and gender was based on a theoretical understanding of the two and the relationship they share. In her seminal text, *Gender Trouble*, Butler (1990) argued that gender and the accepted institution of heterosexuality are socially constructed to serve particular individuals and organizations. Heterosexuality, in other words, both requires and produces limited gender possibilities within an oppositional, binary gender system.

> The institution of a compulsory and naturalized heterosexuality requires and regulates gender as a binary relation in which the masculine term is differentiated from a feminine term, and the differentiation is accomplished through the practices of heterosexual desire. The act of differentiating the two oppositional moments of the binary results in a consolidation of each term, the respective internal coherence of sex, gender, and desire.
>
> *(p. 31)*

Butler highlighted the gendered nature of (homo)sexuality, a relationship further illustrated throughout this book.

Interpretivism served as a logical overarching paradigm to research the experience of teacher candidates as they encountered and made sense of queer issues in their field placements. Interpretivists argue that knowledge and reality do not have an objective or absolute meaning but rather are created in multiple ways depending on the participants and their social context (Abdal-Haqq, 1998; Applefield, Huber, & Moallem, 2000). This theory of ontology and epistemology relates to contemporary ways in which individuals, such as teacher candidates, and institutions, such as schools, handle diverse notions of identity and sexuality. Everyone in society has a unique perspective about gender and sexuality based on prior knowledge, learning opportunities, and experiences. Most individuals have distinct ideas about what it means to be born male or female, display masculinity or femininity, and to desire men and/or women.

Research Context and Methods

In summer 2010, I co-led a cohort of students in a Graduate Teacher Education Program (GTEP) at PSU in Portland, Oregon. I guided and instructed 18 teacher candidates from their initial entry into the program to graduation and early childhood/elementary teaching licensure (although one student in this study sought elementary/midlevel math licensure). Upon enrollment, teacher candidates were required to take an introductory multicultural education course, the only required course that specifically tackled issues surrounding student culture and diversity. As course instructor, I included queer issues in education as a means of determining appropriate support for queer youth and families as well as recognizing the larger hetero- and cisnormative culture that exists in schools. At completion of the five-week course, students were assigned to a cooperating teacher and a school to conduct their yearlong student teaching. I collected data during the first seven months of this field experience.

The study used a multiple-case study design. To holistically examine and interpret how teacher candidates encounter, make sense of, and respond to sexual and gender diversity, I collected data from (a) three individual interviews, (b) two group conversations, (c) multiple direct observations, (d) a self-generated research log, (e) on-site participant journals, (f) electronic prompt/response submissions, and (g) artifacts. Data were collected for seven consecutive months from September 2010 to March 2011. All identifiers of participants have been changed.

Getting to Know the Research Participants: Eight Teacher Candidates Walk Into a Bar

Noelle has a reserved nature. She is more forthcoming in conversation but hesitates with almost every action, which stems from an overall lack of confidence. She is a 23-year-old cisgender, straight, Caucasian female who grew up in generational poverty and only began to unpack the consequences of this when she entered GTEP as a first-generation college student. She approaches the bar and joins Beatrice in ordering a glass of red wine. Beatrice is also a cisgender, straight, Caucasian female. She tries to reassure Noelle that she will be a great teacher, that she is a good person; Beatrice is very maternal. Beatrice is 28 years old, two years older than Aja, a cisgender, bi-curious, mixed-race female. Aja orders a club soda because she's responsible and knows she will have a long drive home. What draws the three women together in conversation is their intense desire to teach.

Ramona and Townes are no different. Ramona, a cisgender, straight, Caucasian female, represents the alternative culture Portland has grown famous for. She's an original hipster without even trying. Ramona is a walking paradox of rebellion and sweetness and orders a whisky neat with a Pabst Blue Ribbon back. Townes is a cisgender, bisexual, Korean American female in her late 20s. She calls the bartender over and requests an IPA. Both women are inquisitive and compassionate. Specializing in math instruction, Townes is the only participant who is working with middle rather than elementary school students.

Three males participated in the study. Jack identifies as a transgender, queer, Caucasian male. His assigned sex at birth was female, but inside his mind and heart, Jack is a man. He is curious about the world, revolutionary in his thinking, and passionate about teaching children. He sticks with water, having given up alcohol years before. Like Jack, Quercus and Moses are in their 20s. They are cisgender, straight, Caucasian males. Quercus is a pensive and analytical person. His parents are international diplomats who have adopted and fostered international children, and this shapes his views on education and the world. Moses, an outspoken self-identified monk, believes that conflict is healthy; he fuels on critical dialogue. Both men order a beer and slouch on their stools. Figure 5.2 delineates the demographics of the participants and their schools.

Assertions

The findings presented in this chapter demonstrate that education is inclusive of queer issues in the sense that they exist. Participants identified them. Critical

Name	Age	Race	Gender Identity	Sexual Orientation	Grade Taught	School	School Characteristics
Jack	29	Caucasian	Transgender male	Queer	1	Willow	In contrast to a neighborhood school, Willow operates on a lottery system to enroll K–8 students with special interests in math and science. Approximately 42% of students in this urban school are identified as talented and gifted (TAG), and there is little racial, ethnic, and linguistic diversity.
Townes	28	Korean American	Cisgender female	Bisexual	7/8	Willow	
Beatrice	28	Caucasian	Cisgender female	Straight	3	Juniper	Juniper is an urban K–8 school with significant cultural and linguistic diversity. Although most student families are from similar working-class backgrounds, they exhibit a wide range of social and cultural capital.
Noelle	23	Caucasian	Cisgender female	Straight	3	Juniper	
Ramona	30	Caucasian	Cisgender female	Straight	3	Juniper	
Quercus	21	Caucasian	Cisgender male	Straight	3	Spruce	Located in a suburban area, Spruce is a K–5 school; 70% of students are White, 16% of the population qualifies for English-language development, and less than 8% qualify for special education services.
Aja	26	Mixed-race	Cisgender female	Bi-curious	4	Spruce	
Moses	27	Caucasian	Cisgender male	Straight	5	Spruce	

FIGURE 5.2. *Teacher Candidate Research Participants' Demographics.* A list of teacher candidates who served as research participants with corresponding demographics including grade levels, schools, and school characteristics.

reflection and collective agency provided a means for making sense of encounters by tracing their roots, postulating their consequences, and judging their merit. A cycle of praxis (Freire, 1970) formed, which was ongoing and transparent and led to the following assertions. The language and composition of each assertion was carefully chosen to form accurate affirmations that could be traced back to the data. The intention here was not to generalize across the field, although the following assertions do align with current literature, but rather to represent the data in a succinct and declarative fashion so as to highlight the scope and depth of the study and also to position it within a critical theory perspective.

Assertion 1: Queerness Exists in K–12 Education

Queer students (and students perceived to be queer) exist and can often be detected by teachers, especially when teachers are given an opportunity to discuss and process queer issues. As early as first grade, queer students (and students perceived to be queer) can begin to feel alienated and/or closeted by school structures (e.g., social dynamics, curriculum, teacher and peer discourse).

Assumptions about stereotypical gender preferences fuel teachers' tendency to separate boys and girls. Discourses of masculinity and femininity are fundamental to social life and inform instructional and management decisions in the classroom. Once in a while, and research (e.g., O'Connor, 2013) suggests with growing frequency, teachers will come across students who defy stereotypical gender preferences. Six of the eight participants encountered such students in their classrooms.

Aja completed her student teaching at Spruce Elementary, where she was paired with a fourth-grade mentor teacher, Mrs. Banksy. Aja described Mrs. Banksy as caring and highly skilled in effective instruction and classroom management. The two encountered a boy in their class, Joey, "exhibiting signs that he might not be sure of or comfortable with his sexuality . . . that he might be gay" (Aja, interview, January 13, 2011). Aja's intuitive assessment was based on nonverbal cues (i.e., flamboyant mannerisms) and his rejection of traditional gender roles (e.g., he reads princess books and wears flashy clothing and stereotypically feminine accessories). A person's sexual orientation is distinct from a person's gender identity and expression, and Aja could not pinpoint whether Joey was gender nonconforming, experiencing some level of gender dysphoria, and/or developing same-sex attractions. She consulted Mrs. Banksy in an effort to make further sense of Joey's experience. In her journal (January 15, 2011), she wrote:

> He's still figuring things out and for me this signals that he's just in a fragile place. We want to make sure we're supporting him. I see other kids picking up on it and I just wonder if that's going to become a problem . . . I'm afraid he might be susceptible to bullying.

Aja's cooperating teacher was likeminded, and the two began talking about ways they could support Joey's positive identity development in the classroom. Aja recalled one particular conversation they shared:

> It was very supportive and we were both on the same page. We agreed that he should be whoever he wants to be, and we just want to make sure that it's a safe environment for him. [Mrs. Banksy] even used the term "safe environment"; it was just great. Maybe he's not necessarily aware of what he's feeling or what kind of confusion he may be experiencing. He might not be fully aware that there is this support here from us but I think he knows that we want what's best for him and that's what makes all the difference.
>
> *(interview, January 13, 2011)*

In a group conversation, Moses connected to Aja's dilemma of a student struggling to understand and accurately express himself. Moses said this about one of his fifth graders:

> I have a student like [Aja] who is kind of in-between having the gender or sexuality . . . in-between what he thinks he should be or his family has modeled, and what he might actually be when he finds himself.
>
> *(February 1, 2011)*

Beatrice and Noelle, who worked as two parts of a triad in their third-grade placement at Juniper Elementary, also encountered a student who expressed his gender creatively. Beatrice spoke of this student as possibly being gay. When asked what she took away from the initial research group conversation, she responded:

> Since having the group meeting and hearing everyone else's experiences, I decided to have a conversation with my CT [cooperating teacher] about one of the students in our classroom. He is by far the tallest student in the class. He prefers to play with the girls in the classroom and I rarely see him interact with boys. His behavior is more feminine and [Noelle] and I are both concerned about this becoming a problem for him with some of the boys in the class. My CT expressed that she was glad he was so much larger than any of the other boys. She felt that this was going to keep him from being teased. I have had this same thought but I have also wondered if, though he is not teased, he is excluded from the groups of boys who play together. I need to spend more time watching my kids at recess to see how he is treated outside the classroom. I want to make sure that he is being supported and not bullied by others in the class.
>
> *(e-mail, January 26, 2011)*

Although Beatrice's intention to support her student was genuine, her operating under stereotypes of gay people to draw conclusions about this particular boy's sexual orientation was problematic. Beatrice's "gaydar," a colloquialism referring to an intuitive ability to assess others' sexual orientation, was triggered because she perceived him to prefer working with females and to display effeminate qualities. In fact, these factors have far more to do with transgressing gender boundaries than same-sex attractions. Confusing gender and sexuality obscures the reality of both; the two need to be carefully teased apart. As previously mentioned, gender encompasses a spectrum of physical, mental, and behavioral traits pertaining to the social constructs of masculinity and femininity. Our gender includes our identity and expression, as well as how others perceive our gender presentation. Sexual orientation, conversely, is characterized by who we are romantically, sexually, emotionally attracted to, whether it be the opposite sex or gender, the same sex or gender, both, or neither. Thus, gender and sexual orientation relate to one another but should never be confused. In effect the two become muddled within heteronormative discourse. Evans (2002) observed, "If to 'be a woman' means, in part, to be a sexual partner with a man, then a man who loves men is feminized. Because woman-desiring-man is normalized, man-desiring-man is 'like a woman' within an historically heteronormative framework" (p. 27).

Townes landed a midlevel student teaching placement where she taught seventh- and eighth-grade math at Willow School. Like some of the other participants, Townes worked as a member of a triad alongside her co-teacher candidate, Travis, and her cooperating teacher, Mr. Kubasak. At the beginning of the school year, staff staged a school-wide assembly to communicate behavior expectations and dress code. Townes and Travis were asked to put on human-size paper doll clothing for a skit. When it was over, Townes described the transphobic and sexist nature of the presentation and considered how it might have affected students in the audience perceived or actually queer.

> When we were preparing for the skit the teachers were joking around about having people cross-dress . . . having Mr. Kubasak wear a really short skirt. It's disrespectful and I said I didn't want to, but I noticed during the assembly that teachers *did* switch their paper doll clothing and pranced around in a way that mocked all kinds of people I know and love. Everyone was laughing and I thought to myself . . . what would it feel like to watch this if I were a boy who likes to wear skirts or dresses? What messages would it give me if I were a girl who tends to dress and act more masculine? I mean these were their teachers, their role models!
>
> *(interview, September 26, 2010)*

During recess duty later that day, Townes observed a teacher and a small handful of students passing around a ballerina tutu that had been used in the skit. They were placing it over their clothing and flamboyantly moving across the soccer field. She was really offended by this mockery of cross-dressing and found the entire scene all too common and constraining. The episode was so familiar, in fact, that it triggered a similar incident she experienced at the university:

> It happened during one of our classes . . . [Quercus] was playing a female role for some skit and everyone was laughing because of how outlandish it was . . . his feminine mannerisms. [Jack] ended up writing the course instructor an email to voice his discomfort with the incident.
> *(interview, September 26, 2010)*

Townes's observations and critique are important. First, she witnessed what hundreds of others saw and provides a counter-narrative that few students could voice in fear of becoming a target of gay baiting. Second, the teachers initiating this mockery seem unaware of how others might perceive it. Perhaps operating under their own rigid definitions of gender performance, these "role models" were inviting others to laugh at them at the expense of alienating some who defy the rigid gender binary. In their essay on teacher knowledge, Petrovic and Rosiek (2007) wrote these words:

> One of the most serious obstacles in preparing teachers to better service LGBTQ students is that they are unaware of the way heteronormative discourses shape their taken-for-granted assumptions about student behavior and feelings. These assumptions influence both their practice and their understanding of their practice.
> *(p. 211)*

Assertion 1 highlights the need for educators to learn more about societal gender norms, which are influenced by family values, media/advertising, peers, and teachers, and to reexamine personal attitudes and biases around gender conformity. Acquiring this knowledge and reframing perspective can help teachers challenge assumptions triggered by "gaydar" and provide support for students based on an accurate understanding of how gender and sexual orientation differ. Given our growing diverse student population and the increased visibility of LGB and questioning students, as well as students who identify and present their gender in creative ways, it is vital that teachers deconstruct rigid definitions of masculinity and femininity and obscure gender dichotomies.

Assertion 2: Gender Dichotomies Are Taught and Reinforced in K–12 Education and Are Harmful to Students

Whether intentional or not, K–12 teachers separate students into a boy/girl gender dichotomy. This rigid binary potentially harms all students by endorsing narrow definitions of identity and is particularly restricting for students who are gender nonconforming.

"I think what has resonated with me most is how often teachers use gender to separate children, to sort and manage them" (Noelle, e-mail, October 1, 2010). Similar observations were made as participants encountered what they came to understand as a gender dichotomy. All participants noticed a dualistic relation of gender within the first two days of school. Gender dichotomy, which is the perception of the two main genders (female and male) as mutually exclusive (even diametrically opposed), surfaced in numerous ways. Constructed and transmitted socially, gender dichotomies define gender identity as entailing specific traits, roles, rights, and responsibilities (Butler, 1990). As Beatrice described, using this binary system to inform instructional practice reinforces dominating patterns of gender and power and can harm students who reside outside socially constructed categories.

> The moment that spoke the clearest to me about social constructions of gender identity in the classroom was when my cooperating teacher talked about the class on the first in-service day. Though she had not yet taught any of the students, she was clearly preparing herself for a certain type of class. From her language I understood that she was concerned about having so many boys. She didn't elaborate on specific male students or behavior issues she had heard from second grade teachers. Her preparation for having a more difficult class was purely based on the number of boys on the class list. This means she assumed that she knew the gender identity of each student before they even entered her room. Since she is most likely the adult that these students spend most of their waking hours with, her perception of their gender and their behavior will likely affect them. As these students continue to build and change their identities, they are in a situation where certain qualities socially assigned to their gender were assumed based on their school paperwork.
>
> *(e-mail, October 1, 2010)*

Jack's cooperating teacher initiated a similar conversation with him at the beginning of the year. He remembered, "It started right off the bat. She made stereotypes like, 'of course it will be chattier and more gossipy, but this is going to be a great class because it's mostly girls'" (interview, September 26, 2010). Mrs. Turner went on to talk about how tidy the room would be because female students love to clean. Jack noted:

> I don't want to negate her observations because she's been teaching for 25 years so I just nod my head and try to debunk her generalizations every once in awhile. I'm like oh yeah, the girls do seem really clean and you know Stephen is a super clean freak too!
>
> *(interview, September 26, 2010)*

Although Jack didn't make any concessions for Mrs. Turner's tendency to categorize students and to make assumptions based on gender, many participants made minor allowances for their cooperating teachers' use of a gender dichotomy as a pattern of practice. Aja, Townes, Quercus, Moses, and Ramona perceived their cooperating teachers' language and actions, which created a divide between students based on gender, as unintentional. In *Language and Power*, Fairclough (1988) explained normalizing discourses as the ways of thinking, doing, and being that become so ingrained in our way of life that we think of them as commonsense.

Over the course of the study, participants named many systems, practices, management techniques, and isolated events that reinforced gender separation. Figure 5.3 shows data that typify encounters participants experienced with gender dichotomy.

Clearly, our categorical blinders restrict what we know and can imagine about gender. Once sorted, anticipated gender norms highly affect students who reside outside, or outright defy, the gender binary. The way in which one individual perceives another individual's gender expression, which again, in mainstream society is filtered through a male/female dichotomy, often leads to assumptions about that individual's sexual orientation.

Jack encountered a male-bodied first grader who defied traditional gender preferences for reading material. Mrs. Turner called the student out on his choice to read a book from *The Rainbow Fairies* series, which visibly embarrassed him in front of his peers. Jack noted that Mrs. Turner would not have asked the same question, or with the same tone of voice, if the student had been reading a book about baseball, for example. Jack found it uneventful that a male student would choose to read a fantasy book, and, in a private conference with the student, Jack encouraged him to continue to read any books he found personally interesting.

Quercus also encountered the prevalence of a gender dichotomy within his elementary education. In a journal entry dated September 27, 2010, he wrote:

> We separate students by boy/girl to serve various purposes. It becomes a tool that may simplify the grouping process for teachers, but it also reinforces the binary notion of gender and sex, as well as various stereotypical inequalities. So the question becomes: Does this harm? And if so, how much and in what ways?

Employing metaphor assisted Quercus in answering his question. In the same September entry he recorded, "Consider a person as a mason. They are the self-determining factor in the construction of their identity. The supplies they use to build this identity are the outside influence . . ."

As shown in Figure 5.4, Quercus concluded that teachers potentially harm students when they use tools to separate individuals into gender binaries. According to him, harm ensues because binary systems and dichotomies limit notions

Gender Dichotomy	Encountered by	Specific Examples
Bathroom passes	Beatrice, Ramona Jack, Moses, Aja Ramona, Quercus	Separate bathroom passes for girls and boys
Instructional activities/ choice times	Beatrice, Noelle Jack, Aja Ramona, Townes	Boy vs. girl teams for academic games; survey/graph gender; directing girls to play with dolls, color/paint, and play board games; boys encouraged to play with blocks, read-aloud vs. read-to-self, and move about the room
Seating charts	Beatrice, Noelle Jack, Moses Aja, Quercus	Seating segregated by gender; like-gender placements to encourage partner participation and collaboration; boy/girl seating to discourage social discourse and off-task behavior; new students getting placed with like-gender students
Transitions	Beatrice, Noelle Aja, Quercus	Boys go first, then girls; "You're not a boy, you can't go yet"; separate boy/girl lines for hallway walking; competitions for which gender group can be quieter, faster, etc.
Academic and behavioral expectations	Beatrice, Noelle Jack, Moses, Townes	Generalizations about boys as loud, rowdy, and physically active; girls as quiet, passive, and gossipy (e.g., "boys give me the most problems," "oh, girls will be girls," "boys aren't supposed to whine, Mikey"; calling on boys more than girls when hands are raised
Color coding	Beatrice, Noelle Jack, Aja	Blue vs. pink name tags, bulletin boards
Division of materials	Aja, Quercus	Separate bins for boy-preferred vs. girl-preferred books, board games, activities
Recess activities	Beatrice, Noelle Jack, Moses, Aja Ramona, Quercus	Gender-segregated activities/playground areas (e.g., girls jump rope and boys play basketball, tag)
Attention signals	Beatrice, Noelle Jack, Moses, Aja Ramona, Quercus	Teachers signaling student attention with words, such as "Okay, boys and girls ..."; order for picking students to provide answers, elicit information (e.g., a girl chooses a boy and then a boy chooses a girl)

FIGURE 5.3. *Participant Observations of Gender Dichotomy as Perceived in the Field.* Representation of data that typify participant encounters with a gender dichotomy. Over the course of the study, participants named many systems, practices, management techniques, and isolated events that reinforced a rigid gender binary.

of who students are, who they think they can be, and who they may ultimately become.

Led by their mentor teacher, Miss Chops, Beatrice and Noelle engaged in collaborative planning. Over the course of the seven-month study, Beatrice maintained diligent notes in her journal, responded to nearly every e-mail prompt,

80 Field Research and Visibility

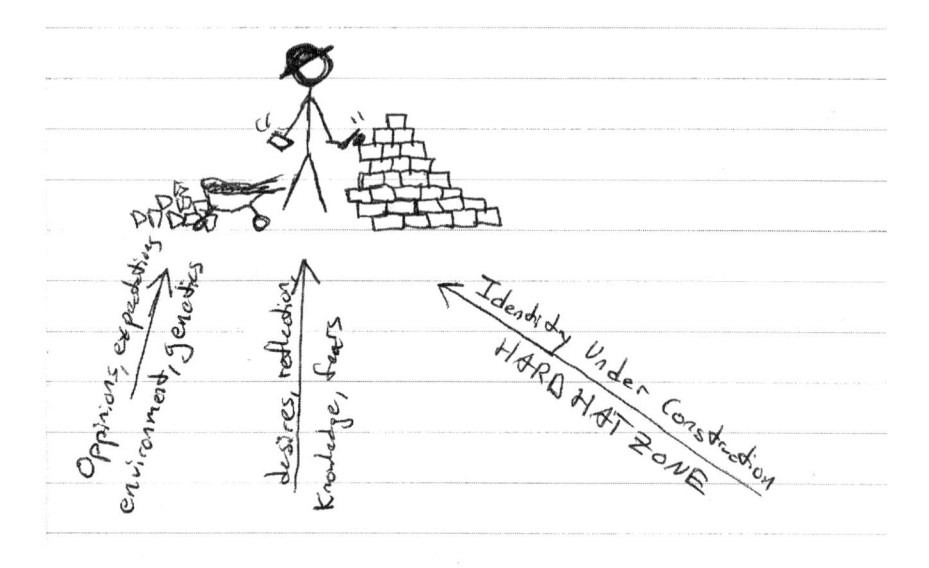

[Hand-drawn figure: A stick figure wearing a hard hat pushes a wheelbarrow of bricks next to a brick wall. Arrows point upward to the figure labeled: "Opinions, expectations," "environment, genetics," "desires, reflection," "knowledge, fears." An arrow labeled "Identity Under Construction" points to the figure. Text on the bricks reads "HARD HAT ZONE."]

• It harms; if it limits who they think they could be. Because it affects who they become. It is a violation of personal rights. So, yes: It harms.

FIGURE 5.4. *Quercus's Understanding of Teachers' Responsibility to Deconstruct the Gender Binary System.* Image and writing representative of a teacher's role in developing healthy student identities given the threat of a gender dichotomy that separates girls and boys in schools across the nation. Taken from Quercus's journal (September 27, 2010).

and engaged in every interview and group conversation. A recurring theme that emerged from all sources of her data set was the notion of gender as a social construct that can be driven by, and also led into, stereotyped assumptions. Beatrice examined instructional language, curriculum, student discourse, and her own assumptions around gender and sexual orientation, to arrive at telling conclusions about the journey of negotiating gender and sexuality in a third-grade classroom.

Beatrice's reflections began on the first day of school. Students were charged with decorating personal name tags. As a preamble to the artistic endeavor, the class engaged in a short discussion about what is, and what is not, an appropriate school illustration. Beatrice recalled boys dominating the conversation with requests to draw weapons, such as army jets and machine guns. Her cooperating teacher silenced the dialogue with a "no weapons" policy. Viewing the end products, Beatrice (journal, September 8, 2010) noticed, "There were as many boys as girls who'd drawn little geometric designs or put a flower on their nametags." This exercise challenged some core assumptions Beatrice held about masculinity as she questioned the authenticity of a male's desire to depict violence. In actuality, the boys seemed very content to abandon their war crafts, which caused her to consider the peer pressure to preserve a stereotypical tough image that male students experience. In a journal entry dated September 8, 2010, she wrote:

> [It] makes me wonder if some of the conversation was happening not because they actually intended to draw anything dangerous but because of the need to seem tough in front of their peers by acting like weapons were interesting to them.

According to Beatrice, her third graders conformed to gender stereotypes because "the desire to be liked by classmates is the focus for most students all day" (journal, September 8, 2010). Schools intentionally divide students by gender for instructional and management purposes. Based on observation, Beatrice felt this gender segregation encouraged students to conform to high levels of stereotypically masculine and feminine norms in order to be liked by their peers and live up to expectations of school culture and global media images.

In addition to fulfilling her duties in third grade, Noelle frequently visited a kindergarten classroom down the hall. She noted, "It is interesting how much gender is being literally taught" (journal, September 17, 2010). She went on to describe one observation of the classroom teacher excusing students to their cubbies according to gender, saying, "Boys first! Let's see who knows they are a boy!" (p. 8). Noelle then watched some girls putting their papers away in their cubbies and being told to sit down because they were not boys. Later that particular day, during an academic activity, kindergartners were again surveyed according to gender.

Noelle's observations reflect common practice in early childhood classrooms whereby adults teach children within a restrictive binary and assume everyone is cisgender. This narrow vision is particularly damaging given that by age two, gender is the first core identity children become aware of (Derman-Sparks & Edwards, 2010). Children's understanding of gender is largely influenced by adult messages that convey what it means to be a "boy" or a "girl." Extending beyond discourse, these messages regulate gender behaviors by establishing what society deems "normal" and rewarding what is acceptable. Rather than forcing children into gender categories based on assumptions about their assigned sex at birth as a means for managing classroom transitions, the teacher Noelle observed should focus on valuing learners in her classroom as individual human beings and revisit the assumption that the gender identity of all children is the same as their assigned sex at birth.

Ramona joined Noelle and Beatrice at Juniper Elementary in a third-grade classroom down the hallway. Like other participants, Ramona started the year writing diligently in her research journal. Unique to Ramona's experience are two separate incidents that involve students confusing gender in an attempt to negotiate and express their identities. The first occurred during Ramona's cafeteria duty. She came upon one of her students, Alfred, who was visibly upset. When asked, he said he was sad because a student from Beatrice and Noelle's classroom called him a "girly sissy" (Ramona, group conversation, October 27, 2010). Ramona glanced down and immediately understood. She saw a pink lunchbox adorned with a myriad of Disney princesses. She asked him if he liked his lunchbox, and when he replied yes, Ramona engaged the girls surrounding Alfred in a conversation that affirmed the boy and perhaps broadened everyone's conceptualization of binary preferences. The conversation uncovered that a girl liked Star Wars, and Alfred could hardly believe his ears or contain his excitement. Scooby Doo and SpongeBob SquarePants then entered the discussion, and again, students were amazed that both boys and girls adored these figures.

Ramona talked about her encounter with Alfred in a group conversation with research participants. Noelle, who teaches the boy who teased Alfred, admitted, "What upset me was that our teacher didn't ask us to address it and this made me mad because I just think it was something we could discuss and learn from as a class" (group conversation, October 27, 2010). When the participant group asked how their cooperating teacher responded, Beatrice nodded in agreement as Noelle explained:

> She just really shut down. I was like ... it doesn't matter who teased him ... it would be a good lesson for the whole class. The CT disagreed and said "no I'll just talk to him" and so she pulled [Joey] out of class. I mean she doesn't even know if it was him that did the teasing!
>
> *(group conversation, October 27, 2010)*

Following this incident, Ramona requested to borrow a book from me called *The Sissy Duckling* (Fierstein, 2002) but never read it to her students, as she intended, because she and her cooperating teacher feared parent backlash.

A final source of evidence to uphold Assertion 2 comes from Moses, who described a staff meeting where the principal mentioned a plethora of toys that were donated to the school and dispersed among classrooms. After the donations were distributed, it was discovered that a kindergarten classroom received all pink toys. The principal shared that one boy in particular was really excited about the shades of pink. Quercus, who was also at the staff meeting, recorded that the principal said, "He is probably so excited about playing with the pink princess clothes" (journal, September 9, 2010). Moses observed, "Everybody laughed at the meeting because it was ridiculous that a boy wanted to play with pink things" (interview, September 23, 2010). Moses suggested the boisterous laughter among the staff was a response to their "discomfort around homosexuality." He said teachers assumed this boy was gay, which disrupted their equilibrium and caused their deflective laughter. It is more than discomfort, however, it is homophobia. It is fear and hatred of what is not deemed straight. Perhaps what made Moses keenly aware of the coping mechanism faculty used was his own uneasiness about queerness. Before participating in the study, he voiced anxiety about the topic. In preparation for our first interview, I recorded the following in my research log (September 23, 2010):

> Moses is thoughtful and articulate. He likes to ask tough questions that challenge people's thinking. With regard to the content of the study, I know that Moses is somewhat uncomfortable. He communicated his discomfort with issues of sexuality during our initial multicultural class that preceded field experience. He explored reasons for his discomfort in a thoughtful and honest way. In a very open forum, he processed his many encounters with aggressive gay men, and the homophobic beliefs he held, all while living as a homeless man in San Francisco in the '90s.

Although the critical encounters that Moses experienced in San Francisco preceded the present study, they informed his recognition of staff laughter as a psychological coping strategy, which is significant for three reasons. First, deducing the root cause of staff tongue-in-cheek rhetoric and corresponding laughter allowed Moses to reflect upon, and make sense of, his prior discomfort surrounding the topic. Second, through dialogue embedded within the structure of the study, Moses came to see his criticism of staff members as a measure of his own growth toward queer acceptance and understanding. Third, Moses joined other research participants in coming to view language as a powerful means to confine acceptance in some contexts and to liberate narrow discourses of gender and sexuality in others.

Assertion 3: Language Is Powerful

Language, in discourse and the media, is a powerful tool often used to bring about emancipation through dialogue and sense-making. But with queer issues related to education, language is often silenced, and the messages people do transmit and receive are often heteronormative and transphobic.

Education is largely housed in discourse and involves being in relationship to others (Evans, 2002). These relationships are flooded in language, which carries historical and social significance. Participants made sense of their encounters with gender and sexual diversity, in part, by characterizing the language they heard within educational discourse and media. Many acknowledged that the implicit, exclusive language used by their cooperating teachers cultivated a culture of silence and fear around nonnormative gender and sexual identities. However, although every participant admitted hearing pejorative language about homosexuality as well as gay and lesbian epithets on the university campus, only one participant heard "that's so gay" at her school site. Beatrice (interview, March 16, 2011) described the encounter:

> Kids were lining up to get fluoride before they came into the classroom when I heard one student say, "That's so gay." I called the boy back and told him what he said was unacceptable and offensive. I didn't know how much to talk to him about it. I didn't know if he knew what it meant.

The 2011 National School Climate Survey (Kosciw, Greytak, Bartkiewicz, Boesen, & Palmer, 2012) revealed that 85% of students report frequently hearing the expression "that's so gay" or "you're so gay" in a derogatory way at school. This staggering statistic requires that teachers equip themselves with effective strategies for interrupting hateful language on the spot. Beatrice was correct in calling attention to, and stopping, the behavior, but branding the student's comment as "unacceptable" is not enough. In fact, students might interpret this teacher response to mean that being gay is not acceptable or that talking about gay identity and culture in schools is forbidden. Petrovic and Rosiek (2007) further articulated "interruption run amok" in their essay on teacher knowledge:

> Stopping name-calling typically translates to some generalized notion of "tolerance." Teachers are happy to accept that they must promote tolerance and even respect for all types of difference. But, in taking this tack, they are also quick to combine stopping name-calling with fear of naming. In other words, while better than nothing, stopping name-calling is quite anemic unless students are educated as to whom they are offending with the name. That person or that group must be named and students must be explicitly educated around the topic.
>
> *(p. 208)*

Rather than silencing dialogue, Beatrice could have asked questions and then followed up with a whole-class lesson on what it means to be gay. Luckily a large collection of materials (e.g., lesson plans, posters, and print materials) has emerged over the past few years to guide teachers in confronting "that's so gay" in schools (see part 3 for examples).

Jack also considered the influence of language on perpetuating hate. "I have friends working in local elementary schools who hear students say 'that's so gay' and 'faggot' on a regular basis. Fortunately, I haven't experienced this yet, but I am sure I will" (e-mail, December 9, 2010). His life on the university campus was another story, where, he said, homo- and transphobic language runs rampant.

Moses (e-mail, December 9, 2010) also observed this phenomenon, and, trying to make sense of it, he wrote:

> Phrases like *that's so gay* are commonplace on campus. The words have lost all meaning, sort of like *lame* and *crazy*. When I call someone "crazy" or "insane," I don't mean to offend the mentally ill. These words have entered our lexicon as multiple-definition words. To decrease their frequency, I don't know what method should be used, other than fear. When I am told about how these words are offensive, I am challenged to change my language or face social excommunication from those who tell me of this. This causes fear, not enlightenment. "Don't say that word, it offends me." This is a powerful statement trying to mold the ingrained habits of the listener. It is an "I statement" of force. It is saying: "I am better than you; you are inconsiderate." The problem is these words are elements of our culture. Adherents to culture are victims of proximity. A Mormon doesn't know that being a Mormon is bunk, as a bigot thinks his offensive actions are honorable and virtuous. We can see their actions as inconsiderate or their conviction to be respectable. Culture creates perspective and virtues are subordinate to a given cultural perspective.

I am not convinced the term "that's so gay" has "lost all meaning," particularly for queer individuals who feel the sting of this rhetoric, but I do believe society is desensitized as a result of the frequency with which these words are uttered. Moses admitted he lacks resources other than "fear" to combat homophobia epithets, but I argue that education—particularly dialogical and dialectic thinking—can have an emancipatory effect far greater and lasting than the punitive imperative he described. Moses's final phrase is especially intriguing as it speaks to the influential power culture has on individuals' thoughts, behaviors, and judgment of others.

Cultural values and social pressures, transmitted by and through discourse and media, were identified by a majority of participants as influencing factors in a highly sexualized contemporary childhood experience. Jack explained, "Skinny jeans are all the rage and outfits marketed to girls are more and more scandalous. This would be fine if girls wore what they wanted and weren't objectified for it, but that's not the case" (e-mail, December 26, 2010). Townes attempted to make sense of similar styles of dress in an eighth-grade classroom.

> I've actually heard other teacher candidates, not participants of the research study, call a specific female student 'slutty,' which is so bad. But, I mean, it does kind of speak to the way girls are socialized to dress . . . low-cut shirts and tight pants or skirts."
>
> *(interview, January 9, 2011)*

Noelle also encountered her third graders striving to obtain a mature, sexualized image. She attributed this to corporate media campaigns and strategic advertising.

> Our marketing tells children what sex or being sexy should look like. Girls see women portrayed as objects, as submissive, and as something for men to enjoy. Boys see men who are portrayed as very tough and authoritative. We thereby push our children into these very untrue (and in my opinion unhealthy) gender roles. I cannot count how many times I turn on the TV to see half-naked and seductive women and can't even figure out what the commercial is trying to sell! But they are definitely selling a powerful image to young girls.
>
> *(e-mail, December 26, 2010)*

Other participants blamed Disney for breeding stereotypes, Hasbro for their *My Little Pony* figures that have evolved over time to be skinnier and more made-up. Still others pointed fingers at video games, which tend to target boys with realistic graphics and hardcore violence. Noelle observed the same group of learners' interest in explicit music. "Take a popular song like "Get Low" and just look at the lyrics," she said (e-mail, December 26, 2010). Following her own advice, Noelle dissected the popular song that describes degrading sex. She noted the following:

> Songs like "Get Low" are everywhere and I hear my third graders singing them so I know that they are exposed to them, even perpetuating them. I have heard 7- and 8-year-olds singing this particular song. Whether or not they understand the terms used is irrelevant because they are still getting a very clear message about gender roles and sexuality. What a horrible message to give anyone!
>
> *(e-mail, December 26, 2010)*

Language also served a vivid and powerful tool in Jack's experience. It was the medium I first used as his cohort leader to communicate my unconditional support to Jack, offering a window into a reality where he could student teach as a man. Language, or rather the silenced words from others, also played a factor in his choice to remain closeted. Jack felt he had no other allies and thus identified as a woman in his placement, which permitted daily spoken reminders of his identity: *Mrs.* Waters. Jack's experience is further discussed in the following assertion related to participant identity development.

Juniper School has an openly out lesbian principal who often brings her partner and their child to school events. Yet despite overwhelming acceptance for the administrator, Noelle said subtle heteronormative discourse and cisgender assumptions were commonplace among staff and students. She documented specific instances in her on-site journal. On September 13, 2010, she recorded a conversation among a group of third graders talking about pop musician Justin Bieber.

> A boy said that the girl next to him couldn't like the music because he [Justin Bieber] was gay. The little girl said she could still like his songs even if he was. This just egged the little boy on. He taunted her saying, "you can't he's gay, he's gay, he's gay."

Noelle felt the student interaction, while imbued in misunderstanding, did not itself present gayness in a pejorative way. I disagree. What does that even mean, "you can't listen to him because he is gay?" Such discourse needs to be challenged. And while the students' quotation cannot carry with it emotion or additional context, the repetition of language certainly implies teasing with *gay* cast in a derogatory light. Noelle felt a need to interrupt or guide the dialogue. She wrote the following in a journal entry (September 13, 2010):

> I wanted to intervene but at the same time the teacher was in ear shot and I observed her do nothing. I never know if it's okay to say something or not. It was wrong, but it's her classroom. Reflecting now, I should have said something but in the moment I looked to the teacher not knowing what to do.

What does a teacher, a student teacher, say in situations like this? How does one interrupt homophobic language and disrupt gender binaries that directly dehumanize some individuals and restrict all people? As teachers, we can employ a simple sequence of reactions to address situations like this. First, it is important to stay calm and state clearly what was observed. Second, we can set perimeters and accurately label what was observed (e.g., that is prejudice; that is hurtful; that is unsafe and disrespectful). Third, we can explore feelings among the students involved to determine where the prejudice or misinformation resides. Finally, incidents like this often signal the need for more specific group or individual learning and development. I can imagine Noelle facilitating an explicit lesson on stereotypes related to being gay or lesbian. This would allow her to assess students' knowledge and experiences and debunk falsehoods on the spot. Teaching Tolerance provides online lesson plans and resources, such as *Unexpected Stereotypes and How to Combat Them* (Schmidt, 2012), which might be a helpful starting place. Yet a single lesson in isolation is not enough to combat the rampant homophobia and heterosexism that exists in our schools. Teachers must find ways to infuse queer-inclusive material throughout the curriculum. More comprehensive strategies on facilitating this learning process and interrupting hateful language are found in part 3.

Although Noelle's students were willing to talk about queerness, even if their rhetoric was saturated in misunderstanding, she found faculty less willing to instigate the conversation. In a journal entry from October 4, 2010, she described a conversation Ramona introduced at a school-wide staff meeting.

> A third grader had come up to [Ramona] and said a guy had given another guy a lap dance and that meant he was gay. She brought it up in the meeting and it seemed to make our [cooperating] teachers uncomfortable so we didn't get any advice on what, if anything, we should do about it. The faculty giggled and played it off as if the student was being inappropriate and disruptive.

The fact that this incident was disregarded at a staff meeting because teachers were uncomfortable with the content fuels the problem. The staff's fear and dismissal perpetuate a cycle of heteronormativity and gender stereotypes. In addition to typifying her encounters, Noelle continually sought meaning from her experiences and reflected on actual (and possible) responses. On November 25, 2010 she e-mailed:

> Students start forming biases very early in life. Imagine how different our world could be if we never created this stereotype of heterosexuality being "normal" and anything else being "abnormal." If we can teach students very young that neither is wrong, neither is better, and somehow perhaps take away the either/or issue all together, then our job of promoting social justice would become a lot easier.

Beatrice encountered a substitute teacher employing instructional language she perceived to transmit heteronormativity. Upon thoughtful reflection, Beatrice noted the repercussions of using exclusive, heteronormative discourse such as "mom and dad" when referring to students' families. This exclusivity, she noted, is avoidable and can ostracize students for various reasons. The substitute teacher also imparted traditional gender roles when introducing vocabulary words associated with a read aloud. She defined *laundry* as something a mom does at home. This struck Beatrice as misogynistic and classist. She thought the narrow definition could alienate students with same-sex parents as well as those not having an at-home mother or access to laundry.

Sexist, heterosexist, and transphobic language also penetrates the curriculum. Beatrice recalls her students watching a *School House Rock* video, *Three Is a Magic Number*. Although she had listened to, and sung, the lyrics as a child, Beatrice was surprised by what she heard, "A man and a woman had a little baby, yes, they did. They had three in the family, and that's a magic number." She wondered how many of her students had families that fit this description. She wrote, "The heterosexual-couple assumption didn't surprise me, but it did bother me" (journal). *Three Is a Magic Number* aired on January 6, 1973. The American Psychological Association removed homosexuality from the association's official list of mental disorders later that year on December 15, 1973. Sadly, almost four decades later, the message lives on: Three is the magic, heteronormative number.

Narrow assumptions about gender also surfaced in Townes's work sample, which is a document written by teacher candidates that helps them connect practice with ideas and skills acquired in their teacher preparation program; work sample components often require teacher candidates to design and implement instruction, assess student learning, reflect on the teaching and learning process, and provide evidence of their ability to facilitate learning among all students. Townes wrote and illustrated a multistep mathematical word problem that featured two skateboarders. Her co-teacher candidate, Travis, specifically wanted two boys skating because there were two skater boys in the class. Townes interjected, "Oh, well I skate and I'm really good at it so let's name one of them a more generally feminine name" (interview, March 31, 2011). If Townes anticipated enlightening her students toward non-stereotypical gender roles (i.e., female skateboarders), she was disappointed when completed student work showed language that signified many students assumed both skaters were male, despite one being named Cheyenne. In the evolution of her own development as a teacher, Townes concluded that future attempts to challenge assumptions surrounding stereotypical gender roles and expectations would have to be far less subtle.

Assertion 4: Teacher Candidates Negotiate Self-Identity in the Learning-to-Teach Process

For teacher candidates, personal identity is constantly being informed by, and shaped through, the learning-to-teach process. Legitimate fear as well as hetero- and cissexism force queer teacher candidates (including straight allies) into closeted classrooms. Requiring explicit and intentional pre-service teacher education on queer issues, as well as opportunities to engage in ongoing dialogue with others relating this discourse to the field, can begin to effectively dismantle perceived cisgender dominance and heteronormativity in education.

All eight participants came to see aspects of their individual identity through the research process. They constantly negotiated their selfhood as it related to sexual orientation, gender, power, race, ethnicity, and the professional roles of teacher candidate and classroom teacher. Regardless of whether their sexual orientations and gender identities are benefited or burdened in society, participants organically contemplated the extent to which they can "own" (and make visible) these aspects of their selfhood within an educational context.

The study showed that, conceptually, claiming one's identity or perceiving an aspect of another person's identity is, in some way, a rite of passage toward becoming a teacher. By analyzing the data, I came to see the notion of identity as intimately interwoven with the concept of visibility. Among participants, it was my perception that we are not able to fully recognize others (e.g., students) or ourselves unless aspects of identity became visually apparent, transparent. That is, when considering queer issues, to "identify" often means to "become visible," to stand out as the *Other* in hetero- and cisnormative institutions. Perhaps what magnifies this visibility, for queer individuals in particular, is the divide between "public" and "private" influenced by "the local" and "the global" (Evans, 2002). It could be that what makes queer issues in education visible is the amount of negotiation it takes to align identity (lived experience and core beliefs) with integrity (actions toward defending that identity).

For his yearlong student teaching placement, Jack was assigned to work with Mrs. Turner, a veteran first-grade teacher at Willow School. Although the two maintained open communication and professional respect for one another, Jack characterized their relationship as "rocky," in part, because Mrs. Turner struggled to understand and accept Jack's transgender identity. At the time of the study, Jack self-injected testosterone weekly and was referred to by trusted friends and family with male pronouns. His identity expression at Willow was a different story. Jack made the conscious and very difficult decision to self-identify as a woman within the field. He was in the initial stages of transitioning and perceived himself "passing" more easily as female, his assigned sex at birth. Thus, his identity was torn: On campus among the cohort he identified as male, and toward Mrs. Turner and their first-grade students he presented as female.

Perhaps most troubling is the cognitive dissonance Jack experienced and transmitted on a daily basis when his students addressed him as "Ms. Waters." "I feel like the kids see me and I really want to be honest with them . . . like they know something is a little different about me" (interview, January 19, 2011). We can surmise the courage it takes to acknowledge that one's assigned sex at birth contradicts one's core gender identity and then explain and defend this to members of a cissexist society over and over again. He knew this program would be difficult regardless of his decision to come out or stay closeted. Although Jack was as prepared as he could possibly be, midway through his journey he confessed that he was discouraged and frustrated.

Most of Jack's encounters with queer issues in the field are unique, owing to his queer identity. Outing himself in the beginning weeks of the program, Jack told members of his cohort, including his cohort leaders, that he was transgender. His disclosure was met with some genuine questions, and he expressed that overall he felt as though his cohort offered unconditional support. Later Jack admitted that it was his peers' overwhelming backing that encouraged him to come out to his cooperating teacher, Mrs. Turner.

> My cooperating teacher said "Can I ask why your voice is so low?" and I said it's kind of a big secret . . . I said, in the rest of my life, I'm a guy and I use male pronouns. I told her it's going to be really weird being *Ms.* [Jack Waters] here.
>
> *(interview, September 26, 2010)*

Jack said Mrs. Turner's reaction to his transgender identity was "cool" at first, but as the year progressed, her support and understanding dwindled. Although he could not pinpoint a specific downturn in their relationship, Jack described one incident that was particularly off-putting:

> [Townes] is so mad at my CT because when they were talking, [Townes] was referring to me as in "blah blah blah *he*" and my CT was like, "oh no [Jack] goes by *she* in school." The way [Townes] describes it, it was after school hours and no one else was around.
> *(interview, January 19, 2011)*

In her exchange with Townes, Mrs. Turner dehumanized Jack in a significant way. As Jack described, this treatment took its toll:

> I really have to psych myself up every night before I go in to another day of school. I say to myself, "It's okay, I'm going do this and it's going to be great!" For me it's about the kids. It's really hard though and I feel like I would have so much more energy to bring if I could just be myself.
> *(interview, January 19, 2011)*

All research participants agreed that it was unfortunate and unfair for Jack to closet his trans identity. Within group conversations it was unanimously decided that presenting as a woman brought violence to Jack and presented a missed opportunity for his students, the school, and the greater community to learn and grow. A related lesson learned as a result of making sense of Jack's experience was a collective criticism of the educational system as a whole. Whether their own identities were suppressed, or the queer students they cared for in the field were targeted, participants came to observe schools as hetero- and cissexist institutions that forced some people to shed their integrity at the door. A critical examination of school discourse and contemporary media included in Assertion 3 provided ample means for their defense.

Although his relationship with Mrs. Turner was rocky at best, the connection he shared with his first graders can be characterized as influential, inspiring, deep, and meaningful. Still, he wondered how this connection could have been enriched if he had presented as his true self. When I asked Jack if he felt empowered to make his own decision, if he felt he had support from GTEP to make a decision about his gender presentation, he responded:

> I felt like I had a lot of support from you actually. The only reason I considered coming out was because of your support. I hadn't even considered it at first and then you told me you had my back and that you'd totally be there for me. That was really encouraging and exciting to me and I was

like yeah I can do this. And then I just decided not to because you weren't my university supervisor at the school and I didn't get that support from anywhere else.

(interview, January 19, 2011)

Townes has been in relationships with men and women and understands what it is like to be the *Other*. She empathized with Jack's need to feel supported.

It's like having that person who has your back . . . it's feeling secure if and when teachers or parents question the way you present yourself. Someone at the university, and involved with the field site, carries the authority and has connections in schools to take a stand and say, "No, it isn't a problem to be who you are." I think it is disappointing that this didn't happen for [Jack].

(interview, September 26, 2010)

Townes's desire for advocacy at the leadership level, for someone to assert "It's not a problem to be who you are," is important because personal identity is constantly negotiated throughout the learning-to-teach process.

The study included two whole-group conversations. The notion of identity dominated the initial discussion when Quercus declared:

To identify something, you have certain ownership in that identity. For example, I spent a lot of time around Baptists growing up . . . I mean I was in that community. Although I never identified as one, I identify as someone who had an experience with them so when people speak poorly of them, I often get offended . . . not because I don't agree, but because the people talking about them might not have that full experience. So to stereotype genders and orientations, especially ones you don't identify as or seek to understand, is a bit destructive. How do you really know if you're not that way? Coming to see gender and sexuality on a spectrum more and more it's harder for me to know. I visited [Jack's] school and noticed that I am the only student teacher in our cohort that doesn't have a nametag on the classroom door, but then I saw [Jack's] nametag and I was like, maybe I'd rather not have my name on the door if it doesn't actually respect who I am or fully identify me because it said "[Ms. Waters]," which is maybe a minor thing, but what if it's not because it's the little things that often matter most.

(group conversation, October 27, 2010)

When asked if it was "a minor thing," Jack confessed that indeed the name tag on his classroom's front door greeted him as a daily reminder of his closeted identity. I walked through this closet door on February 28, 2011, to conduct an observation. A guest instructor was teaching a Spanish lesson, a language in which gender serves a grammatical purpose. The division of nouns into masculine and feminine categories teaches students subliminal messages about dichotomous classification and stereotypical gender expectations. When I entered the classroom, Mrs. Turner, who was observing the lesson at her desk, pointed to Jack and said, "She's over there." After my brief visit, I recorded the following reflection.

> There were no students—those she is aiming to "protect"—in earshot and yet [Mrs. Turner] felt it necessary to invalidate Jack's identity. This made me very angry because I feel like it was a conscious and purposeful action to underscore Jack. This is demoralizing to me personally and professionally as an educator who has spent all year trying to inspire and encourage teacher candidates to teach who they are. This is not based on touchy feely philosophy or any other subjective quality . . . it is a simple and researched fact. When we teach who we are, we sustain our selves in this vulnerable profession.
> *(self-generated research log, February 28, 2011)*

Moses and Townes talked about their closeted identities as well. When asked if he felt comfortable embracing his true self in the field, Moses, who is a practicing Buddhist, wrote:

> Alternative ways of being are made to hide and feel ashamed. I feel ashamed. I don't belong, and I don't dare tell the school I'm in about my beliefs. I wouldn't even tell our cohort about them out of fear. If I feel this way, I assume that those who are more readily stigmatized feel even worse.
> *(e-mail, March 3, 2011)*

Although Moses's veil drapes outside the margins of gender or sexual orientation, he does give voice to the paralyzing effect of shame and fear. Shame motivated Moses to hide just as fear caused Townes's hesitance in revealing an aspect of her identity, her bisexuality, which she predicted was unwelcomed at Willow. However, over the course of the year she befriended a teacher at the school, Ms. Powell (who did not host a teacher candidate), and in a group conversation Townes explained how she engaged in dialogue to emancipate her queer identity.

> [Ms. Powell] gave me a ride to school and she outed herself because I told her that I had had a girlfriend before my current boyfriend. We wouldn't have had that conversation on the [Willow] campus. I mean none of that would have happened! It's uncomfortable to have to edit myself in that way

and to be like . . . if I talk about my partner [*waving hand in front of face to dry tears*] . . . it's just like it's really frustrating . . . [*crying*] . . . because it makes you afraid that you're going to say something wrong. It's just frustrating that you have to edit yourself.

(group conversation, October 27, 2010)

Offering a counter-narrative, Beatrice outwardly reflected on her heterosexual identity, which admittedly grants her numerous invisible privileges. She articulated her heterosexual identity negotiation, a process that is likely to be ignored or relegated to unconsciousness in a heterosexist society as a result of "normative" assumptions about heterosexuality (Fassinger, 2000). Putting words to her experience, Beatrice used the study, in part, to deepen her understanding of majority and minority group identity development. In an e-mail (November 25, 2010), she wrote:

When I look back at my evolving views on homosexuality, I see that while I accepted the homosexual relationships some of my friends began in high school, it was not until a few years ago that I really started to question the view of heterosexuality as "normal." I was very comfortable with homosexuality, but my experience with it had not ever caused me to really think about my own decision to identify as heterosexual. I think there is a big difference between understanding homosexuality as normal/good for a specific person who has identified themselves as such, and seeing homosexuality and heterosexuality as equally normal/good options for everyone.

Beatrice had identified her heterosexual privilege years before, but the process of her negotiation was made visible when given the space and prompting provided within the research study.

Moses experienced a sensitive negotiation of his gender and faced overarching assumptions surrounding gender expression within his triad at Spruce Elementary. He shared teaching responsibilities with a male mentor teacher and female co-teacher candidate named Nel. His cooperating teacher, Mr. Scotti, provided solid leadership, guiding the three in effective collaboration that directly fueled student learning. Despite this triad's ability to orchestrate a healthy working relationship over the course of the year, Moses remembered a couple of instances that could have potentially caused tension.

I have noticed that [Mr. Scotti] seems to give [Nel] more of the clerical tasks and me more one-on-one or group instruction opportunities. I think that's because he knows I've worked with low behavior kids, but it also seems like we're going to give the girl the secretarial tasks and the guy the real tasks.

(interview, September 23, 2010)

Moses also came across a situation that targeted his gender. In an interview on January 7, 2011, he described an event concerning a first grader with a habit of missing her mother and generating tears in an effort to be sent home. According to Moses, when the classroom teacher, Mrs. Henning, told him and Nel about this girl, she said, "If we help her throughout the day, then [Nel] will probably want to work with her more because she's a woman." Moses attempted to make sense of this later:

> I don't know if it was accurate. The truth is we don't know how the student would respond to a man. Maybe she'd think there would be stricter rules and know that she couldn't just break down and cry and I know that it's gender charged or whatever, but I didn't think it was necessarily true that [Nel] would be the better person to work with her. I wanted to help out and join in but seeing as how I was a man, I was blocked off from it.
> *(interview, January 7, 2011)*

Located down the hall at Spruce Elementary is Quercus's fourth-grade classroom. He also worked in a triad; Mrs. North served as his cooperating teacher, and Megan was his cohort colleague and co-teacher candidate. The three engaged in collaborative planning and shared instruction and management responsibilities in the classroom. The composition of his triad model affected Quercus in ways that he hadn't anticipated and that also directly relate to the research study. Early in the program, he pointed out that he was the only male teacher candidate paired with a female cooperating teacher (Jack's exclusion was a result of him choosing to present as female in his field placement). The additional four male teacher candidates in the cohort (who are not all represented in this study) were unintentionally matched with male cooperating teachers. Although Quercus valued the members in his triad, he attributed an initial inefficient negotiation of his "teacher voice" and authority to the gender imbalance. Mirroring the behaviors of his immediate colleagues (namely Mrs. North and Megan), Quercus discussed the conflict he experienced in his stereotypical feminine approach to classroom management:

> I see people instinctively as equal . . . we're all very different, but I try to approach people as much as I can as equals. I try to treat them as I would like to be treated. I did this last term in the field . . . and it didn't work. I attribute some of this to me being male and behaving with some reservations. I didn't want to take over . . . I ended up taking on a traditional feminine approach. It's really interesting how students voice their confusion when you don't match their gender role associations.
> *(interview, January 12, 2011)*

Interestingly, Quercus seems to both perpetuate and call into question gender stereotyping. He claims that females act with reservation more often than males and implies that women are incapable of, or unwilling to, take control of a classroom. These stereotypical images of women are outdated in today's American society and are being debunked in elementary classrooms across the nation. That he finds students' comments about what he perceives to be gender-defiant behavior "interesting" makes me wonder about the content of these messages. Did students voice confusion, or did Quercus, highly aware of his self-identity and perceived identity, reject nonnormative tendencies to position himself far from the closet?

Quercus first broached the topic of gender roles and assertiveness in the initial group conversation, which led research participants to consider their identity as teacher candidates. Townes responded angrily when Quercus said that Megan, the co-teacher candidate assigned to his practicum classroom, had yet to find her "teacher voice" (group conversation, October 27, 2011). Later, in an individual interview, Townes recalled the encounter:

> When [Quercus] said that [Megan] needed to work on her teacher voice, it really upset me because I felt like the trend is for girls to be more submissive, more passive, and more polite than boys. So when I heard him say that so nonchalantly, it really upset me. I was like no . . . you don't understand, we women are having to break conditions that we have been taught for so long . . . that in some way we have accepted from way back in elementary school . . . and from interaction through interaction through interaction since.
>
> *(January 9, 2011)*

Townes admitted that at the time of the group conversation, she struggled with the same issues Quercus accused Megan of experiencing. Townes's university supervisor, Steve, had recently conducted a formal observation of her and Travis in their classroom. According to Townes—and supported by her observation evaluation—Steve praised Travis for asserting himself as a poised and strict presence but suggested that Townes strengthen her management skills and work on commanding more control over student attention. She specifically remembered Steve challenging what he referred to as her "nurturing nature."

Steve's critique conflicted with how Townes was raised, how she was socialized. As stated previously, Townes is Korean American. She was adopted by a Caucasian family when she was a baby and grew up with brothers and sisters of varying racial and ethnic identities. Townes is extremely passionate about mathematics and possesses sophisticated knowledge in the subject. In her first individual interview, Townes voiced frustration with living this stereotype (i.e., an Asian-American girl who excels at math). As a student, she resented people who assumed math came easy for her, and she spent most of her childhood masking her interest in math in an effort to be unpredictable and popular.

Females are supposed to be cute and little and passive compared to male peers. I see girls in my class now and it reminds me of the way people treated me when I was that age. I used to hide that I was good at math. I relate to the pressure to be attractive ... you don't want to be too much of a nerd or too smart ... you don't want to fall into that stereotype because for some reason it's not attractive.

(interview, January 9, 2011)

For Townes, the normed concept of "teacher as authoritarian" was positioned against her core nurturing quality and infused with historical and social messages related to gender performance. Townes held this tension by interrogating rigid social gender expectations that reinforced female = nurturing and by challenging the notion that paradox is a black and white *either–or* construct versus an opportunity to join what seems contradictory as *both–and* (Palmer, 1998). In other words, both Steve and Quercus contended that Townes must either claim authority *or* be nurturing. Why can't these seemingly contradictory entities both be true within one person's identity? Steve and Quercus also attributed value to authority, asserting that it is superior to the ability to nurture, which Townes interpreted as a misogynistic view. Townes examined these constructs of identity only when made visible through discursive analysis (with regard to Quercus) and an on-site observation and debrief (with regard to Steve).

Townes realized that her own gender construction was strongly influenced by societal norms. This thought was in mind as she reflected upon the ways her seventh- and eighth-grade girls interacted with peers. Over the course of the year, she came to many generalizations based on observable behavior. One particular student, a seventh grader named Sarah, exemplified Townes's assertion that girls tend to dilute their intelligence and focus more on social rather than academic aspects in order to impress friends, increase popularity, and attract crushes. One day Townes overheard her voice concern about riding the bus home because, according to Sarah, every time she took public transportation, the police got involved somehow. As Sarah began to recall details, a male student spoke up and said, "Stop acting so stupid." The girls at the table laughed, and she engaged in conversation with the boy as she now had his full attention (interview, January 19, 2011). Townes's point was that Sarah often masked her intelligence (she is incredibly bright) behind a veil of makeup and skimpy clothing as well as mannerisms that perpetuate the image of a mature, feminized socialite. In fact, her projection of this socially constructed and highly reinforced identity was so revealing that Townes's cooperating teacher expressed visible shock when Sarah won a prestigious school-wide math award.

Finally, a broader issue Townes encountered that urged her to negotiate her role as a teacher candidate was the unequal distribution of attention delivered to male students. Townes often tried to make sense of this, and although she never determined whether it was intentional or not, she noted that the imbalance persisted throughout the study. She also became aware of her cooperating teacher's habit of interrupting females mid-sentence to request that they speak louder. Townes offered that Mr. Kubasak probably doesn't understand that girls are socialized to speak quietly and that many educational settings encourage girls to appear introverted. When asked how she would serve as a role model to counteract this, she said:

> Regarding gender and sexuality, I hope to push the envelope of what is socially accepted. I'm going to be standing in front of students as a real-life female who is good at math and who is opinionated. Essentially I really want to be a subtle example of something students, girls in particular, can return to later and be like . . . I remember her, she was licensed to be articulate and opinionated, and lead the class as a good mentor.
>
> (interview, March 31, 2011)

Findings from the present study assert that legitimate fear and hetero- as well as cisnormativity force queer teacher candidates into closeted classrooms. A high frequency of the following words were coded in the data: *Fear, afraid, scared, apprehension, worry,* and *concern,* all experiences of fear. All of the eight participants experienced fear as the major emotion responsible for impeding their willingness and future likelihood to stand against hetero- and cissexism in education. Participants were induced by a perceived threat in addressing queer issues in the classroom, regardless of their individual sexual and/or gender identities. Moses, who identifies as a heterosexual male, responded to an e-mail prompt that asked him to predict how his colleagues would react if he were to come out as a gay man at school. He wrote, "Open minds aren't always the majority here [at Spruce]. I'd lie in fear if it was my choice. Better to be the shy guy than the gay guy" (October 14, 2010). Moses went on to characterize the fear that motivated his response. Job security topped the list, but a desire to be liked and accepted among others was also a contributing factor to his resolution.

Jack, on the other hand, did not live in the hypothetical. He experienced fear in a myriad of ways every day. He felt apprehension and concern about presenting himself as a lie to his students. He worried about accidently going into the boy's bathroom out of habit. He panicked when students' parents looked at him questioningly. Indeed, Jack lived in fear every day—fear his secret would always come out, fear it would never come out. Part of Jack's fear was rooted in the vulnerability of his role as a teacher candidate. In fact, all participants were afraid to elicit unwanted controversy in taking a stance against heteronormativity given the infancy of their professional careers. Research demonstrates this fear sometimes does not subside with experience. Taylor (2002) explained the phenomenon:

> For schools to be transformed from sites where homophobia is learned and practiced into ones where students can unlearn homophobia, teachers must act as "change agents" who recognize and confront the homophobia of school culture. Since homophobia is a form of prejudice that still enjoys a robust social acceptability in many mainstream communities, this takes courage and commitment on the part of teachers, and most, unless provoked, choose not to undertake the challenge. In many school districts, classroom teachers cannot address homophobia or make a positive reference to lesbians or gays without fear of losing their jobs; if teachers there can summon the courage to intervene in cases of homophobic bullying, that is perhaps all we can ask of them. But even in districts where there is explicit administrative support for anti-homophobia education, the prospect is so intimidating that few teachers attempt it. Those who do are often lesbian or gay themselves.
>
> *(pp. 220–221)*

Townes spoke candidly about an incident she experienced among a group of teachers at her placement site and, in doing so, named her own fear. "They were talking about getting a substitute teacher and I said, 'Get a cute one.' Then someone said, 'Do you want a boy or a girl?' and I was like, 'Oh. I don't care'" (interview, March 31, 2011). Townes regretted saying the words as soon as they left her mouth. "They were definitely put off by my comment, but then, they had asked me. Should I have lied? In that second I felt like, I wonder if it is okay for me to say that."

Participating in the study raised the issue of censorship for Quercus as well. For him, queerness can serve as a relevant and educational resource for interdisciplinary teaching in school. While reviewing queer youth risk statistics, Quercus said:

> You know I look at these numbers and I'm seeing fractions! This would be so great to include in a math class, but we teach with our hands tied behind our backs. And if we openly address an issue like this without really building that support, then we're at risk of losing our jobs. I mean think about if we taught these things, if we used these real-life statistics in our reading and writing and part of our social studies, think about how empowering that could be.
>
> *(group conversation, February 1, 2011)*

According to the data, all participants shared similar trepidation when faced with an issue related to gender and/or sexual diversity. Most followed in the footsteps of their cooperating teachers and decided not to address the matter in an explicit way for fear of upsetting or defying their cooperating teachers or outing themselves in some way. Others made subtle attempts to deal with the issue but were still acting out behaviors that were by and large motivated by fear.

Overall, the research study showed that teacher candidates' personal identity was constantly being molded through the learning-to-teach process. Hetero- and cisgender hegemony forced queer teacher candidates (including straight allies) into closets wallpapered with fear and shame. Providing explicit and intentional opportunities for teacher candidates to discuss queer issues, as was offered in this study, can increase awareness and drive action toward dismantling queer oppression. Findings from the current study also suggest that teacher candidates greatly crave these learning opportunities.

Assertion 5: Teacher Candidates Possess a Desire to Learn About and Act as Queer Advocates and Allies

Teacher candidates want to explore how gender and sexual diversity manifest in schools and seek ways to support queer students and colleagues. Teacher candidates who are encouraged and given tools to identify and make sense of queer issues in the field begin to voice a professional responsibility to address, if not outright counter-teach, issues that arise in schools that are homophobic and/or transphobic.

In designing the methods for this study, I anticipated that the participant group would likely become somewhat of an intervention. Indeed, by engaging in continuous critical, and at times collective, dialogue, as well as undergoing the process of negotiating meaning, participants came to identify, make sense of, and respond to queer issues in revolutionary ways. The impact of the study on participant experience, and their ability to make sense of their experience, came up early (and often, over time) in individual and group conversations as well as e-mail prompts and journal entries.

In the third and final round of individual interviews, I asked participants what if anything (positive or negative) they were taking away from participating. Although answers varied, all responses reflected positive outcomes for participation. Jack and Noelle spoke to the necessity of talking about gender and sexuality in order to desensitize, or normalize, such rhetoric in educational contexts. In our concluding interview, Jack shared, "It is good to talk about this stuff with other teachers because the more we talk about it, the less scary it is for everyone and the sooner we can get on with supporting our students in ways they deserve" (March 17, 2011). This was certainly the case for Noelle, who upon completion of the study articulated her desire to help queer youth as a means of promoting social justice.

> As a pre-service teacher it is scary to start considering all the things we do not know ... things we are afraid to talk about. We are about to be thrown into the world of teaching and there is no way a year-long program can prepare us for everything we need to know and be able to do. We do have

something on our side though ... we have a crazy passion to teach and to fight for social justice in this world. Participating in this study has helped me find this passion and redefine its meaning for me. Because of this I am an asset to gender-nonconforming and gay and lesbian youth who would perhaps not otherwise find a teacher they could trust.

(e-mail, March 11, 2011)

Beatrice and Ramona voiced their willingness to continue to build awareness around students as complete individuals with distinct gender and sexual identities. This realization challenged their prior assumptions about child development and student acknowledgement of societal gender norms and sexual identity. Beatrice admitted that her participation in the study helped her identify, and then adequately support, a student in her class whom she believed was actively questioning his sexual orientation identity.

> The way he talks, the way he compliments my clothes or my earrings when nobody else is in the classroom ... I think that wondering about or experimenting with his sexual identity or gender performance based on certain clues like that would have just slid by me before.
>
> *(interview, March 16, 2011)*

For others, participating in the study helped shape ideas about education and the role of the teacher. It provoked constructive dialogue with cooperating teachers, students, university instructors, and cohort colleagues—both in and outside the study. Arguably, the most invigorating conversations included the two planned meetings referred to in the research design as *group conversations*. On such occasions, all participants and I gathered to talk about issues of relevance with regard to sexual and gender diversity. Shortly after the second conversation, Noelle wrote:

> I think the group meeting went really well. It seems we all had thought-provoking ideas to share, more so than at our first group meeting. We sure are developing our critical minds! What I think I took away more than anything was how much of a role we, as future teachers, play in issues around gender and sexual diversity in the schools we teach.
>
> *(e-mail, February 3, 2011)*

Reflecting on the process, Aja contributed this:

> It provides a forum where it's like ... here is some information and a loose framework for how we can look at these issues with others. On my own I would not know how to have these conversations. I needed guidance to engage in important discussions and to self-reflect in a critical way.
>
> *(interview, March 16, 2011)*

Critical reflection was identified by a handful of participants as a major component of the study. It was also viewed as an effective tool for aiding the process of sense-making of ideas about education and the role of the teacher in relation to gender and sexual diversity. In fact, the space and intentionality set aside for reflection was what first attracted Quercus to participate. In our initial interview, he explained, "I jumped at the opportunity. Inside I was like, I definitely want to do this for the opportunity to reflect . . . the opportunity to pay attention to those sensitivities are so important" (September 26, 2010). Quercus also found his journal particularly helpful in getting to deeper levels of self-understanding. "I take notes in my journal of things that stand out, like quotes, observations. I constantly find myself naming, reflecting, acting . . . that whole process" (interview, September 26, 2010).

This notion of praxis typified Aja's experience as well. When asked if and how the study impacted her student teaching experience, she said:

> I've reflected a lot. Given all the journal entries and the different meetings we have had, it's really helped me to focus on things with a different lens and I do see things differently. The study helped me learn different ways that I can incorporate inclusivity into my practice . . . ways I can support students and that's really the heart of it for me, to learn how to be a better teacher.
> *(interview, March 16, 2011)*

Research participants viewed the study as a means to learn, analyze, and reflect on inclusive practices and critical pedagogy. Findings that inform Assertion 5, *Teacher candidates possess a desire to learn about and act as queer advocates and allies*, not only described how the study affected participants but also related to the ways in which they made sense of queer issues positioned within teacher preparation programs. All eight participants attended numerous graduate-level courses while completing their teaching and learning responsibilities in the field. Their experiences on campus, as consumers of university coursework and instructional methods, comprised a substantial amount of coded research. Presented here is a synthesis of the ways in which participants made sense of queer issues related to components of teacher education.

With a magnified lens, all participants voiced a need to explicitly cover queer issues in greater detail on the university campus. Jack believed that increased attention to these issues could help prepare teachers to see their role as influential and to acknowledge that bringing up the issues does not have to be as controversial as one may think.

> I think it is really important for straight and cisgendered people to tackle homophobia and transphobia in their classrooms and at large because there is the threat of queer and/or trans teachers losing their jobs for bringing up

these issues and being told they are pushing their own agenda onto others. Having conversations with students about gender dynamics is really important and can often come up organically by reading a story, talking on the playground, or directly responding to students' comments like "I don't want to sit next to all these girls!"

(e-mail, November 11, 2010)

In addition to voicing an overall need to address queer issues in teacher education, participants noted the importance of approach in introducing the topic. Expressing her needs as a social learner, Beatrice clarified, "Talking about these issues and knowing I have a support system are more important to me than having certain strategies worked out" (e-mail, November 11, 2010). Still, other participants, such as Aja, requested concrete tactics.

I really want to make sense of these issues and figure out how to mediate and address them positively and constructively so we can have teachable moments instead of moments when things go wrong and we look the other way because we're uncomfortable.

(interview, September 30, 2010)

Educating teacher candidates on basic laws, such as antidiscrimination legislation, is another suggestion that emerged from the data. Other recommendations included helping pre-service teachers break down and map their own gender and sexuality on a spectrum, incorporating more readings on critical theory in courses, and engaging in more dialogue about children and social development. Another idea is for the program to offer courses on conflict and resolution in education and/or classes on developing communication skills.

In a group conversation (February 1, 2011), Moses argued that the university must take ownership by requiring a field assignment that develops the practice of such strategies, the implementation of what Aja described as "a teachable moment." The following is a transcript of the dialogue as it unfolded.

MOSES: I think there should be some sort of lesson plan assignment presented with cohort members as our students, just to get a feel for what it would be like. To get a feel for the awkward things that would come up so when we go to do it in front of a class and it doesn't blow up in our faces. I'm sure that if I were to do it in front of us, I'd make several mistakes and say the wrong thing because I do that, but it would be a lot easier to do it a second time.

NOELLE: That's a really good idea.

TOWNES: Yeah, that would be so cool if we had GTEP backing us and that was a required assignment out in the field.

BEATRICE: That would be really cool!

RAMONA: Yeah. We could be like . . . sorry, we have to!

MOSES: (*Laughing*) It's a field requirement! Yeah, that would make sense. It would change something. (*Looking at me.*) Make it required!!

TOWNES: But GTEP has partnerships that they build with these elementary and middle schools—

AJA: Well, if the school restricts us from completing the assignment, then maybe GTEP doesn't want to partner with that school anyway.

MOSES: Can you make it a requirement, like can we make it happen?

OLIVIA: For you?

MOSES: Sure.

OLIVIA: I am hoping that this research informs future practice here at PSU, so you know, who knows what the future will hold . . .

MOSES: I want to go over to [Spruce Elementary] and say I *have* to do this!

After reflecting on the group dialogue, Moses reiterated his point in an individual interview.

> At the very least it should be mandated for student teachers to develop and execute a lesson in the field because if we don't get used to doing it now while we are building our repertoire of lessons and our feelings of how we are in the classroom, then our efforts to address gender and sexual diversity will be weak and abandoned when we go out into a school and teach on our own.
>
> *(March 16, 2011)*

In addition to making sense of specific assignments, participants agreed that issues of social justice should transcend an isolated, introductory multicultural course, which, in the case of GTEP, preceded active field engagement. According to Beatrice, the timing of the course presented itself as a missed opportunity. "It was more like an academic/social interest than a this-is-how-it-directly-relates-to-my-students interest" (March 16, 2011). Aja observed, "Multicultural and urban education was an amazing class, but one class is not enough, especially given the importance and prevalence of these issues" (e-mail, March 16, 2011).

Another theme shared by participants focused on the language and word choice among GTEP faculty and staff. Representative of similar data offered by her co-participants, Noelle wrote:

> I think the faculty needs to be very aware of what they say about gender and assumptions they make around relationships and families. You [Olivia] are very conscious of the things you say, but other faculty members are not

so careful. Often I have seen stereotypical gender roles taught and added to stereotypes. I think that they should be more aware of how they talk and remember that members of their audience come from all walks of life.

(e-mail, November 11, 2010)

A final element coded within this fifth assertion is the need for intentional, transparent, and inclusive field placement assignments. Jack felt that his harmful experience with Mrs. Turner could have been prevented had the program conducted more informed school visits and acquired a sense of how the cooperating teacher would respond to issues related to nonnormative gender presentation and sexual orientation in the classroom.

Over and above assessing individual cooperating teachers' dispositions toward social justice and queerness, Moses recommended that GTEP examine schools more closely as it continues developing meaningful partnerships. The following statement also implies his suggestion for the university to consider school demographics and to seek placements that reflect the diversity found in schools across the nation.

Unfortunately, a quasi-democratic, two-party, pseudo-capitalistic environment makes it difficult to find truly democratic institutions that are open-minded. Teachers from these close-minded mental places need more preparation, but the best prep would be, in my opinion, an immersion. The person(s) would need to be around diversity. They need to socialize or work with queer students or dyad-moms/dyad-dads and understand their humanity.

(e-mail, November 11, 2010)

This final assertion—claiming teacher candidates want to explore how gender and sexual diversity manifest in schools—is particularly interesting to me as a teacher educator. I witnessed participants encouraged to identify and make sense of queer issues. They validated *and* challenged one another, which deepened our understanding of queer phenomena in public education.

Conclusion

The assertions in this chapter are important for many reasons. First, they provide insights into the way things are. They reflect a current reality for school stakeholders, a truth participants came to recognize as institutional hetero- and cissexism in their field placements. Locating and naming the system of attitudes, bias, and discrimination that further disenfranchises queer people contributes to the congruent literature cited in Chapter 2 (e.g., hooks, 1994; Sears & Williams, 1997; Sedgwick, 1990).

Second, the assertions are significant because they focus on outcomes for K–12 learners. Core themes attended to the presence or lack of support and empowerment, which participants believed influence youth's sense of human agency in school. Negative attention themes were indicative of the vulnerability that youth felt at school whereas positive support gave rise to students' sense of belonging and self-pride.

Participants of the study also developed an increased awareness of self. Assertions that speak to the identification and sustainability of the person within the profession are important because teaching stems from our inwardness, and knowing ourselves is as important as employing sound instructional strategies and knowing our students well (Palmer, 1997). The acknowledgement of queerness in the classroom, as well as within the study, triggered participants to consider their own sexual orientation and gender identity, which established a deeper sense of self-identity.

A final reason is that the assertions acknowledge that concentrated efforts toward deconstructing hetero- and cisnormative institutions require resources, such as time. This recognition can move the field toward identifying which resources are needed and how these resources might be utilized.

Reflection Questions

1. How does sexual and gender diversity show up in your professional work? In what ways do queer individuals and culture directly affect you?
2. Review each of the five assertions. Which of these stand out to you most? Why? In what ways might one or more of the assertions affirm or contradict your experience in education?
3. Is there a particular research participant you connected with? What did you find meaningful about his or her experience or perspective?

Recommended Resources

Books About Queer Issues in Education

DePalma, R., & Atkinson, E. (Eds.). (2009). *Interrogating heteronormativity in primary schools: The No Outsiders Project*. Oakhill, VA: Trentham.

Epstein, D. (Ed.). (1994). *Challenging lesbian and gay inequalities in education*. Buckingham, UK: Open University Press.

Larrabee, T.G., & Morehead, P. (2010). Broadening views of social justice and teacher leadership: Addressing LGB issues in teacher education. *Issues in Teacher Education, 19*(2), 37–52.

Sadowski, M. (2010). Setting LGBTQ issues within wider frameworks for pre-service educators. *Issues in Teacher Education, 19*(2), 53–63.

Articles About Queer Issues in Education

Athanases, S.Z., & Larrabee, T.G. (2003). Toward a consistent stance in teaching for equity: Learning to advocate for lesbian- and gay-identified youth. *Teaching and Teacher Education, 19*, 237–261.

Cahill, B., & Adams, E. (1997). An exploratory study of early childhood teachers' attitudes toward gender roles. *Sex Roles, 36*(7/8), 517–529.

Grossman, A.H., Haney, A.P., Edwards, P., Alessi, E.J., Ardon, M., & Howell, T.J. (2009). Lesbian, gay, bisexual and transgender youth talk about experiencing and coping with school violence: A qualitative study. *Journal of LGBT Youth, 6*, 24–46.

Hermann-Wilmarth, J.M., & Bills, P. (2010). Identity shifts: Queering teacher education research. *The Teacher Educator, 45*, 257–272.

References

Abdal-Haqq, I. (1998). *Constructivism in teacher education: Considerations for those who would link practice to theory.* Washington, DC: Office of Educational Research and Improvement. (ERIC Document Reproduction Service No. ED426986)

Applefield, J.M., Huber, R., & Moallem, M. (2000). Constructivism in theory and practice: Toward a better understanding. *High School Journal, 84*(2), 35–53.

Bridge 13 Program. (2006). *Bridging our differences.* Retrieved from www.prideproject.org/bridge_13

Butler, J. (1990). *Gender trouble: Feminism and the subversion of identity.* New York: Routledge.

Derman-Sparks, L., & Edwards, J.O. (2010). *Anti-bias education: For young children and ourselves.* Washington, DC: National Association for the Education of Young Children.

Evans, K. (2002). *Negotiating the self: Identity, sexuality, and emotion in learning to teach.* New York: Routledge.

Fairclough, N. (1988). *Language and power.* London, UK: Longman.

Fassinger, R.E. (2000). Gender and sexuality in human development: Implications for prevention and advocacy in counseling psychology. In S.D. Brown & R.W. Lent (Eds.), *Handbook of counseling psychology* (pp. 346–378). New York: John Wiley.

Fierstein, H. (2002). *The sissy duckling.* New York: Simon & Schuster Books for Young Readers.

Freire, P. (1970). *Pedagogy of the oppressed.* New York: Continuum.

hooks, b. (1994). *Teaching to transgress: Education as the practice of freedom,* London, UK: Routledge.

Kosciw, J.G., Greytak, E.A., Bartkiewicz, M.J., Boesen, M.J., & Palmer, N.A. (2012). *The 2011 National School Climate Survey: The experiences of lesbian, gay, bisexual and transgender youth in our nation's schools.* New York: GLSEN.

O'Connor, C. (2013, March 3). Pediatricians see growing number of cross-gender kids like Coy Mathis. *Denver Post.* Retrieved from www.denverpost.com/ci_22706559/pediatricians-see-growing-number-crosss-gender-kids-like

Palmer, P.J. (1997). The heart of a teacher. *Change Magazine, 29*(6), 14–21.

Palmer, P.J. (1998). *The courage to teach: Exploring the inner landscape of a teacher's life.* San Francisco, CA: Jossey-Bass.

Petrovic, J.E., & Rosiek, J. (2007). From teacher knowledge to queered teacher knowledge research: Escaping the epistemic straight jacket. In N.M. Rodriguez & W.F. Pinar (Eds.), *Queering straight teachers* (pp. 201–231). New York: Peter Lang.

Schmidt, S. (2012, August 28). *Re: Unexpected stereotypes and how to combat them*. Retrieved from www.tolerance.org/blog/unexpected-stereotypes-and-how-combat-them

Sears, J.T. (2005). *Youth, education, and sexualities: An international encyclopedia*. Westport, CT: Greenwood Press.

Sears, J.T., & Williams, W.L. (1997). *Overcoming heterosexism and homophobia*. New York: Columbia University Press.

Sedgwick, E.K. (1990). *Epistemology of the closet*. Berkeley: University of California Press.

Taylor, C. (2002). Beyond empathy: Confronting homophobia in critical education courses. *Journal of Lesbian Studies, 6*(3/4), 219–234.

6
TEACHER EDUCATORS QUEER THEIR PRACTICE

In This Chapter

- Methodology and findings from a three-year study that examined how teacher educators confront and work through educational issues related to queerness.
- An introduction to the Curriculum and Instruction (CI) LGBTQ Task Force, which was formed to investigate school climate and lead queer inclusion efforts within the department.
- A narrative sequence of events initiated by the CI LGBTQ Task Force to provide direction to faculty across the nation who are hungry for queer inclusion in their teacher preparation programs.
- A look at one tangible outcome of the task force, a course now offered through the department called *LGBTQ Advocacy in K–12 Classrooms*.

Research Goals and Approach

The research in Chapter 5 illustrates that by developing agency within group conversations and ongoing sense-making and support, participants were able to contribute a group impact. Acquiring this influence was likely unique to those who participated in the study; however, if presented with a framework for queer inclusion, teacher educators could begin to imagine and produce a far greater collective impact. Indeed, before teacher candidates can be guided toward acquiring the knowledge, skills, and dispositions necessary to expose the deep injustice of queer oppression, teacher educators must be mentored through this process. The Queer Inclusion in Education Framework in Chapter 3 proposes that as teacher educators work toward queer inclusion by developing a willingness and ability to understand and meet the needs of queer students, transformative action in teacher education ensues. This chapter describes such a transformation among faculty in the CI department at Portland State University (PSU).

Members of the CI LGBTQ Task Force wanted to examine how faculty responded to ongoing professional development focused on queer content. Specially, we wanted to investigate faculty members' experience working with queer teacher candidates as well as faculty's ability and willingness to infuse sexual orientation and gender diversity into their coursework and instruction.

The purpose of our inquiry was to collect information to inform the direction and actions of the task force and to align our support with faculty needs. We engaged in participatory action research, which is the "systematic collection and analysis of data for the purpose of taking action and making change" (Gillis & Jackson, 2002, p. 264). The cyclic process of research, reflection, and action involved in participatory action research also prompted members of the task force to investigate our individual roles by asking questions like these: What brought me to this work? How does this work influence my life and professional practice?

Research Context and Methods

PSU is located in the heart of downtown Portland, Oregon. The university's total enrollment is 30,000. PSU's Graduate School of Education (GSE) is the largest and most comprehensive school of education in Oregon. The GSE is comprised of several departments, including the CI department, and offers several degree options, such as doctor of education, master of education, and MA/MS in counseling, curriculum and instruction, educational leadership, and special education. Multiple teacher licensure programs, including the Graduate Teacher Education Program (GTEP), are also offered within the GSE.

Members of the CI LGBTQ Task Force collected a wide variety of data sources for three consecutive years from 2010–2013. We collected and analyzed data from (a) self-generated notes and formal meeting minutes from CI faculty meetings in which the task force presented, (b) artifacts provided by faculty at CI faculty meetings in which the task force presented, (c) focus group sessions with current LGBTQ-identified teacher candidates, (d) task force members' ongoing reflective writing, (e) task force monthly meeting agendas, notes, and reflections, and (g) GSE faculty written responses to CI LGBTQ Task Force presentations.

Introduction to the CI LGBTQ Task Force

In fall 2010, the chair of the CI department, Christine Chaillé, came to a faculty meeting with one simple question: "What would we have done?" A teacher candidate from a nearby university made national headlines when he was forced to discontinue his student teaching for disclosing that he was gay. He told a fourth grader who asked if he was married that he was not. When the student asked why, Seth Stambaugh replied that it was not legal for him to get married because he would choose to marry another man.

Posing that simple question, "What would we have done?" led to organizing a task force to brainstorm and implement policy change and instructional practices. Prior to this conversation, the invisibility of queerness took several forms within the GSE. It was my perception that universal denial of the need to address queer issues and the subtle marginalization of queer faculty and students was largely unquestioned until this moment.

At the beginning of fall in 2013, the CI LGBTQ Task Force was composed of three founding members as well as one individual who joined year two and one who joined year four. The founding members—Chaillé, Audrey Lingley, and I—recalled our initial gravitation to this work. Chaillé, who was serving her third consecutive year as department chair at the time she raised the issue, explained in these terms:

> When the Seth Stambaugh case surfaced, it seemed like an opportunity to engage in what could be a difficult conversation. While I knew that I, and many of my colleagues, both gay and straight, had responded thoughtfully to issues involving teacher candidates who were gay, encounters with homophobia in the schools, or education about LBGTQ issues in our public schools, we had never had discussions as a faculty about how each of us had responded, nor had we even discussed whether we should have some program-wide consensus and work together on these issues.
>
> *(personal communication, April 5, 2012)*

Chaillé has courage and integrity. She is not afraid to take a hard stance on what she believes in. Leading by example, she asked faculty to engage in difficult conversations that were emotionally and politically charged. She also followed through on her initial commitment to address queer issues by providing support, leadership, and resources. She offered the task force 15–25 minutes at most of the monthly department meetings over an 18-month period. During this time the department was taking on a massive program revision and negotiating severe budget cuts in the midst of union upheaval, so the unique gift of time as a limited resource was not lost on me. Chaillé, who set the agenda for department meetings, communicated the imperative for addressing LGBTQ issues in teacher education by dedicating so much time to the topic.

Another founding member, Lingley, was a doctoral student beginning her graduate assistantship at the time Chaillé raised up Seth Stambaugh's experience. Lingley happened to attend the faculty meeting by chance and e-mailed Chaillé a few days later to inquire if she could serve on the task force, even though she was not a faculty member. When asked what initially drew her in, Lingley conveyed that queer activism has always been a part of her life.

> I had been an active advocate for gay rights for 20 years; my queer coming of age emerged within the AIDS activist organization ACT UP in the early 1990s at Oberlin College. I wrote my master's thesis in 1994 on why addressing LGBTQ issues in K–12 education was important for the academic achievement of all students. Until meeting and marrying my husband in the early 2000s, I'd had to actively negotiate being a visibly queer teacher (I had a long-term same-sex partner) in middle and high school classrooms in both openly accepting urban and barely-tolerant suburban contexts. Once I married a man, however, my queerness became less apparent; I looked more like a straight ally, without a same-sex partner. Passing for straight did not lessen my level of commitment to explicitly addressing an issue that was easily swept under the rug in K–12 education.
>
> *(personal communication, April 5, 2012)*

As for me, not accepting the invitation to join the task force was never an option. I needed this forum and community to process and understand my own evolution as a queer doctoral student and educator. My experience in education, up to that point, had been rough. I came out as a lesbian three months before joining the Peace Corps, where I was forced into the closet for complex cultural reasons. When I returned from rural South Africa, I secured my first American teaching job within a conservative school district. Over time I came out to close colleagues, but I filtered conversations strategically depending on who was in the staff room. Heteronormativity ran rampant, and cisgender dominance ruled the school, masking any awareness of *Other*. Highly disenchanted, I left K–8 teaching to enroll in PSU's doctoral program to study queer issues in education. I secured a position as a graduate assistant and then became a fixed-term faculty member in summer 2010. Chaillé's invitation to join the task force surfaced shortly thereafter, and I was hooked.

Anita Bright joined the task force in fall 2011 as a newly appointed tenure-track faculty member. Later she recalled her first memory of hearing about the task force and described her eagerness to participate.

> Entering my new role at PSU, I was eager to become engaged with my new community and to learn more about the ways advocacy, allyship, and social justice were both envisioned and actualized at this level. After several decades in K–12 settings, wherein many topics were off-limits, I was excited to stretch my wings and see how things might be different. At my first faculty retreat, one of the women in the room (Olivia, then a doctoral student and fixed-term faculty member) stood up and made a short announcement

about the LGBTQ Task Force and explained that anyone was welcome to join. I knew I both needed and wanted to be involved in various things that were meaningful to me, and this seemed perfect.

(personal communication, April 5, 2012)

The final member of the task force, Rurik Nackerud, was a doctoral student and adjunct faculty member. He joined the task force because he wanted to be more involved with queer issues affecting current PSU faculty and students.

LGBTQ Task Force Chronology and Faculty Development

The CI LGBTQ Task Force began meeting monthly in winter 2010. We framed two goals to guide our efforts:

1. Provide teacher educators with skills, dispositions, and knowledge that empower them to act as advocates for LGBTQ K–12 students and K–12 teachers.
2. Provide a conceptual framework for teaching, researching, and writing about LGBTQ issues in education and unpack what queer education looks like: what it is, what it is not.

Coming up with the goals was easy, but deliberating on ways to approach these goals proved more challenging. Lingley and I developed what we called a *Spectrum of Visibility* (see the Companion Website at queerinclusion.com) to help prioritize task force initiatives. Maintaining and dismantling hetero- and cisnormativity served as bookends to an assortment of actions scattered on this continuum, actions such as developing a mission statement, reviewing program admissions and application language, increasing inclusive print media (e.g., safe space posters), identifying a queer faculty mentor, developing explicit queer inclusion in course curricula, encouraging faculty professional development, conducting and analyzing queer research, making queer inclusion a part of university-school partnership criteria, and offering a course on queer issues in education. What we found was that the *Spectrum of Visibility* actually served as an activity of sorts that catapulted important dialogue and helped the task force, and then faculty, join in the conversation. By discussing (and sometimes disagreeing about) which actions should be plotted where on the continuum, faculty revealed current levels of understandings and personal assumptions around queerness, oppression, and advocacy. This helped us develop a shared knowledge bank and vocabulary.

Putting our doctoral candidacy skills to work, Lingley and I channeled our inner academics to conduct an annotated review of the literature on LGBTQ issues in teacher education. We set sail in uncharted territory and hoped to discover how others in teacher education infuse queerness into their courses and programs. We were utterly disappointed when we found next to nothing. Still, what did exist was helpful in getting us started. Larrabee and Morehead (2010) argued for a contextualization of LGB issues in education within broader conceptual frameworks of social justice and teacher leadership. Sadowski (2010) demonstrated how placing LGBTQ issues within the larger ideals often reflected in a school's mission statement is an effective strategy for empowering educators to advocate for LGBTQ youth. In their article, "Visibility Matters: Policy Work as Activism in Teacher Education," Horn et al. (2010) conducted an electronic assessment of all 57 Illinois teacher education programs to determine levels of LGBTQ (in)visibility. The authors' list of recommendations for teacher education programs (discussed in Chapter 2) was of particular importance to the task force.

Task force members blazed a trail by conducting original research with CI faculty to expose teacher educators' perspectives, concerns, and hopes around queerness. We documented the entire journey, including a significant initial experience at a department meeting held in May 2011. Faculty took turns reading direct quotations that captured Jack's (see Chapter 5) experiences in GTEP, a program housed in the CI department. The following are two of the ten quotations from Jack, which were shared in that setting.

> Not a day goes by when I don't debate whether I can go through with this—having to choose to present myself as a lie to get a job—a job that's challenging enough as it is. I think maybe I'm whining too much or asking too much that I get to be who I am and teach.
> *(individual interview, March 17, 2011)*

> I do feel really isolated a lot of times in the program. I love my cohort and I love everyone in the program. I really want to hang out with people outside of class but I don't because often times I just want to be around queer people and I have so little time that I'm like I'm in school, which is the most heteronormative nightmare ever, you know like every day so that's really hard.
> *(individual interview, January 19, 2011)*

Direct quotations from Jack were used to situate teacher candidates' needs at our own front door. The task force thought it would be powerful and relevant for faculty to give voice to the testimony of a current transgender GTEP student. After reading the statements aloud in a round robin fashion, faculty sat in silence for five minutes writing to the prompt, "What issues does this raise for you?" Faculty members' written responses were coded, and four categories emerged: goals, concerns, observations, and personal reflections. As shown in Figure 6.1, faculty expressed a wide range of reactions.

Within this same forum, we asked faculty if we should commit to examining LGBTQ issues. Of the 20 respondents, 19 said yes, and 1 did not respond. Of the 19, 6 followed their affirmative with a qualifier regarding how to proceed

Themes	Examples From Faculty Responses
Goal The faculty member articulated a specific or general goal related to addressing LGBTQ issues.	"Preparation of Cooperating Teachers and University Supervisors for such situations and responsiveness." "Identifying and bridging university and community resources that support LGBTQ adults and youth." "What can we do to equip students like Jack—or for that matter *all* student—to be teacher leaders that promote social justice in schools and among the educational community?"
Concern The faculty member articulated a specific or general concern related to addressing LGBTQ issues.	"Do we create a safe 'space' or 'learning environment' that allows students and faculty to engage this sensitive issue here at GSE/PSU?" "Is it safe to come out with all the crazy/angry homophobes with homophobic parents out in our classrooms?" "Huge 'knowledge gap' in many of us. We don't know what to do. And silence often creates uncomfortableness." "I worry about how 'traditional' some school settings/stances are and want to know there would be support for them."
Observation The faculty member wrote a neutral statement expressing a particular pedagogical, political, or social stance or a speculation about LGBTQ people/issues.	"An intense sense of loneliness and vulnerability for Jack." "When 'one' is hurt, we are all hurt; when 'one' is unseen, we are all invisible!" "Is society in general ready to face reality about these issues?"
Personal Reflection The faculty member directly reflected on his or her own practice or experience.	"I feel ... less comfortable or knowledgeable about trans issues."

FIGURE 6.1. *Initial Faculty Meeting to Establish Queer Relevance.* A sample of faculty responses to the prompt, "What issues does reading Jack's quotations and considering queer inclusion in teacher education for the first time raise for you?" Recorded in a CI department faculty meeting on May 9, 2011, and subsequently arranged into four major themes.

(e.g., yes, but we do x first). When asked one final question, "What do you need, want, hope for regarding this topic?" faculty responded:

- Case studies and actual student voices
- Creation of a safe space for faculty dialogue

- Theoretical literature
- Pragmatic literature
- Topic to be part of our regular professional development
- Curricular materials to use in courses
- Clarify department's intentions and goals with this issue
- Develop a policy position
- Support for balancing personal perspective with professional stance
- Structured opportunities for student-to-student networking and mentoring.

To gather more precise information, we concluded the activity by asking faculty to record priorities on an index card. We requested each faculty member choose one of three areas of focus—professional preparedness, program clarity and commitment, and curriculum—to articulate a specific priority within that category. Faculty contributed three priorities for *professional preparedness*, one of which read, "Defining or identifying measurable goals can be difficult without some sort of baseline data. A survey maybe? A book club—with readings/discussion groups." *Program clarity and commitment* coded four responses, such as, "Clear policy is most important" and "Policy for our LGBT GTEP students as they are teaching in schools." A majority of the faculty wanted to focus on *curriculum*. Some tangible ideas produced by faculty included "Create a resource library for university faculty (articles, books, curricula, instructional approaches)" and "Concrete curriculum development is a really worthy goal. It will push us beyond our shared tendency to talk talk talk and will make us do something. Maybe a resource like an FAQ about 'what to do if' scenarios."

Although most faculty wanted to dive right into curriculum development and the (re)production of queer resources, members of the task force decided that generating a commitment statement was an important precursor. One thing was certain: It appeared that the faculty wanted to continue the discussion. Thus, the following month the task force organized a brown bag colloquium. The objectives of this interactive exchange were to (a) disseminate my research (see Chapter 5) as a means for examining the ways GTEP students encounter and make sense of LGBTQ issues in the field and on campus, (b) discuss personal and professional experiences and/or responsibilities in response to study findings, and (c) co-construct a resolution statement that represents CI advocacy for queer K–12 students and teachers. Fourteen CI faculty members attended this voluntary session making it the most widely attended of its kind during the year. Our agenda was twofold:

1. I presented research findings and assertions to frame an urgent need to both support queer teacher candidates and to interrupt hetero- and cisnormativity in schools.
2. Participants divided into small working groups to begin co-constructing an LGBTQ resolution statement.

The task force asked brown bag attendees to address the following prompts to aid in the second agenda item:

- What do we stand for as a department? Do we strive to be *tolerant* of LGBTQ individuals? To *accept* LGBTQ individuals, to be *inclusive* of LGBTQ individuals and issues? Do we strive to demonstrate a *visible opposition to homophobia*? Or something else entirely . . . ?
- Finish this sentence: The Curriculum and Instruction Department within the Graduate School of Education has a firm commitment to . . .
- Finish this sentence: Whereas some educational institutions discriminate against LGBTQ individuals, the Department of Curriculum and Instruction . . .
- When it comes to the topic of sexual orientation and gender identity and expression, what should be taught in K–12 public schools as well as teacher preparation programs?

The task force analyzed faculty responses and used the feedback to construct a draft that we brought to the next CI department meeting. After rich discussion about language and intention, faculty made slight revisions to the draft and unanimously approved the following statement in January 2012.

Curriculum and Instruction Department's LGBTQ Resolution Statement

As part of its commitment to social justice and human dignity, the Curriculum and Instruction Department demonstrates LGBTQ advocacy through inclusive policies and practices that are both intentionally proactive and strategically responsive.

Our next step as a faculty was to operationalize the resolution statement. The task force used momentum generated from our first two conversations to present a framework for taking inventory of current practices and policies. Specifically, we sought to collect faculty input on how they believed the CI department was currently and potentially "intentionally proactive" and "strategically responsive" with regard to queer-inclusive policies and practices. Small groups were supplied with a blank grid (see Figure 6.2) to guide their discussion. One pattern across faculty responses was the need to document (i.e., make visible) and enforce (i.e., make happen) queer teacher candidates' right to student teach in a safe and affirming placement. In other words, all participants wanted to ensure that teacher candidates, such as Jack, recognize that the department "has their back."

The quadrant that elicited the most response was *intentionally proactive practices*. Faculty were eager to discuss current and potential practices they deemed deliberate and proactive toward queer justice and inclusion. Here, faculty voiced desires to "prepare teachers to address homophobic language in schools," "within methods courses include examples in which LGBTQ are represented in literature or readings," "emphasize teacher dispositions needed for equitable treatment of

	Policies	**Practices**
Intentionally Proactive	*Example:* Teacher candidate's have the option of being removed from a placement that does not support LGBTQ inclusivity.	*Example:* Cohort leader/advisor skillfully supports LGBTQ Teacher Candidate negotiate the intersections between personal and professional identity transformation during GTEP.
Strategically Responsive	*Example:* Partnership agreements include language about Portland State's commitment to LGBTQ advocacy.	*Example:* In GTEP courses, LGBTQ people are explicitly identified as a group of learners within a diversity/equity context.

FIGURE 6.2. *Implementing an LGBTQ Resolution Statement.* A blank grid provided to CI faculty in winter 2012. Small groups were instructed to use the handout to brainstorm how the CI department was currently and perhaps intentionally proactive and strategically responsive with regard to queer-inclusive policies and practices.

LGBTQ students," and "uncover instructional strategies and curriculum implications for including LGBTQ issues." The Companion Website features a complete list of faculty responses to the activity depicted in Figure 6.2 as well as downloadable resources to facilitate the drafting of a resolution statement.

The elevated level of faculty engagement throughout this activity was striking. People seemed to appreciate that we were *doing* something with the resolution statement, a statement they now felt ownership over. This brainstorming and sorting exercise helped us continue to make sense of the words we put on paper and ultimately generated a product that would bring these words to life. Pulling apart the statement and using its exact language (i.e., policies and practices, intentionally proactive and strategically responsive) to operationalize possibilities for action also provoked some faculty to recall the *Spectrum of Visibility* document introduced the previous year. This opportunity allowed us to reflect on our efforts and progress over the past year. We were, at this point in our process, speaking a similar language. There was 100% buy-in, and faculty were beginning to envision, articulate, and act in transformative ways.

As previously mentioned, the task force was offered 15–25 minutes at most monthly department meetings over an 18-month period. Norming queer dialogue resulted in CI faculty's growing comfort with the topic. This prompted the task force to reach out to campus stakeholders to build more global partnerships. I met with the coordinator of the university's Queer Resource Center, and Lingley shared our work with PSU's chief diversity officer. We also wanted to elevate our visibility within the larger GSE. In addition to CI, the GSE houses the following departments: Continuing Education, Counseling, Educational Leadership and Policy, Child Development and Family Services, and Special Education. In spring 2012 the task force requested an opportunity to present at a GSE faculty meeting and was allocated 30 minutes to share our resolution statement, extend our support and agency across departments, and facilitate an activity that would both provide insight into our process thus far and allow us to gather more data. The activity required small groups of GSE faculty to brainstorm ways LGBTQ issues come up in their particular work/department. Specifically, faculty were asked to (a) form groups of three to five people (striving for diverse departmental representation), (b) use three minutes of silent time for personal reflection/writing, (c) discuss responses to the prompt ensuring everyone had an opportunity to share or pass, and (d) reconvene as a whole group to share big ideas and debrief the process.

Faculty responses were eye-opening. Again, participants were asked to respond to the question: "How do LGBTQ issues come up in your particular work/department within the GSE?" I began my analysis by transcribing all responses verbatim and landed on four distinct coding categories: current practices, desired practices, questions, and personal experiences. Some responses included department affiliations (e.g., in special education we ...) and described specifics (e.g., use case study, require a particular assignment) while other responses were unowned (i.e., no department attached to claim) and vague (e.g., we are inclusive and honor all diversity).

For *current practices*, a member of the Special Education Department wrote, "It's a civil rights issue. I cover an extensive/inclusive definition of 'family' in my *Survey of Exceptional Learner* course. I also cover issues pertaining to bullying, targeting students who are different." Members of the Counseling Department small group offered their view:

> All aspects of human sexuality show up in our practice; students seem to "know" this, but it is quite different when an individual student is actually presented with sexuality issues with a client in practice, whether LGBTQ or otherwise. Some students are particularly interested and ask/advocate in classes and program.

These two submissions identify a professional disposition to address queerness on some level within their departments. The approaches, as described here, vary in specificity but communicate an overall awareness that inclusivity is important. Consistent with the Chapter 5 findings, the second quotation illustrates that faculty recognize that graduate students desire training on how to best support queer individuals.

Members of the Educational Leadership and Policy (ELP) department, who teach and prepare school administrators, acknowledged their efforts to be LGBTQ inclusive:

> We examine all the manifestations of diversity with a lens of equity and with a focus on law. We teach our students about processes to ensure equity, how to communicate the focus to all stakeholders, and how to use disciplinary and/or complaint procedures when staff or students attempt to deny the rights of our students or staff through discriminatory practices, policies, or actions. We definitely include LGBTQ and allies and other issues in our discussions.

Providing what reads almost like a policy statement, these faculty members clearly defend their stance on equity and fairness and collapse queer issues into this cause. Another small group wrote of the ELP curriculum:

> We cover identity in *Developmental Perspectives in Adult Education*, a course all students in our programs take. We also use case studies of real-life events, such as the anti-gay church group protesting outside a school; we ask students how schools should respond in situations like this.

Other GSE faculty members are not so confident. Two separate groups recorded that queer issues are not addressed, to their knowledge, within their departments. One group wrote, "It doesn't show up. Sometimes this issue becomes a separate class-setting priority rather than a departmental concern. Therefore, it gets silenced and the problem either becomes invisible or gets forgotten within our work!"

Then there were some faculty whose confidence in addressing queer issues fell somewhere in between. One CI teacher educator told a story about a teacher candidate who, she felt, handled working with a transgender student really well. A member of the small group recorded this statement:

> There is a risk of avoiding topics that feel "hot" or "sensitive" just sticking our head in the sand when we worry that discussing, taking on, addressing topics could result in conflict being misconstrued, as biased. In order to address an issue regarding a possibly gay or trans student, we have to acknowledge that we think the student might be gay or trans—what if we are wrong? Might we be causing harm by raising the idea with a student who does not identify that way—it's tricky.

Compared to the ELP statement claiming they attend to all matters of diversity, this CI faculty member clearly identified and began processing an essential wondering. Without asserting one statement or departmental faculty is superior, I wonder if the contrast between these two statements lies in the amount of intentional time and scaffolding devoted to faculty development on the issue. The first statement, and many other responses offered by non-CI department faculty, may seem declarative bordering on defensive while most responses from CI faculty raised questions, critiqued current self-practice, and refrained from vague assertions that queerness was being addressed. Perhaps departments outside CI are further along with queer-inclusion efforts despite not having a department-wide focus on the issue. Or maybe this is comparing apples and oranges given the diversity of professional preparation needs across departments. One final remark: This observational comparison might be counterproductive all together; perhaps the focus should remain on the fact that people connected around this issue and generated active, on-topic conversation.

The second category identified in analysis was *desired practices*, gaps in knowledge, experiences, and/or resources that inhibit faculty from practicing queer inclusion. Some desired practices, as voiced by GSE faculty, included:

- Definitions of culture and diversity
- How to help facilitate students who change genders
- How to prepare teacher candidates for conservative K–12 environments
- How to address name calling
- Gender difference as a topic to address with K–12 students
- Curriculum/support for inclusive language practices for all teachers in the classroom/everywhere to not perpetuate heterosexual power (normalizing).

Eight items appeared in this category across all group submissions. Although the list was not exhaustive, it does point to specific needs across departments. This list also reveals that faculty differentiated gender and sexual orientation and articulated distinct needs for both. It seems the entire GSE faculty would like more information and resources to support queer (university) students and to prepare all practitioners for their professional roles within in a diverse, inclusive society.

Questions composed the third category. Two distinct groups posed questions. One group asked, "Should the GSE take more of a leadership role in districts to inform them about LGBTQ issues? How do you do an equity audit of curriculum with LGBTQ issues in mind?" The other group, addressing their question to task force members specifically, wondered:

> Would you share your work to assess/monitor Oregon Department of Education and school district policies regarding this issue? In particular, support to LGBTQ teachers and students. We need a list of the school districts that stand up for their LGBTQ employees.

At the onset of our GSE presentation, the task force introduced a suggestion box for faculty members to deposit confidential questions/comments. The one note submitted inquired about partnerships and implications for local schools and districts. This person wrote:

> You've done a lot of great work on this issue. I feel it should be shared/ worked on with other departments in the GSE. Could we consider taking it further—expand the task force to include districts and K–12 schools?

These questions, submitted by faculty from a range of departments, are similar in the sense that they all recognize the field (partnering K–12 schools and school districts) as a key component in advancing the conversation and creating positive change. A focus on semantics uncovers an element of taking a stance. The first respondents posed the following question: Should the GSE take more of a leadership role? Their use of *should* might denote an open and honest question to initiate dialogue, or it might represent an ambivalent stance on the issue. The second submission, in the form of a request, is less ambivalent about whether the GSE should take up the issue, but the authors seemed to dodge participation by requesting that the task force conduct the work. Finally, the third question asserted a desire to expand the task force with opportunities for the entire GSE to participate in efforts toward queer inclusion.

The last category was *personal stories*. Although all comments and questions were informed by individual personal experience (combined with group dynamics as faculty interacted with each other and the subject), some group members chose to articulate personal stories as a way to communicate their experiences with queer issues in education. One group submitted the following anecdote:

> In class discussions of policy issues in one of my classes, I spoke about the Seth Stambaugh case. Unfortunately, I used an example of why people are sensitive to the issue of sexuality and teachers and used another recent example of a teacher dating a student. I inadvertently linked being gay with child abuse. A student objected online. We had a great conversation the last class after I apologized for my lapse. It alerted me to the importance of how I talk about issues and to not assume that my students understand my intention. I need to be clear and to not link LGBTQ issues and other issues of discipline or school policy. They are not the same.

This quotation represents the sensitive and necessary nature of this work. It also exposes a common myth associating queerness and perversion to exacerbate the generalization that talking about queerness automatically means talking about sex. What I really appreciate about this admission is the faculty member's willingness to work through discomfort and conflict in the moment. Resurfacing the painful experience later with colleagues demonstrates humility and a desire to learn from mistakes.

Teacher educators also used the *personal stories* category to explore self-identity as a multifaceted and interlaced construct. Faculty of color explored the interstice of race, sexuality, and gender in new ways. Discourse asserting (and then debunking) queerness as "the new black" came into context when faculty critically examined queer and racial civil rights movements toward equality. International faculty shared how their unique cultural and ethnic backgrounds contributed to their understanding and evolutionary thinking of gender and sexual orientation. For them, acculturation is a process—their lived experience—whereby cultural identity, race, ethnicity, class, gender, and sexual identity are fused. Many of these transnational teacher educators used the conversation facilitated by the task force to raise the notion of multiple group identity and to assist faculty in supporting students who were *Othered* before they were queer.

Inviting faculty to engage in the prompt "How do LGBTQ issues come up in your particular work/department within the GSE?" presented imperative, and often neglected, dialogue. It also supplied the task force with a formative assessment on broader GSE practices, questions, and personal stories. (See the Companion Website for a complete list of faculty responses as well as the handout used to facilitate small-group discussion.)

Lingley and I recorded observational notes during the GSE activity. Lingley wrote, "Small group discussion began immediately. There was little to no individual think/write time despite our oral and visual instructions." Perhaps a lack of silent, personal reflection indicated that faculty members were eager to jump right into discussion. Or it might be the nature of the topic or the group of individuals that deterred people from individually contemplating their experiences before engaging in dialogue. Finally, it could be that faculty felt pressure to address the prompt within the narrow time frame.

My notes made reference to the concluding discussion. "We allowed five minutes for whole group discussion. It was slow to get started yet we had to end with three raised hands." In other words, the conversation was just gaining momentum when our time came to a close. The power of our presentations within CI meetings resided in the fact that they were consistent and regular. Over time the CI faculty refined their ability to jump in and out of the conversation, accessing similar reference points and language. However, as a larger faculty, many of whom had never previously discussed queer issues in their professional practice, we simply did not have enough time. In a subsequent task force meeting, we reflected on the activity and agreed that it successfully planted a seed within all departments and started the conversation. The biggest challenge, or shortcoming, of the activity was limited time. We did not allow for an adequate debrief, which was unfortunate as faculty were eager to further process their small-group discussions.

Following the GSE presentation, the task force, once again folding inward to the CI department, revisited faculty's desire to develop and use queer curriculum. We wanted to provide teacher educators with the library of resources we had collected over the previous two years, but we felt it was vital to first elicit and honor faculty knowledge. Within small groups, CI faculty discussed and recorded responses to the following prompts.

- What entry points can you identify for LGBTQ issues within the department's current curriculum? For instance, a field-based assignment connected to *Integrated Methods I: Reading, Language Arts* that requires students to read *And Tango Makes Three* (Richardson & Parnell, 2012) and facilitate a discussion about family diversity with K–8 students. Or including text or video about transgender youth in *Multicultural and Urban Education*.
- Describe any stories or experiences you have with queer issues (in education) that might help colleagues. Think of these as case studies that can offer faculty knowledge and guidance.
- Brainstorm and list any specific teaching methods and/or materials that would be good resources to include in our LGBTQ resource binder.

A focus on curriculum entry points, stories or experiences, and methods and/or materials we theorized would allow faculty to think more deeply about their current practices and critique curriculum they encountered daily.

As before, faculty was highly engaged, with 46 responses produced in just 15 minutes. Of note, faculty identified the following entry points for LGBTQ issues within the department: classroom management (bullying); literacy methods courses (banned books, LGBTQ children's books); including the LGBTQ resolution statement in all program handbooks and course syllabi; destabilization of heteronormative language (e.g., *partner* instead of *husband/wife*; *family* instead of *mother/father*); and use of persona dolls affected by queerness in early childhood education classes.

Brainstorming future entry points for queer inclusion proved easier than reviving past stories and experiences with queerness. Still, a pair of faculty who identified as *Other* noted that they have experienced multiple conflicts surrounding language, culture, social status, cultural capital, issues of power, and inclusion/exclusion. "For us," they wrote, "LGBTQ cannot really be separated from these conflicts, or acts of discrimination." Other small groups said they had encountered the following: a student teacher who changed gender during the program, a group of students who presented a project on collections of LGBTQ literature, and personal fear with self-identifying as a queer professor.

Finally, noteworthy responses to the final item, a brainstormed list of specific queer teaching methods and materials, included using "Reclaiming Identity" by Tonningsen and other narratives from *Stories of the Courage to Teach* (Intrator, 2002) as a required reading, the *It Gets Better* video series, and GLSEN. (See the

Companion Website for a full list of faculty responses to all three prompts as well as the handout used to facilitate the small-group discussion.)

For months leading up to the next CI faculty meeting, task force members worked on a department website to house queer content and resources for faculty and staff. This website included information about the task force, resources on vocabulary and sexual and gender identity development, curriculum for teacher candidates broken down by levels (elementary, midlevel, and secondary), ready-to-go graduate-level assignments, local laws and policies affecting schools and queer individuals, research and literature, film and audio resources for classroom use, and a comprehensive list of web resources.

To resituate our purpose in providing and using such resources, the task force felt it necessary to bring in student voices. I had spoken with two current teacher candidates earlier in the year and elicited the following quotations, which were visually projected and read aloud during the CI meeting. A GTEP student who identified as gender nonconforming and lesbian said:

> As a student at PSU, I have always felt safe and supported by the on-campus community. As I prepared to step off campus and into my student teaching classroom, I worried about how my perceived gender-nonconformity would be met, not only by my cooperating teacher, but also by the students and parents with whom I would spend the year. More explicit attention to the issues that GLBTQ student teachers may face—along with the assurance that the GTEP community was prepared to defend me should issues arise—would have gone a long way towards easing the intense anxiety I felt as I prepared to transition into the classroom.
>
> *(October 7, 2012)*

The second quotation was from a cisgender, straight GTEP teacher candidate who was placed in a third-grade classroom with a student who, going into the school year, had transitioned from male to female.

> In the courses I have had thus far, I can't say that GTEP has prepared me for meeting the needs of trans and gender-nonconforming students. I would love to receive information or resources on how to address gender issues that may arise surrounding the identities of students. This is particularly relevant for me this year as I am struggling to adequately support the girl in my classroom who recently transitioned.
>
> *(October 8, 2012)*

After the quotations were read aloud, the task force shared a progress report detailing queer-inclusive efforts completed to that point. We consistently provided updated progress reports for several reasons. First, we wanted to be transparent and continue to elicit faculty buy-in. Second, we needed faculty to be informed so they would feel welcome and able to contribute should they decide to attend a monthly task force meeting. Third, we aspired to provide a chronological account of our accomplishments so faculty would recall the process and transmit our work beyond the department. Fourth, we wanted faculty to be invested in, and proud of, the many queer-inclusive actions taken within the department.

Sharing the quotations and providing a progress report consumed 5 of our 30 minutes at this particular meeting. The next agenda item was to introduce the website. I provided a quick tutorial to orientate faculty before giving them 15 minutes to explore the website in pairs using iPads. Guided by a handout (see Figure 6.3), faculty recorded observations and then articulated their goals for queer advocacy. One pair wrote, "We appreciate the opportunity to explore the

Name(s): _____

Exploring the CI LGBTQ Advocacy Website

Come back to. . .	I have a question about. . .

Remember to use. . .

In Class   In Advising

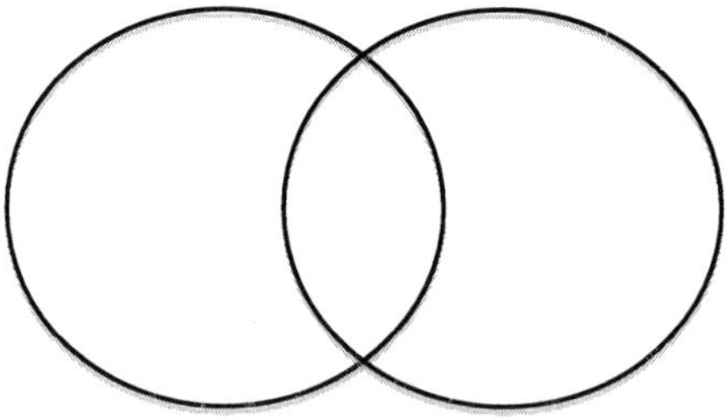

Personal 2012–2013 LGBTQ-Inclusive Goal Setting
1. What do you plan to do (big or small) to uphold the CI LGBTQ Resolution Statement?
2. What will you do this term . . . next term . . . in classes . . . in advising . . . in everyday interactions with students to demonstrate LGBTQ advocacy?

FIGURE 6.3. *Handout to Guide Faculty in Exploring the Departmental LGBTQ Website.* After receiving a brief orientation to the LGBTQ faculty website, pairs completed the handout by recording observations and articulating goals for queer advocacy.

website. We need more time to see the specifics of each section, but we think our initial goals will be in the areas of course assignments and readings." Another pair recorded, "We will bring LGBTQ liberation to the forefront of social justice conversations and efforts." The program coordinator of GTEP shared, "In working with partnerships this year, I will include our resolution statement/ideas in conversations about ways to support teacher candidates and K–12 learners." Finally, another participant within a dyad recorded this statement:

> I will look to infuse my classroom activities and my advising to individual students with information, problem-posing, and awareness strategies to support both the LGBTQ teacher candidates themselves, and assist all candidates in supporting and educating their K–12 students around the variety of issues they encounter.

We concluded the activity with a 10-minute whole-group discussion to gather input about the website and to allow faculty to reflect on goal setting. Task force members collected handouts completed by each pair. These were scanned and e-mailed to the authors with answers to their questions (if applicable). This provided the task force with data and faculty members with electronic residue of their commitment to use the website as well as their immediate goals for LGBTQ advocacy. The following is an e-mail sent to faculty members who worked on the task together (May 15, 2012):

Hi Henry and Thule,

I hope this email finds you well. Attached is a copy of your work from our CI meeting this month. You might remember the LGBTQ Task Force facilitated a brief partner activity for which you explored our department's *LGBTQ Advocacy in Education* website and articulated personal goals for queering your practice (see attached).

Henry, you asked how we could better include supervisors, cooperating teachers, and adjunct educators in this conversation. This is a great question that the task force will discuss in our June meeting. I look forward to any input you have on this given your unique position at the axis of such fieldwork. Thule, you asked if this is infused in our ongoing GTEP program revision. This question is vital! I have had my finger on the pulse of this while we've engaged in revision dialogue, but you remind me to bring this to our upcoming task force meeting and to GTEP program coordinators' attention. Thank you!

Please consider members of the CI LGBTQ Task Force as a resource next year as you work toward your goal(s). We would also love to hear feedback on how your work regarding LGBTQ advocacy is received by your students.

Sincerely,
Olivia

As the 2011–2012 academic year came to a close, task force members began brainstorming goals for the following year. I submitted a proposal for a university diversity mini-grant, and in winter 2013 it was approved. The task force was awarded $800 to design and produce posters for a visibility campaign. The purpose of the campaign was to bring awareness to the task force and increase overall GSE enrollment and hiring of queer individuals and allies. Up to this point, the task force had been highly active, with support and involvement from the larger CI department, but most of our efforts involved behind-the-scenes work within faculty meetings. We needed to bring our advocacy to the forefront. We hoped that in addition to communicating our commitment to queer social justice, the campaign would aid in our recruitment and retention of queer and straight-ally students and faculty.

I worked with the GSE diversity committee to gather ideas for poster content and settled on four tableaux, each showcasing our CI LGBTQ resolution statement (see Figure 6.4). It was important to select a range of focus grades to represent queer inclusion from early childhood to graduate-level education. We were also mindful to use authentic subjects who had close ties to the CI department. In retrospect I wish we had showcased a teacher candidate or cooperating teacher who presented their gender creatively. This lack of representation constituted a

FIGURE 6.4. *LGBTQ Task Force Visibility Campaign.* Four separate posters mounted in the halls of the Graduate School of Education to increase recruitment and retention efforts of queer faculty and students and to raise awareness about the Curriculum and Instruction department's commitment to interrupt hetero- and cisnormativity in education.

vital gap. Prior to mounting our posters, the task force was granted 10 minutes to present at a GSE faculty meeting. We revisited LGBTQ Task Force goals and CI's resolution statement before briefly sharing some accomplishments to collapse the time since our last GSE presentation. We closed with a teaser by projecting images from our visibility campaign, encouraging faculty to be on the lookout for their debut. As of this date, the walls of the GSE have four sets of each tableau (single posters measuring 11x17 inches), and the feedback from students and faculty has been overwhelmingly positive.

Additional mini-grant funds were used to purchase resources to queer faculty's professional library and to supplement the LGBTQ advocacy department website. We purchased two sets of The Bully Project educator's DVD and toolkit and two sets of a DVD produced by Welcoming Schools called *What Do You Know? Six- to Twelve-Year-Olds Talk about Gays and Lesbians*. We also stocked our shelves with books, ranging from children's literature that infused queer themes to academic texts on queer theory and activism. We shared these resources at a CI faculty meeting and viewed the Welcoming Schools video. Directly after the meeting, I was approached by a faculty member who wanted to use the video in her class that night.

At our last CI meeting in spring 2013, the task force again had the floor. I prepared the story of an encounter I had with a teacher candidate and planted two faculty members in the crowd with queer stories of their own. We started our 20-minute presentation with my story: A teacher candidate had recently told me about an experience she had with her third graders. Two students approached her, and one spoke up, "Ms. Lemons, Juan says you gay." Caught off-guard, Ms. Lemons replied, "Excuse me?" to which Marco restated, "Juan says you gay." Ms. Lemons responded by maintaining eye contact, slightly tilting her head, and uttering "huh." She then attended to a student raising her hand across the classroom. When I asked if she was satisfied with her response to the encounter, she said, "Sure. I mean I guess I don't know how else to answer in a way that affirms who I am *and* secures my placement in the program and school."

Faculty member Owen, whom I had spoken with prior to the meeting, followed with his own account of an interaction with a current male teacher candidate:

> Just prior to entering the program, a student in my cohort transitioned from female to male. I reached out to him to ensure that his needs were being met by me and within the program. At first I feared this conversation because I don't have all the knowledge and all the answers, but after the fact I felt so empowered and my student felt supported. We now have an understanding and remain open with each other.

The final person to share a story at the faculty meeting was Chaillé, our department chair, who recalled an encounter with a doctoral student who also served as her graduate assistant. He was new to the program, to the university, and was also new to living as an out gay man. Apparently he was negotiating his identity and assessing whether his new academic home would embrace his gayness. In a moment of panic, he sought services at the university's Queer Resource Center. It was closed, but there was a posting outside the door with PSU queer allies, and at the top of the list he saw a name that allowed him to breathe again: Christine Chaillé.

The three vignettes opened the door for others to share their stories. Faculty participation amazed me! Perhaps it was the two-plus years of effort we had put in to surface and work through queer issues as they related to education, or the increasing numbers of queer self-identification among students, but stories multiplied, and staff body language (affirming nods and utterances) demonstrated an elevated understanding and relevance. Of note, many faculty members perseverated over the initial story I shared. They specifically wanted guidance on how to advise queer teacher candidates about what they should and should not share about their gender and/or sexual orientation. They wanted the task force to validate or critique Ms. Lemon's response and provide language for such encounters. An interesting conversation ensued on state and local school district policies, the sharing of teachers' private versus public lives, and the nature of teacher-student relationships. As a group we did not generate concrete universal understanding, but the conversation was a meaningful step toward better supporting our teacher candidates in the field.

At about this same time, I was approached by a transgender teacher candidate enrolled in the two-year GTEP program. Although Jason admitted he was transgender, he identified first and foremost as male. He told me he was very anxious about the upcoming confirmation of his field experience placement. Jason was particularly nervous because his legal name does not match his preferred/actual name, and he worried that the school administrator, upon receiving his paperwork, would out him to the staff and his cooperating teacher. In his head the situation went something like this:

> *Principal:* (Looking at the list of teacher candidates) I see here we are supposed to have a Jennifer with us. Jennifer, are you here? (Looking at Jason) And who are you? I don't see your name on my list.

Upon hearing Jason express his apprehension about the program and his placement, I met with the GSE field placement coordinator. Chaillé joined our conversation. In this meeting, it was clarified that administrators do not receive paperwork containing students' legal names. Our dialogue moved into ways we can better support transgender and gender-nonconforming students in our programs. This conversation, however, remained shallow because we were three cisgender, gender-conforming females. How could our privileged identities inform us about the unique needs of transgender and gender-nonconforming students and what they may experience or need from a teacher preparation program? We needed to capture the voices of individuals with this lived experience. In addition to Jason, I knew of two other then current transgender GTEP teacher candidates. I sent all three the following e-mail (May 31, 2013):

Hi you three,

I hope this email finds you well. I am writing because I am interested in getting us four together to discuss how the CI department (more specifically GTEP) can improve its support and outreach for transgender and significantly gender-nonconforming teacher candidates. I imagine part of this discussion could focus on admissions and information, field placements, and staff education.

As members of the CI LGBTQ Task Force, Christine Chaillé and I asked ourselves, "What we can do to support current transgender students, recruit more transgender and gender-nonconforming students, and educate faculty such that we, as a program, increase awareness and advocacy?" But alas, Christine and I are gender-conforming, cisgender individuals. Our hearts are in the right place, but we need insider perspective in order to make a real difference.

So, I wonder if you might be willing to get together as a group and chat for an hour or so. This is not tied to a research study and you will not be asked to put your name behind anything discussed. I simply want to know, from your perspectives, what faculty could do to make GTEP more welcoming and supportive. I imagine the discussion to be pretty informal with the exception of some note-taking on my part so I can capture some information that is needed to implement (immediate) change. My suggestion is that we meet together as a group of four, but if you would feel more comfortable meeting with me one on one or submitting something in writing rather than meeting face to face, then that's okay too.

Thanks for your consideration,
Olivia

The three teacher candidates were willing and excited to meet. The four of us came together in early summer 2013 and talked for 90 minutes. Upon meeting, they all realized they had mutual friends in common, or as one of them said, "It's a small community!" Our discourse straddled the fine line between tragedy and humor; one moment people were cracking jokes and everyone would laugh, and the next minute someone was sharing a highly intimate and heavy experience. To guide our discussion, I had prepared three prompts and a graphic organizer unpacking various components of GTEP (see Figure 6.5). The prompts were intended to address tensions as well as to provide space for teacher candidates to offer suggestions.

This discussion illuminated many things for me. My notes uncovered four categories: field placements, queer ally visibility at onset of program (including website

Discussion Questions
1. When or where have you experienced anxiety in our Graduate Teacher Education Program (GTEP) as a result of your gender identity and/or perceived gender expression?
2. When or where have you experienced frustration in GTEP as a result of your gender identity and/or perceived gender expression?
3. Moving forward, how can GTEP best support you and future transgender and gender-nonconforming students? What concrete recommendations can you suggest?

Some Elements to Consider

Field Placements
- School matching
- Cooperating teacher matching
- Paperwork
- Initial meeting

Admissions
- Website
- Correspondence and communication
- Paperwork

GTEP

Curriculum and Instruction
- Acknowledgement/visibility
  - Instructional activities
  - Syllabi
  - Course texts
  - Inclusive language

Orientation and Getting Started
- GTEP paperwork: Forms, handbook, information handouts
- Initial cohort meeting or retreat
- Cohort community building
- Safe and supported opportunities to disclose

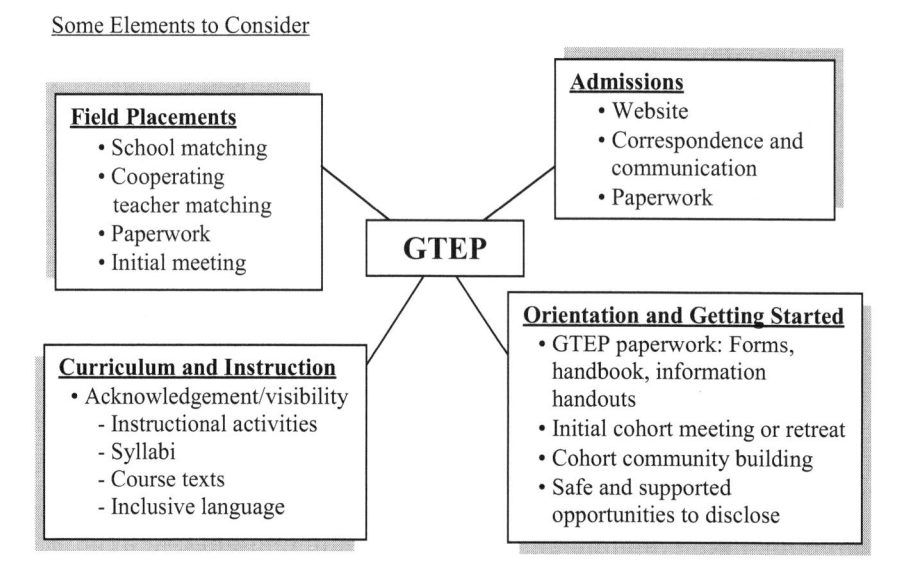

FIGURE 6.5. *Transgender Focus Group Discussion Guide.* A tool presented to three transgender teacher candidates on June 25, 2013, to guide initial discussion centered on faculty and program responsiveness to their needs.

development); faculty development and training (including positive models and missed opportunities); and a student queer task force. A synopsis of each category follows. (See the Companion Website for a complete account of this transgender focus group discussion as well as the graphic organizer used to facilitate the conversation.)

All three transgender candidates said field placements caused them the most anxiety in GTEP. One candidate would have appreciated the space to voice concerns about health, safety, and comfort within a K–12 placement (e.g., having a point of contact who invites this dialogue). Other suggestions for decreasing anxiety included providing concrete help up front, in part by acknowledging the unique needs of queer candidates and demystifying the process of securing field placements; PSU forming partnerships with specific schools and creating a district map with "temperature ratings" that help faculty and students gauge LGBTQ-safe and supportive schools; and the presence of CI's LGBTQ resolution statement and Q&A on the field placement website.

Candidates also emphasized their desire to see more queer-inclusive language, including explicit acknowledgement of transgender identity, while researching programs and applying to GTEP. One noted, "Trans cannot be assumed . . . it must not disappear behind lesbian and gay rhetoric. Transgender is often an afterthought in contemporary queer discourse and this makes us invisible."

The group discussed the possibility of a queer web link—embedded on the GSE's homepage as well as all program application sites—that would provide potential and current (queer) students with essential information. We brainstormed the following category headings (see the Companion Website for sample detailed content):

- CI LGBTQ resolution statement
- LGBTQ task force meeting information
- Queer liaison/contact person and available office hours
- Admissions Q&A for queer students
- LGBTQ information and resources for current students.

The group also discussed the need for faculty development and training on transgender and queer issues. "Faculty must be taught to think about gender in more complex ways," one student voiced. It was determined that faculty members need to explore inclusive ways of building cohort communities at the beginning of the program. Starting the cohort (or a course) with introductions that include stating preferred pronouns would be "constructive," as one student put it. According to the group, a demonstration and an example script of how this activity can be facilitated should be supplied to faculty to ensure the exercise is done sensitively (i.e., the point is not to single out transgender and gender-nonconforming students). In addition, only one individual in the group was aware that the GSE had a gender-neutral bathroom. The students suggested I mention this in faculty development, asking teacher educators to inform candidates of the gender-neutral bathroom at the onset of the program, thus ensuring one simple way to support transgender students. Jason said, "In fact, some cohort leaders organize a scavenger hunt for us to become familiar with the university and department, and the gender-neutral bathroom should be added to their existing list of spaces."

The group identified positive models that they observed within the GSE and also discussed missed opportunities among faculty and within classes. Two candidates felt the overall school culture was inclusive and that the GSE's commitment to social justice was transparent. One candidate, Everett, really appreciated that Owen, his cohort leader, was proactive and asked for a meeting to discuss his unique experience within the program. Owen offered Everett resources (CI

LGBTQ Task Force contact information) and unconditional support. Another candidate appreciated how an instructor opened up during the first session of *Multicultural and Urban Education* and offered pieces of her personal background and identity. As a result, the candidate felt they (this student preferred plural pronouns) could be authentic in class, and they viewed their instructor as an immediate ally. This same student said their cohort leader was very honest and up front with them by saying, "I know I have a lot to work on. I have a lot to learn about gender and transgender, but I want to learn and I'm here to support you." The student really appreciated their cohort leader's honesty and humility.

Missed opportunities were also identified. One candidate was triggered by narrow and exclusive language in an introductory GTEP course. The activity equated sex with gender, and our group discussed an overall need to educate faculty on the distinctions between sex, gender, and sexual orientation. Of the three, Jason struggled the most in the program; he was unhappy with it and felt isolated and unsupported. As the only (transgender) male in his cohort, early on Jason grew tired of gender-specific language and assumptions about heterosexual partnership.

Our final discussion point focused on a student queer task force. At the meeting, I introduced my idea of creating a queer/straight alliance within the GSE for teacher candidates. To me, this meant advertising a monthly meeting at a regularly scheduled time and place for current candidates interested in queer issues in education. I imagined that attendees might identify as lesbian, gay, bisexual, transgender, gender nonconforming, questioning, queer, intersex, straight allies, or folks interested in social justice. It would offer community among queer students in otherwise multi-isolated cohorts. It might also allow people to discuss experiences and challenges about being queer in K–12 school settings and thereby meet a unique need of their teacher preparation. I believed meeting agendas should be set by the students to adequately meet their social, academic, or both needs. The group liked the idea and thought calling it the Queer Task Force was a good idea.

LGBTQ Advocacy in K–12 Classrooms

Parallel to my engagement with the transgender focus group, I finished a one-credit course called *LGBTQ Advocacy in K–12 Classrooms*. Lingley and I had offered the spring course as an extension to our task force work. We met several times over the year to develop the scope and sequence from scratch. Our course description read as follows:

> This course is designed to provide a forum to explore issues of gender and sexual diversity for professionals in (or preparing for) K–12 school settings. This course will provide students with knowledge and skills to facilitate

increased understanding of others and of self around issues of identity, context, sexual orientation, and gender. Using constructivist approaches, participants will develop a personal framework for encountering and making sense of gender and sexual identity as they manifest in K–12 schools.

We identified four course objectives:

1. Reflect on personal biases to deepen own understanding of gender and sexual orientation, which are culturally and socially constructed.
2. Investigate legal responsibilities for addressing gender and sexual orientation in K–12 schools.
3. Identify instructional and curricular resources for addressing gender and sexual orientation in K–12 schools.
4. Develop a personal framework for encountering and making sense of gender and sexual identity as they manifest in schools.

Students could choose undergraduate or graduate credit for the elective course. Offering the course at a time when enrollment across campus (as well as the nation) was down and classes were being cut left and right due to low registration was risky, but we were overjoyed when 19 students registered for the class (4 undergraduates and 15 graduates). Our roster included individuals from a myriad of campus programs (e.g., counseling, teacher preparation, women's studies) and practicing professions (e.g., counseling, administration, and teaching).

Lingley and I distributed two surveys to gather initial information from course participants. The first survey, which was voluntary, collected information about student demographics and current comfort levels in addressing gender and sexual diversity. Participants (n = 16) submitted this survey. A majority of class participants (n = 11) were age 25–34. We asked students to complete the following statement using a Likert scale of never, seldom, sometimes, and often: *My teacher education courses have . . . acknowledged LGBTQ identity, culture, history*. Responses varied: 14% said often, 43% reported sometimes, 35% chose seldom, and 7% disclosed never. Upon reviewing these data, Lingley and I noticed two flaws with the question. One, we asked students to account for various criteria within one question (LGBTQ identity, culture, *and* history), and two, we failed to collect data on whether or not experiences were had on our campus or at another institution.

Items 5 and 6 on the survey asked students about their comfort levels in addressing gender and sexual diversity in their current (practicum or professional) placement. Using a Likert scale, we asked participants to reflect on the following statements: *I am comfortable addressing gender diversity in my current teaching placement* and *I am comfortable addressing sexual orientation and family diversity in my current teaching placement*. With regard to gender, 12% strongly agreed, 44% agreed, 26% mildly agreed, 6% disagreed, and for 12% the question was non-applicable.

Pertaining to the latter, 19% reported great comfort addressing sexual orientation and family diversity noted by their *strongly agree*, 38% agreed, 25% mildly agreed, 6% mildly disagreed, 6% disagreed, and for 6% the question was non-applicable.

This survey had a small sample size, and although the goal was not to generalize, within the context of the course, results provided us with important information. For instance, we were surprised by how many people were comfortable (on some level) addressing gender and sexual orientation in their current work. Given their sense of ease, we were relieved that we had inserted a question to elicit what participants wanted from the course: "Why this course, for you, at this time?" There was a wide range of response, but one common theme emerged. As one student said, "I need to know what I am allowed to talk about in my placement with regard to LGBTQ." Another student put it this way:

> I want to give this issue a voice, but I need to find ways to refine my own voice. How do I talk about these and other social issues in a way that helps and doesn't get me fired? I want to gain knowledge and skills about how to articulate and navigate these issues.

The other survey, the *Getting to Know You Survey*, provided us with information to meet course expectations and individual student needs. We provided the following prompts on this required survey.

- Please list two things you want to learn in this course.
- How do you learn best most of the time (lecture, whole-class discussion, cooperative learning, audiovisual or interactive activities, project-based learning, reading, and other)? Please rank your preferences.
- Do you usually feel comfortable asking questions or speaking during class discussions?
- Describe any supports or accommodations you will need to succeed in this course.
- Describe your current professional context/interest in education. Include information about past professional experiences in schools/learning communities (e.g., summer camp, tutoring, youth service agencies, etc.) that you want us to be aware of as we make decisions about curricular resources.
- What do you enjoy doing in your free time?
- In the space below, draw a diagram of your favorite classroom seating layout.

Most noteworthy for the scope of this chapter is the first item. As shown in the following, class participants offered diverse sources of motivation for taking the course. After careful analysis I organized responses to the prompt (list two things you want to learn in this course) into the following categories: engage in dialogue; provide ally support; acquire and use knowledge/information; and dispositions, teaching, and curriculum.

Engage in Dialogue

- Ways to talk about LGBTQ issues without losing my job;
- I want to know what my limitations will be as a teacher when it comes to talking to my class as well as individual students about LGBTQ subjects;
- Progressive, respectful, and contemporary language that supports/honors LGBTQ community;
- Learn how to converse about sexual orientation;
- How to create an inclusive learning community in all of my own classes down the road;
- How to talk to adolescents about LGBTQ issues in class.

Provide Ally Support

- Ways to support students being bullied or stereotyped;
- How to most effectively intervene to help make school more inclusive for LGBTQ kids;
- How to prevent bullying by educator;
- How to advocate for LGBTQ students in middle and high schools in oppressive environments;
- How to advocate more effectively for my students;
- How to advocate more effectively for myself as a LGBTQ staff member;
- Learn how to advocate for the LGBTQ community in the field of social services;
- How to further advocate for LGBTQ youth in school and beyond;
- How to advocate in a library setting where there are many students all the time;
- How to become a better advocate;
- Ways through my work that I can be supportive and welcoming (i.e., environment, school documents, language, resources, etc.);
- How to be a strong advocate in schools that I'm observing in, student teaching in, and my own classes;
- How to better communicate with and advocate for LGBTQ families in my current and future classrooms.

Acquire and Use Knowledge/Information

- Any information available to learn more about LGBTQ community and families as I am slightly inexperienced;
- School contexts in which individuals advocate for students and faculty/community regarding LGBTQ issues;
- Develop basic competency around history, theory, and practice in support of LGBTQ community;
- Get a better understanding of what's going on with or happening with children (as opposed to adult LGBTQ);

- Resources for/How to facilitate conversations with students about gender/family diversity;
- Resources for students who may come to me for advice;
- Current Oregon law relevant to LGBTQ folks;
- Additional resources to offer school communities seeking understanding.

Dispositions, Teaching, and Curriculum

- Foster confidence/courage to do hard work around LGBTQ issues;
- How to approach gender in elementary school classrooms;
- How to place materials for learning in all realms;
- How to coach people into integrating more about LGBTQ in their curriculum;
- How to convince district-level leaders that LGBTQ education is as important as straight education (when it comes to health, wellness, visibility, and acceptance *not* tolerance).

The class was organized into three separate sessions. We met from nine in the morning to noon on the first Saturday of each month during the term. We organized content into three themes and addressed one per session.

1. What's happened before?
2. What can I now know?
3. What happens next?

The class topics, objectives, activities, and readings/assignments for each session corresponded with the essential questions listed earlier (see Appendix C for course outline and schedule and the Companion Website for the class syllabus).

Lingley and I brainstormed this three-part structure based on the course objectives and our understanding of processing LGBTQ content as it relates to education and advocacy. We wanted the first session to honor the knowledge and experience of participants entering the room. After a brief framing of the class using queer and critical social theories, and introducing basic terms and concepts (e.g., queer, cisgender, identity development, heteronormativity), we facilitated an intuitive art exercise to provide time and space to reflect on personal assumptions, values, and beliefs about queerness and to prepare students for their upcoming *Memoir/Self-Inventory* assignment.

As a prelude to offering queer-inclusive curriculum in Chapters 7 and 8 of this book, the *Memoir/Self-Inventory* assignment description read:

> Operating under the assumption that gender and sexual orientation are socially and culturally constructed, this assignment invites you to mine your own constructions for the purpose of increasing your ability to be intentional in speech and action as an educator. In your essay, thoughtfully reflect

upon the genesis and evolution of your beliefs about gender and sexual orientation. We suggest that rather than crafting a chronological narrative, you identify one or two themes or patterns that emerge from the retrospective look, and use descriptions of critical events or influential persons to illustrate those themes. In recognition that many of our beliefs about gender and sexual orientation may be unexplored assumptions, we will engage in intuitive learning activities in our first class session as pre-writing for this essay.
(LGBTQ Advocacy in K–12 Classrooms *syllabus, pp. 3–4*)

We used class time for the intuitive art exercise mentioned earlier, which can also be described as a pre-writing activity and small-group discussion (see the Companion Website for the intuitive art exercise lesson plan) so students could explore potential themes related to their beliefs about gender and sexual orientation. Everyone received an 8- by 10-inch piece of white cardstock and oil pastels. Students had 20 minutes to create a visual representation of their individual constructions of gender and sexual orientation by exploring current beliefs, the genesis and evolution of their beliefs, and/or critical events that shaped their beliefs. Lingley and I reminded students to focus on *self* rather than doing a sociological critique. Although the assignment required that they not organize their memoir by chronological events, we stated that they might find structuring a chronology helpful as a pre-writing activity. Then they could analyze their timeline for themes. Next, we informed students that after 20 minutes they would meet in groups of three to share their visuals and talk through their beliefs and/or the evolution of those beliefs as part of beginning to "write" their memoir. We encouraged students to allow images to intuitively emerge, even ones that didn't seem to make sense, as sometimes it is in the explaining afterward that new insights become clear. Students worked in silence, and we were careful to provide a rationale for this aspect of the process. Earlier in the class, Lingley and I shared our own personal stories about being queer educators, and the act of silencing, or being silenced, was a theme among both our experiences. We intentionally noted that, for the purpose of this activity, we requested a silence that allowed us to go inward while still being in community. It was an opportunity to explore silence as a source of strength and shared support instead of as a source of shame and alienation.

The art pieces were incredible, only outshone by the thoughtful and courageous dialogue that ensued in the small groups. The final product submitted by students for the *Memoir/Self-Inventory* assignment, a 2- to 3-page essay, was equally powerful. The following are excerpts of the final essay from two students, one of whom said in the final day of class, "The memoir was almost cathartic."

> *Student 1.* The majority of my childhood was spent negotiating my gender identity under the watchful eyes of my mother. We had different ideas of who I would be and how I would present myself to the world. As a teacher, I deal with questions about my gender every day. Whether it's

direct questions from students I know or stares and comments in the hall from students I don't know, it's just become normal. I'm really comfortable with myself now and talking with students about gender has become something I enjoy and even seek out at times. Recently, however, students have been asking questions and making comments about sexual orientation. In the minds of most, it seems, gender nonconformity and sexual orientation are inextricably linked. In these moments I panic. I revert back to the assumption of deviance, put my head down, and do everything I can to get out of the situation alive.

Student 2. As I reflect on my experiences and mine them for insights about the origins and content of my ideas surrounding gender and sexual orientation, feelings of separation, distance, and *Otherness* shade my investigation. This is simultaneously disturbing and unexpected: These are my perceptions; it is my history, so why have I so frequently felt uncomfortable, as if I were wearing ill-fitting shoes? At school I learned what I would later labor to unknow. I absorbed an image of the world, a world where gay men want to be women or gay women want to be men. I learned that some (my) expressions of sexuality and gender are deemed pathological, deformed, sub-human, or worse.

The second session, which posed the essential question, "What can I now know?" focused on information sharing. In preparation for class, students read essays from two chapters ("Heterosexism" and "Transgender Oppression") in *Readings for Diversity and Social Justice* (Adams, Blumenfeld, Castañeda, Hackman, Peters, & Zúñiga, 2013). The texts addressed privilege, homo- and transphobia, and advocacy. Guided by questions Lingley and I developed, students formed small groups and engaged in dialogue. Afterward, I facilitated an interactive lecture centered on the three Oregon state laws, recently passed, that have an impact on LGBTQ advocacy in schools: the Oregon Equality Act (2007), which forbids discrimination based on sexual orientation and gender identity/expression in public and charter school education; the Comprehensive Sexuality Education Act (2009), legislation that requires public school districts to provide age-appropriate sex education courses in all K–12 schools and "use culturally and gender sensitive materials, language, and strategies that recognize different sexual orientations and gender roles"; and the Oregon Safe Schools Act (2009), which strengthens and enhances anti-bullying policies for K–12 public schools in Oregon and identifies sexual orientation (including actual or perceived gender identity) as a protected class.

As we expected, this class activity proved to be relevant. It equipped course participants with concrete protection in addressing queer issues. In their initial surveys and many of the memoirs, students expressed a desire to advocate for queer youth and address gender and sexual orientation in their teaching but feared losing their job or outing themselves. As one student put it, "Having guidelines and policies written down takes the pressure off. If a parent does complain, you can point to the policy ... the subjective becomes objective, the rare or abnormal, with time, becomes the norm."

The final class focused on advocacy and transformative action as we tried to answer the question, "What happens next?" Lingley and I assigned an essay called "Becoming an Ally: A New Examination" (Evans & Washington, 2013) that students read in preparation for class. The authors offered a four-level framework for reflecting on allyship: "awareness, knowledge/education, skills, and action" (p. 418). We asked students to discuss in small groups where they would place themselves in general using this framework. We encouraged them to consider if their position changed depending on the school context (e.g., faculty meeting vs. classroom vs. one-on-one meeting with student or parent).

In session two, several students had requested tangible lessons or activities to teach counter-normative sexuality and gender in schools. In response, Lingley and I prepared two formal activities that we modeled in this final session. Due to time constraints, we facilitated the activities simultaneously and asked students to choose one. We provided a synopsis of both activities so students could make an informed decision, and we made lesson plans for both activities available. I taught a lesson called the *Timeline Activity*, which is described in detail in Chapter 8.

Lingley facilitated the parallel activity called *Gender-Based Violence/Gender Binary Awareness* (Scheepstra, 2013). We invited students to choose this second activity if they wanted to experience an activity that they could replicate with middle or high school students, although it would benefit faculty/staff as well. The lesson focuses on helping others deconstruct the gender binary. To begin, students formed small groups and discussed how a "real" woman and "real" man look and act. After culminating a written account of participants' thoughts about women and men, Lingley talked about how these are perceptions and not truths. The notion of stereotypes emerged, and the group explored where these messages come from. Lingley then drew a continuum on chart paper and wrote "real men" and "real women" at either end of the binary. She asserted that gender is more fluid, that many people place themselves in a different place on the continuum than at either extreme. She handed the small group of students an envelope filled with portrait photos to sort and place on the continuum. She roamed the crowd and asked students to think of reasons why they placed the photos where they did. After 15 minutes, the group came together to discuss the activity. Lingley asked which photos were the easiest and the hardest to place and why. Then she steered the conversation toward gender-based violence, asking "Who is most at risk of being harmed and why? What names do we call people who don't 'fit in'? How are the 'real' women/men perceived?" These prompts led to dialogue around the myriad ways in which people choose to perform gender or express who they are. To close, Lingley juxtaposed gender identity, which is a more static form of identity, an emotional state of mind. Students reported learning content and acquiring facilitation skills during the course of the lesson demonstration. (See the Companion Website for a complete *Gender-Based Violence/Gender Binary Awareness* activity lesson plan and materials.)

Course participants split themselves equally between the two activities. When these concluded, the entire class came together to debrief the learning experiences and to share other activities, lesson plans, and teaching ideas. The entire group contributed to a conversation that resulted in a comprehensive list of websites and resources.

We concluded the course in two parts. First, we voiced appreciations and "take-aways" as a group. This forum provided an opportunity for participants (including Lingley and me) to preserve the moment and express what we had learned and valued from this experience. One common theme was people's gratitude toward having a safe space within a public education setting to talk about queerness as it relates to education. Multiple individuals also commented on the sense of agency provided. One person said, "I have learned a lot as a result of the spectrum of lived experience, and it is empowering to know there are all us allies out there." Another student declared, "It reduces my sense of isolation as a queer teacher."

In addition to stating what they valued about the course, students expressed where they felt structure and content fell short. A handful of students nodded in agreement when a fellow classmate said that sessions should have been spaced closer together. Rather than meeting for three hours once a month, some students would have preferred to meet three times within one month. Another student suggested including a journaling component and said it would have helped him process and reflect course content and readings more thoroughly on an individual level. Other participants seemed to like the idea.

After conducting this brief class discussion, Lingley and I invited participants to complete an electronic personal assessment. The first two items used a Likert scale:

1. I am comfortable addressing gender diversity in my current teaching.
2. I am comfortable addressing sexual orientation and same-sex family diversity in my current teaching.

The remaining questions were open-ended.

3. What brought me to this course initially?
4. How, if at all, has my understanding of gender and sexual orientation changed over the term?
5. What assets do I now carry with me into my practice as an educator?
6. What, if any, fears do I have about being an advocate for LGBTQ students, teachers, and families?
7. What do I see as the greatest promise this work holds for me? For my students/colleagues?

Responses to the first two items demonstrated a shift in student perspective over the course of the class. These were the only two questions we presented on both the initial and exit survey. Whereas before students engaged with the class 6% disagreed with the statement "I am comfortable addressing gender diversity in my current teaching" and 12% noted the statement was non-applicable, after the course 100% of participants responded that they agreed on some level (i.e., 19% mildly agreed, 10% agreed, and 19% strongly agreed) that they felt comfortable addressing gender diversity. In other words, some might not have recognized the capacity and relevance of queer advocacy in their work prior to the course, or they might have felt underprepared to address issues pertaining to gender in their profession, but something changed during their participation. Similarly, on the initial survey, 6% disagreed with the statement "I am comfortable addressing sexual orientation diversity in my current teaching" and 6% noted the statement was non-applicable, yet after the course 100% of participants responded that they agreed on some level (19% mildly agreed, 50% agreed, and 31% strongly agreed) that they were comfortable addressing sexual orientation.

Replies to item 4, "How, if at all, has my understanding of gender and sexual orientation changed over the term?" were overwhelmingly positive that individual transformation occurred. One student wrote, "My understanding has been enriched . . . learning the further degrees of gender and sexual orientation has answered questions I didn't know I had." Another responded, "My understanding has certainly evolved. I have not only improved my awareness, but also spent time in the other stages of becoming an ally: knowledge/education, skills, and action. Well, action is next—but I feel more competent than ever." Finally, a third student wrote:

> I think taking the class with several LGBTQ people present, and hearing their perspectives, taught me how vulnerable many people in this group feel as public employees trying to advocate for themselves and their students. It helps me acknowledge my place of privilege and gives me a sense of duty to take action as an ally.

Question 5 of the exit survey stated, "What assets do I now carry with me into my practice as an educator?" Responses included: acute recognition of oppressive environments and new resources that can be accessed when needed; affirmation that we are not alone; tangible queer activities for administrators/staff; and memories of assignments and experiences that can be used/modified to fit one's own practice. One student wrote, "One thing I do not carry with me is quite as much worry or concern about the consequences of addressing queer issues."

Still, worry and concern were residual emotions felt by some participants at the conclusion of the course. Item 6 asked, "What, if any, fears do I have about being an advocate for LGBTQ students, teachers, and families?" Participants noted fear of saying the wrong thing, upsetting someone, alienating themselves within an oppressive environment, not acting as an advocate, negative parent/guardian response to LGBTQ advocacy, fear of being exposed as queer, lack of education or language in certain situations, fear of conflict, and realization that often queer students suffer in silence, forcing some teachers to simply not see what is in front of them. One class participant wrote:

> I'm afraid of being exposed—an object of difference or controversy in the community of my school—and possibly of losing my job. I'm also wary of my own emotional reactivity surrounding these issues. To some extent this course has addressed both of those fears.

The final question that Lingley and I posed was, "What do I see as the greatest promise this work holds for me? For my students/colleagues?" Student reaction was insightful and encouraging.

> *Student 1.* The biggest promise for me is that, as I continue to engage in this work, I will feel more and more comfortable presenting my true self to my class. For my students, this means they get a better teacher and a classroom community in which they feel free to be themselves. For my colleagues, this means they get a more involved, passionate coworker.
> *Student 2.* Change is in the air! There are many people in the profession who have a similar goal in mind. If I can keep that in mind and think of myself as one of many, I will feel far stronger for my effort.
> *Student 3.* I really see the greatest promise as more students STAYING ALIVE as a result of this work!!!!! I also see more people being kinder to queer kids and more understanding. I also like the idea of having safer places to work. I really also see so many people that are just confused about LGBTQ issues that could get clarity and feel less threatened.
> *Student 4.* My ideal would be to create a learning environment that doesn't tolerate or uncritically accept psychological or physical violence against its own members. The promise might be to teach in a school where any of the students or faculty that cared to could be as open about their life experience and sexuality as any other.
> *Student 5.* The greatest promise this work holds for me is the opportunity to help LGBTQ students and faculty feel empowered in coming out and advocating for themselves. That I will be able to show all of my students their personal value and ultimately, save some lives.

Lingley and I did not require anything of our students that we ourselves were not willing to do. So, shortly after our class concluded, she and I co-constructed an account our experience as course designers and instructors. What follows is a transcript of this conversation.

OM: In the process of preparing for and teaching this course, what did you learn about queer advocacy in education?

AL: I think my biggest takeaway was that people want this. Teachers want this, and there is a hunger and desire to be given language to negotiate sexual orientation and gender identity issues in K–12 settings.

OM: I had a similar thought. My journey of working on my dissertation was done in isolation essentially, and this class helped me realize—through student discussion and feedback as well as my own observations—that queer advocacy in education is elevated when people come together in community.

AL: The other thing I learned in terms of the field of queer advocacy in education is that because there is still a tabula rasa, there are whole ideas and constructs being put together through this process of giving language to dynamics that have been experienced as shameful and so therefore private or silenced in some ways. For me, that was part of the empowerment and excitement frankly of doing this work—there is a blank slate making this work important because we're creating constructs that can be used in classrooms if you subscribe to the idea that language shapes action.

OM: What, if anything, were you nervous or fearful about in designing and teaching this course?

AL: I am stumped by the words *nervous* and *fearful*. I get nervous whenever I'm teaching so that is true. But I was more excited than anything. So if I tweaked your question to what was my personal experience in designing and teaching this course, then I have to say I was excited to integrate experiences I have had inside and outside of education with some professional capacities I was developing at Portland State. So it felt like yet one more example of Parker Palmer's philosophy of teaching with identity and integrity. Designing and teaching this course was a gift on so many levels . . . it was a gift to me personally, it was a gift to me professionally, it was a gift to be able to collaborate with you, and it was a gift to be able to do this raw and difficult work with the students, with the adults who were there.

OM: I like that word *raw* because it did feel authentic in the sense that students were unfiltered with their language. Not that they weren't thoughtful or intentional with their words, they were, but nothing felt forced or as if students were editing their thoughts to be politically correct.

AL: Were you nervous about anything?

OM: Well, sure. I was nervous about who the students would be and their reasons for being there. I thought we might get two participants, we might get 50, and as long as they stayed, they were going to get something out of it, so that's great, but I was nervous that maybe their intention was just to satisfy a credit, in which case, as instructors, would our job be more focused on . . . would we risk what could be perceived as trying to recruit people, which has such a stigma in these types of discussions? In other words, would we be charged with convincing people that queer issues in education are important? And on a personal level, I wondered if that would propel me into the closet as a way of maintaining a sense of objectivity. For me it is easy when I teach about issues of social justice to take the stance that racism is wrong, that sexism is unjust because, in part, these are widely held beliefs and universal values. But often when I hear a homophobic comment or confront someone whom I perceive to be homophobic or transphobic, even in a subtle way, as a gay woman with an androgynous wife I sometimes accommodate their thinking and validate where they are at in the process. I don't do this as easily with other forms of diversity. So I guess in not knowing who was going to be in our class, I was somewhat apprehensive about how that would impact my negotiation of queer visibility.

AL: Right. The experience of you and me going to the movie theater and watching the AIDS Coalition to Unleash Power (ACT UP) documentary at the same time that we were designing this course really reminded me of how I came out at a time when gay people were dying and being allowed to die because they were gay. There was so much anger and grief that propelled the political nature of coming out in the late 1980s/early 1990s. This significant time in my identity development combined with the fact that I now have a husband—that I am married to a man and thus have this social cover that you don't in some ways—is bound to political activism and makes me ready for a fight. And so for me I didn't have the same concerns as you did about teaching the class because my attitude was "bring it on!" If I can play a part in helping someone else feel assertive in their school community, if students could borrow some of my 1991 ACT UP political anger, then I was going to go for it. I think this is where the ten years between us make a difference actually.

OM: Speaking of our students, what resonates with you about our first class introductions? What struck you about the responses to our prompt, "Why this class, for you, now?"

AL: The word *rawness* comes to mind again. It was a room basically full of 20 strangers, and what struck me was how close the emotions were to the surface while at the same time it was never experienced as a group therapy moment even though in some ways what was happening was professionally therapeutic on some level for everyone. There was this sense of professional commitment combined with an open heart, and that is so beautiful when that happens in a classroom and very uncommon for a first meeting.

OM: I had a similar reaction. In the past I have facilitated this type of question at the beginning of courses to elicit formative feedback and often hear the disassociation with which some students speak from. "Oh, I needed this class." The most connected response I would stumble upon was students claiming to be interested in the course title or description. But never have I sat in a class where 100% of the students spoke with such conviction about their decision to register for a course, and I don't think that was paired with explicit expectations of what they'd get from the course either. Anyway, I think for a lot of people it was pretty courageous just showing up and on top of that to articulate why . . . well, that was huge.

AL: Yeah, we had a diverse group, which made planning interesting.

OM: Totally. I left our first planning session thinking that we would have to carefully edit what we were teaching and what students were learning by proxy. The class was one credit, and we had so much material to go over, and we imagined that everyone would be at different spots in terms of their comfort and experience with these issues. One of the hardest things for me personally was having the power to decide what is important and putting that in front of students.

AL: In combination with differentiating instruction on multiple levels in multiple ways.

OM: And building community, which has to happen when you're talking about these issues, but again it's one credit so where is the time . . . that's the tension.

AL: But in looking back, when I think about the most important and memorable moment of teaching this course and the challenge of meeting people's expectations and their needs—their professional needs in combination with being able to differentiate instruction and build community—I think the field observation assignment [see Chapter 8 and the Companion Website for a full assignment description] in particular was a way for people to make decisions for themselves about their own professional needs and the context within which they were working. The assignment also allowed them to apply the content from the readings and the ideas we discussed in class, which in a way was fairly novel. It deeply integrated theory and practice and was manageable given the one-credit nature of the class. I think out of all the assignments that one was the most authentic in terms of being challenging but also flexible.

OM: I find it interesting you say that because listening to students debrief their field observation assignment was my most memorable experience because of the array of diversity among observers, perceptions, and critiques. I thought it was such a rich conversation that, as you say, bridged theory and practice. For me it added a lot of context to my dissertation work that looked at ways sexual orientation and gender identity surface in schools. In class I remember listening in on Angela's conversation about her field observation assignment in a middle school cafeteria where she was student teaching. Her mentor teacher asked her why she was observing students during lunch, and Angela told her about the assignment. This adult quickly ushered all the queer and questioning students who were around and said to Angela, "Okay, here they are, interview them." Angela said, "That's not what this assignment is about. I am not here to tokenize these people!" It put Angela, who is working through her own identity as an ally, on the spot. For me, in that moment listening to her, I remember thinking that's why we're doing this work, that's why this class exists because in talking about these issues we're educating younger generations, and hopefully in 20 or 30 years with this continued work, we won't have those types of situations where to examine heteronormativity, we have to go directly to the queer kids. No, let's challenge everything else! And Angela got that. As someone who is newly introduced to this work, she unpacked that in a way that I think the class really supported.

AL: Right, I think so, too.

OM: In retrospect, what would you do differently as a course instructor?

AL: Well, we received explicit feedback from some students wanting to meet with shorter periods of time in between . . . instead of meeting once a month for three months, many students seemed to want to meet three times in one month. I think our intention behind meeting three times over the course of the term was to give people time to work on some of the assignments outside of class and for the content to simmer, incubate. But in responding to students, I would be curious to experiment with teaching a one-credit class over the course of six weeks, maybe we could meet every other week as opposed to stretching it over ten weeks.

OM: What do you think about the other piece of explicit feedback we received in our final class, the suggestion that journaling be included as a class component?

AL: If we were to do this over a six-week period, it could help keep students actively engaged with the material, but then I don't think we're talking about a one-credit class anymore.

OM: Yeah, I agree with you. I think it would be interesting to experiment with the class schedule. My recollection is similar to yours in the sense that we wanted to allow time for processing, but I think logistically the weeks in between classes hindered students' productivity and also created more work for us as instructors who had to remind people to turn in their assignments especially toward the end of the term. I don't think it was because students were disengaged with the content . . . I think it was just the end of the year, only a one-credit course, and the structure of it didn't align with their needs.

AL: And journaling?

OM: It's not something I immediately go to as a teacher educator. I value reflection, but my journaling experiences as a student in higher education were never facilitated in a way that I viewed as authentic. For me it always felt like jumping through a hoop, like writing something for someone else or just filling the pages to meet my quota. I resented it. Maybe I was just never taught how to journal in that forum. Certainly I can see how offering some optional prompts or teaching students how to utilize a journal for personal growth would be worthwhile.

AL: Although I enjoy face-to-face teaching and learning, I would be curious to explore a hybrid model of the class where perhaps it could be bumped up to two credits. There could be in-class meetings, but a journaling component could be added, for example, as a blogging assignment. Or with so many people owning smartphones these days, students could take pictures of things they see that are related to the course content . . . provocative things they could capture and post.

OM: Well, that kind of happened organically in class.

AL: Yeah, it did.

OM: A couple times people brought something in to share. Remember when Sam brought in pictures of different public bathroom icons and we talked critically about how social images play into or defy a rigid gender binary? This kind of show-and-tell became more popular as the term went on. People got to know each other better, and I think they also began noticing more examples related to our class.

AL: So I think we could offer the course for two credits and put in a hybrid component.

OM: You know, one thing I'm thinking of right now is how well we held the line of being inclusive of gender and sexual orientation. I think we helped our students understand the connection between the two, especially around common misconceptions that confuse them, and also how they are distinct. I feel like everyone in our class—whether they were cisgender, transgender, queer, straight, and everything in between—I feel and hope everyone felt acknowledged both in community with others and as individuals with unique needs. I think a class like this could have easily not done that.

AL: Yeah, I agree. Between the two of us we don't model a tremendous amount of diversity, but we do model some. On that note a major takeaway from teaching the class was how much more I learned about the experience of being transgender and the academic field of transgender studies. I feel like this is an area that offers the most promise for educators being able to understand heteronormativity, sexual orientation, gender identity development, and the area of collision between gender identity and gender expectations. I really came to appreciate this learning because I don't know that many people who are transgender and because I grew up at a time when it was stigmatized and viewed as a mental illness. I feel like I had an embodied experience of that stigma being reduced through the act of having to prepare for and teach this class.

OM: How would learning and teaching about trans and gender issues help teach people about heteronormativity, particularly in schools?

AL: So, here's my totally raw, unedited answer. Once the freak status is removed from being transgender, people can emotionally and intellectually engage with what it means to transcend gender performance. With the status being removed, I was able to engage at a much deeper level than I ever have before around what it means to have this internal experience in the world of not being in alignment with gender performance expectations.

OM: Yeah, and this can be teased apart. When you talk about gender performance and transcendence, you can also acknowledge and start questioning attraction, emotional connection, and sexual orientation.

AL: Exactly. Transgender people make it possible for everything to be up for discussion. It's a huge gift actually for women and for gay people to have that kind of permission granted . . . it can all be up for grabs.

Conclusion

The CI LGBTQ Task Force offers one example of agency within an institution. In a few short years, this group of four individuals led a faculty in drafting and approving a resolution statement. We also facilitated efforts to bring this policy to life by providing ongoing faculty development and curriculum including a website with consolidated materials and resources, organizing a visibility campaign, and offering an elective course on queer advocacy in education. On a personal level, task force members grappled with individual roles by answering questions like these: What brought me to this work? How does this work influence my life and professional practice?

This chapter provides a rather transparent representation of our process in hopes that it might inform and guide others. The task force learned many lessons along the way, and we witnessed transformative change, and that is progress toward something huge and meaningful.

Reflection Questions

1. How are queer issues surfaced or suffocated in your particular work?
2. How are queer issues addressed among administrators or leaders within your school or department?
3. What, if at all, do you fear about addressing queer issues with your school faculty or colleagues within your department?
4. What challenges do you identify as potential inhibitors of creating a queer-inclusive environment within your school or department? What steps can you take to overcome these obstacles?
5. What outcomes could result from addressing queer issues among your school staff or within your department?

Recommended Resources

Books and Articles About Queer Issues in Teacher Education

Horn, S.S., Konkol, P., McInerney, K., Meiners, E.R., North, C., Nuñez, I., ... Sullivan, S. (2010). Visibility matters: Policy work as activism in teacher education. *Issues in Teacher Education, 19*(2), 65–80.

Larrabee, T.G., & Morehead, P. (2010). Broadening views of social justice and teacher leadership: Addressing LGB issues in teacher education. *Issues in Teacher Education, 19*(2), 37–53.

Petrovic, J.E., & Rosiek, J. (2007). From teacher knowledge to queered teacher knowledge research: Escaping the epistemic straight jacket. In N.M. Rodriguez & W.F. Pinar (Eds.), *Queering straight teachers* (pp. 201–231). New York: Peter Lang.

Rands, K.E. (2009). Considering transgender people in education: A gender-complex approach. *Journal of Teacher Education, 60*(4), 419–431.

Sadowski, M. (2010). Core values and the identity-supportive classroom: Setting LGBTQ issues within wider frameworks for preservice educators. *Issues in Teacher Education, 19*(2), 53–63.

Tonningsen, K. (2002). Reclaiming identity: Sharing teacher's truth. In S. Intrator (Ed.), *Stories of the courage to teach: Honoring the teacher's heart* (pp. 94–99). San Francisco, CA: Jossey-Bass.

Whitlock, R.U. (2010). Getting queer: Teacher education, gender studies, and the cross-disciplinary quest for queer pedagogies. *Issues in Teacher Education, 19*(2), 81–104.

References

Adams, M., Blumenfeld, W.J., Castañeda, C., Hackman, H.W., Peters, M.L., & Zúñiga, X. (Eds.). (2013). *Readings for diversity and social justice* (3rd ed.). New York: Routledge.

Evans, N.J., & Washington, J. (2013). Becoming an ally: A new examination. In M. Adams, W.J. Blumenfeld, C. Castañeda, H.W. Hackman, M. Peters, & X. Zúñiga (Eds.), *Readings for diversity and social justice* (3rd ed., pp. 411–420). New York: Routledge.

Gillis, A., & Jackson, W. (2002). *Research methods for nurses: Methods and interpretation*. Philadelphia: F.A. Davis Company.

Horn, S.S., Konkol, P., McInerney, K., Meiners, E.R., North, C., Nuñez, I., ... Sullivan, S. (2010). Visibility matters: Policy work as activism in teacher education. *Issues in Teacher Education, 19*(2), 65–80.

Intrator, S.M. (Ed.). (2002). *Stories of the courage to teach: Honoring the teacher's heart*. San Francisco, CA: Jossey-Bass.

Larrabee, T.G., & Morehead, P. (2010). Broadening views of social justice and teacher leadership: Addressing LGB issues in teacher education. *Issues in Teacher Education, 19*(2), 37–53.

Richardson, J., & Parnell, P. (2012). *And Tango makes three*. New York: Simon and Schuster.

Sadowski, M. (2010). Core values and the identity-supportive classroom: Setting LGBTQ issues within wider frameworks for preservice educators. *Issues in Teacher Education, 19*(2), 53–63.

Scheepstra, T. (2013). *Gender-based violence/gender binary awareness activity for middle/high school students and faculty development*. Unpublished curriculum, Ontario Institute for Studies in Education (OISE), University of Toronto, Ontario, Canada.

PART III
A Toolkit for Queering Practice

7
ACTIVITIES AND MATERIALS FOR FACULTY DEVELOPMENT

In This Chapter

- Strategies for engaging faculty in initial conversations centered on gender and sexual orientation; conversations that can establish relevance, ground common language, debunk stereotypes, and illuminate current forms of knowledge and experience among faculty.
- Considerations for assessing school climate, analyzing current policies, evaluating current student/teacher candidate supports, and taking inventory of faculty development needs.
- Tangible activities for department leaders and/or queer task force members to use for ongoing faculty development with the hope that departments will borrow and adapt the content and methods presented here to fit the unique needs of their institutions.

Introduction

As in K–12 school environments, heteronormative discourses are widespread at colleges and universities (Evans & Broido, 2002; Nixon & Givens, 2007; O'Connor, 1998). Schools and colleges of education are no exception, and scholars overwhelmingly agree that teacher education programs are plagued by silence when it comes to LGBTQ concerns (Bower & Klecka, 2009; Clark, 2010; DeJean, 2010; Hermann-Wilmarth & Bills, 2010; Jennings, 2007; Szalacha, 2004; Vavrus, 2009). Yet, as I have argued thus far, education, particularly teacher education, serves as a catalyst for change with extraordinary emancipatory potential. Education provides the means to challenge heteronormative culture in which persons are assumed to be heterosexual unless some evidence to the contrary is presented. Likewise, schools serve as a site where modern perceptions of gender can be disassembled and rebuilt to represent more fluid and complex constructs related to, but not conflated with, sexuality. The Queer Inclusion in Education Framework presented in Chapter 3 (Appendix B) shows that before such transformation can be realized among preK–12 youth and adolescents, teacher education must be reformed. This chapter applies what it means to make over teacher education with a queer perspective by providing ready-to-use materials to guide faculty toward more inclusive practices. Informed by the framework, these activities and resources are designed to increase the knowledge, skills, and dispositions of teacher educators through critical reflection and identity (re)negotiation.

Strategies for Facilitating Initial Conversations

Approaching the topics of diverse sexual orientations and gender identities, particularly as they relate to education, can be sensitive. For reasons already mentioned, schools have historically transmitted heterosexist ideology that connects to a wide distribution of narrow gender expectations. Facilitating queer conversations among teacher educators adds further complexity because, in part, most faculty are products of such education. Also by the time most of us reach adulthood, we have largely sophisticated our values and views of gender and sexuality. However, it is noteworthy that when it comes to sexual orientation, the literature convincingly finds that individuals with higher levels of education tend to be more tolerant (Bobo & Licari, 1989; van den Akker, van der Ploeg, & Scheepers, 2013). In other words, instructors and academics in teacher education (who hold advanced degrees and have unlimited exposure to education, critical thinking, literature, and intellectual discourse) have a higher likelihood to be open and accepting of diverse sexual orientations. Still, beginning the conversation is never easy. Exploratory, critical, constructive discussion among teacher educators can only occur in a climate where everyone feels respected and safe in taking risks.

It is important to structure initial conversations about gender and sexual orientation within the work of the institution, department, or program itself. Igniting relevant discourse that connects with teacher educators' local and professional lives is important. The facilitator's approach is also significant. Faculty leading the initial discussion should exhibit openness and humility; they should present a safe invitation to consider, discuss, critique, reflect, and act. Five focus areas for facilitating initial conversations include the use of discussion questions, case studies, informative literature (i.e., research and statistics), language and terminology, and debunking stereotypes.

Discussion Questions

Discussion provides a means for bringing personal stories and experiences with queer issues to the forefront. This is important for teacher educators, as Sumara (2007) observed:

> Because all of us have been socialized by heteronormativity, we are all, to some degree, homophobic. Identifying as gay does not prevent one from being homophobic. As teachers who are public leaders, we have an obligation to learn about the structures that create our identities and our ways of experiencing and expressing them. As we do this work on ourselves, we will gain some insights into how we will work with our students.
>
> *(p. 54)*

Beginning an initial conversation about queerness in small groups is a safe way for faculty members to exchange current levels of understanding. Prompting discussion with specific questions can guide participants' thinking, maximize interaction, and keep the conversation going and on point. Here are possible discussion questions:

- What messages did you receive as a student about sexual orientation and gender in the classroom? Here, think about the "hidden curriculum," which is a byproduct of an education—lessons that are learned but not openly intended, such as the transmission of norms, values, and beliefs conveyed in the classroom and the social environment.
- How do sexual orientation and gender (identity and performance) emerge in your professional work?
- In what ways are you directly affected by queer individuals and culture, and how might this impact your practice working with students?

Again, these are initial questions to *begin* thinking about the complex ways we view gender and sexuality and how these views influence the professional practice of teachers. The facilitators may choose to keep the entire discussion confined to small groups, or they might provide an opportunity for whole-group processing. Posing the question, "Would anyone like to voice a learning outcome, appreciation, concern, frustration, or question based on your small-group discussion?" is an effective way to debrief and can also supply the facilitators with important feedback about the activity to inform next steps.

Case Study

Case study is another method for broaching the topics of sexual orientation and gender for the first time. It is particularly helpful for providing context to individuals who have little knowledge about queer issues, limited exposure to queer people, and/or do not see the relevant connection between queer issues and education. As people begin to speak openly with each other and apply the context to their lives and professional experience, the discussion provides evidence to reluctant individuals that the topic is worthy of discussion.

Several approaches for case-based learning are possible and effective for discussing queer perspectives related to education. The facilitators must decide whether to conduct the activity as a whole or small group, or small-to-whole group. Given that this activity is suggested as an initial entry point for discussing queer issues, I recommend beginning in small groups unless the faculty have a great deal of experience engaging in courageous conversations. It should also be noted that case studies can be used with any number of pedagogical techniques, such as problem-posing (described in Chapter 8) and the Socratic method, to promote forceful questioning and critical thinking.

In preparation for the activity, the facilitators should read the study/studies and think through each case. They should also articulate what they hope faculty will achieve through discussing the cases. A learning objective such as "Participants will discuss ways that sexual orientation and gender surface in teacher education and apply these to their practice" will guide faculty and hold them accountable for their learning. Finally, the facilitators must develop probing questions to deepen the small- and/or whole-group discussion and encourage individuals and groups to think beyond their initial responses. This expands the conversation and forces participants to explore the reasoning behind their conclusions.

Cases can be presented to faculty in a variety of forms (print, video, hypertext, audio, role-plays). Facilitators can author the text; retrieve cases from published literature, such as the ones that follow; or invite teacher educators to engage in participative case writing. However they are delivered, cases need to be realistic, and uncommon terms (e.g., cisgender, heteronormative) must be adequately defined. The facilitators may choose to have everyone analyze one study or distribute several studies at once.

What follows are five possible case studies for teacher educators to consider.

Teacher Candidate in Transition: Skylar, a teacher candidate you instruct (and possibly advise in the field), approaches you after class asking for a moment of your time. He opens up and tells you that up until last year he identified as a woman (his assigned sex at birth), but now he has socially transitioned 100% to living as a man. He confesses that he is nervous about navigating his field placement and asks for your support and guidance.

- What clarifying and probing questions do you ask Skylar?
- What support, guidance, and resources do you provide?
- Now, imagine Skylar has transitioned from male to female. Does this change your perception, support, or plan of action? Why or why not?

A Colleague Comes Out: Shortly after a faculty meeting, your close friend and departmental colleague approaches you in your office. You notice she is visibly upset. When asked what's wrong, your colleague admits she was just set up on a blind date by the department chair, who assumes she is straight. Now your colleague feels like she either has to come out to her boss, which she was not previously prepared to do, or go on the blind date.

- What do you say to console your colleague?
- What, if any, advice do you give her?
- What, if any, further action do you take as an ally in a heteronormative work environment?

Homophobic Remark in Class: In the middle of your interactive lecture, a teacher candidate raises his hand to respond to a comment made by another student. He says, "I'm not homophobic. In fact I have a lot of gay friends, but I do think young kids should not be exposed to homosexuality . . . not that there's anything wrong with it." You notice some of the students cringe in their seats as the room goes silent.

- What do you say in response to the teacher candidate's comment?
- How do you address the awkwardness in that moment?
- What follow-up action might be necessary?

Unfortunate Oversights: A teacher candidate makes an appointment to speak with you early on in the term. She is taking your course centered on social justice and is concerned about a line in the required text, *Anti-Bias Education* by Derman-Sparks & Edwards (2010, p. 95), that misidentifies transgender as a sexual orientation (". . . be sure you understand that sexual orientation [e.g., heterosexuality, homosexuality, transgender] does not develop from the activities children do, it is based in a child's particular biology"). The teacher candidate also expresses her discomfort regarding the first class session when you projected the class roster, as seen from your university account, to verify course participants' e-mail addresses and contact information. This student had recently changed her name with the university, but if she hadn't, she would have been mortified to see her "male" birth name displayed.

- How do you acknowledge to this student what you have heard?
- How might this encounter alter your practice?
- What questions does this issue raise for you?

Experience as a Sexual Minority: You identify as gay, lesbian, bisexual, or pansexual. You teach and advise a core group of 30 teacher candidates throughout the year. You notice early on that they are genuinely interested in you as a person, your life outside work.

- What goes into your decision making for determining what, if anything, to share about your sexual orientation?
- What fears do you have in coming out to your students?
- What fears do you have in remaining closeted to your students?

Informative Literature

A third strategy to facilitate initial conversations on queerness is the use of informative literature. Teacher educators can be guided to interpret and make sense of global research that situates the issue as well as local trends that establish relevance. The Gay, Lesbian and Straight Education Network (GLSEN)'s website is a great resource with free downloads of their National School Climate Survey (published every two years) as well as links to local and state data. In addition to quantitative research, teacher educators can be encouraged to read and discuss research literature that features narrative, qualitative sources of data and experiences. This book, for example, can serve as a platform for engaging in sustained conversation much like a book club functions. (Other examples of literature that serves a similar purpose can be found under "recommended resources" at the conclusions of each chapter in this book.)

Language and Terminology

To work with future K–12 teachers on conceptualizing gender and sexuality in more complex ways, teacher educators must develop a vocabulary of gender and nonnormative orientations. Thus, focusing on language and terminology is a fourth strategy for effectively introducing sexual orientation and gender into faculty discourse. The power behind this approach lies in its ability to naturalize queer discourse and safely establish common vocabulary as a point of reference. Often people are afraid of engaging in dialogue centered on aspects of identity and social justice, particularly around categories from which they derive privilege. This is, in part, due to fear of saying something offensive, saying the "wrong" thing. Too often this human response stifles engagement and silences discourse. For example, a faculty member might be reluctant to talk about a student who is transgender because, in doing so, the faculty member feels the need to compare this person's experience with someone who is not transgender and yet the only word that comes to mind is *normal*, which the faculty member feels will be perceived as offensive and transphobic.

When terms and acronyms such as *cisgender*, *queer*, and *LGBTQ*, as well as concepts like heteronormativity, gender variance, and homo- and transphobia, are defined and discussed, then and only then can faculty begin to internalize their meanings, articulate their impact, and challenge basic assumptions about the world. When combined with action to alleviate queer oppression, this cycle of praxis operates to disrupt Chapter 5's third assertion: Language, in discourse and the media, is a powerful tool often used to bring about emancipation through dialogue and sense-making. But with queer issues related to education, language is often silenced, and the messages people do transmit and receive are often heteronormative and transphobic.

There are many ways to introduce language and terminology to faculty. One method is to provide a handout with terms and definitions related to sex, gender, and sexual orientation (see the Companion Website for a range of materials). Faculty can read the content and then discuss terms that are new, vocabulary and/or definitions that contradict prior knowledge or experience, and definitions that need further explanation to aid comprehension. In addition to straightforward vocabulary resources, many published materials can help faculty differentiate the complex constructions of sex, gender, and sexual orientation. Two such resources are *Gender Gumby* (Sexual and Gender Minority Youth Resource Center, 2013), which demonstrates the fluidity of gender and sexuality, and the *Societal Discomfort Zone* (TransActive, 2011), which distinguishes between biology, gender identity, and sexual orientation (see the Companion Website for materials and facilitation guides). When teacher educators are given resources, time, and a safe space in which to explore and make meaning of language, then faculty can come together in community to confidently articulate and comprehend queer issues.

Debunking Stereotypes

A fifth possible strategy for facilitating initial conversations is the exercise of surfacing and promptly debunking queer myths and stereotypes (e.g., being lesbian, gay, bisexual, and/or transgender is a choice; queer parents are not as good as a father and a mother; gay relationships don't last). Stereotypes represent assumed knowledge of an entire group based on an experience with (or information about) a member (or members) of that group. Queer individuals are stigmatized with a variety of negative and inaccurate stereotypes (Herek, Widaman, & Capitanio, 2005; Valentine, 1993; Wright & Canetto, 2009). Confronting stereotypes can serve as a valuable starting point because it extracts personal assumptions and biases, corrects misinformation that is often reinforced by media and culture, and yields accurate vocabulary, concepts, and statistics that aid learning.

Numerous methods and tools are available to identify and break down stereotyping. One idea is for facilitators working with teacher educators to write the following labels in large print on separate pieces of chart paper and then post them around the room: "lesbians," "gay men," "bisexuals," "transgender people," and "queer teachers." Next, teacher educators—with black markers in hand—walk around to each poster and silently scribe all the stereotypes that come to mind when they read the labels. After ample time has been given, the facilitators initiate dialogue, making sure the posters are still visible. A slight variation to this activity is offering teacher educators index cards rather than using large chart paper. Participants write down a stereotype they have heard about LGBTQ people, and then the facilitator shuffles the cards and invites a few people to select one and read it aloud. The group then discusses the origins of the stereotype as well as how they think a person might feel to be typecast in that manner. Regardless of the method, it is important for facilitators to do the following:

- Direct the conversation so that it is open and honest yet does not condone or affirm existing stereotypes;
- Recognize that most, if not all, participants have been stereotyped in their lifetime; use this to connect participants rather than allowing the differences to divide the group;
- If applicable, acknowledge that laughter is an expression of human emotion that can help us deal with pain or difference but that it is not appropriate to laugh at terms or comments written for this activity.

What follows are potential debrief questions for facilitators to pioneer the discussion.

- How did it feel to write the stereotypes (and see them in print)?
- Where do they come from? How are they perpetrated?
- How do intersections of identity influence stereotypes (e.g., sexual orientation and gender interacting with issues of racial or religious identity)?
- Where do we hear queer stereotypes most often used?
- How do these stereotypes influence our work as educators?
- What experiences do you have with confronting these stereotypes in the classroom?
- What can we do in our practice to avoid perpetuating stereotypes about queer culture and individuals?

Special attention should be paid to dismantling gender stereotypes as well. Rands (2009) wrote extensively about gender-stereotyped education and its power to reproduce the gender oppression matrix in the classroom. This matrix, representing the specific forms privilege and oppression take, consists of two connected forms of gender oppression: *gender category oppression* and *gender transgression oppression*. The former is oppression based on the gender category in which one is perceived to be—socially and culturally viewed as male *or* female. Whereas this oppression is based on identity, gender transgression oppression is oppression based on gender performance. For example, a girl who dresses in a traditionally feminine way is both oppressed based on her gender category and also privileged based on her gender conformity. Unpacking the complexity of gender oppression and the stereotypes that uphold this oppression is extremely important. Rands's article, "Considering Transgender People in Education: A Gender-Complex Approach" (2009), can be instrumental in this endeavor.

Anti-queer bias is multidimensional, and to garner greater understanding of it, teacher educators must name and challenge stereotypes that perpetuate prejudice and fear. Regardless of how this activity, or any initial conversation, is presented, it is important not to rush the process. Facilitators should rely on the knowledge and experience of teacher educators and allow faculty continuous opportunities to own the process and to point to colleagues as a source of long-term support.

Methods for Evaluating Current Practices

A postscript to initiating queer dialogue among teacher educators is turning the focus inward to inventory and critique our own current practices. Described in the following are four methods for evaluating current practices including (a) assessing school climate, (b) analyzing current policy and diversity statements, (c) evaluating current student supports, and (d) eliciting faculty development needs. This ongoing work further develops the knowledge, skills, and dispositions required of faculty members engaged in an inclusive process for promoting diversity education.

Assess School Climate

"The school climate—the impressions, beliefs, and expectations about school as a learning environment—play a critical role in the academic development of the student learner, and administrators and teachers clearly strongly influence that impression" (Perkins, 2007, p. 6). Faculty can assess school/department climate in a number of ways. First, the faculty, or a subset of faculty such as a queer task force, can brainstorm questions they seek to ask staff and/or students in the form of an anonymous survey.

Using a Likert scale, statements for faculty and staff to respond to might include these:

- I have access to information and resources to support lesbian, gay, and bisexual students.
- I have access to information and resources to support transgender and gender-nonconforming students.
- I feel comfortable addressing gender in my classes.
- I feel comfortable addressing sexual orientation in my classes.
- I include topics of gender variance in my teaching.

- I include topics of diverse sexual orientations in my teaching.
- I feel confident recognizing homophobic language in class.
- I feel confident interrupting homophobic language in class.
- I feel confident recognizing transphobic language in class.
- I feel confident interrupting transphobic language in class.

Statements for teacher candidates to respond to might include these:

- I have access to at least one faculty member whom I identify as a LGBTQ ally.
- I have access to information and support surrounding gender and sexual orientation within the department or my program.
- My instructors address gender in required coursework.
- I feel comfortable when my instructors bring up the topic of gender.
- My instructors address sexual orientation in required coursework.
- I feel comfortable when my instructors bring up the topic of sexual orientation.
- When homophobic language occurs in class, my instructors address it.
- When transphobic language occurs in class, my instructors address it.
- I have opportunities to explore how gender potentially affects my role as an educator.
- I have opportunities to explore how sexual orientation potentially affects my role as an educator.

If faculty are unwilling or underprepared to design an assessment tool, there are plenty of such tools available online that can be altered to meet the individual needs of any institution or department.

Analyze Current Policy and Diversity Statements

Analyzing department policy, diversity statements, and conceptual frameworks is another way to evaluate practice and work toward cultivating a teacher education program that invites those who identify as queer to disclose their subject positions in safe and meaningful ways. Written policies and statements ensure that all individuals who come into contact with the school, department, or university are treated with dignity, respect, and equitable opportunities. Such documents also guide faculty by clearly articulating a sense of vision and purpose. When we review a current policy, it is important to note the year in which it was written as well as the overall language and tone. Is the policy (or statement) explicitly queer inclusive, and, if so, does the language accurately and equitably reflect diverse sexual orientations and gender variance? It may be necessary to consult with others outside a department or program; luckily, most universities house an equity or diversity office that can serve as a valuable resource.

Evaluate Current Student Supports

A third method for analyzing current practices requires teacher educators to examine the support that is offered to teacher candidates. Department leaders and/or queer task force members can lead faculty in analyzing curriculum, website content, orientation materials, and instructor language to determine queer inclusivity and visibility. As it relates to curriculum, teacher educators can be encouraged within a faculty meeting to review several departmental syllabi to discuss language and content. Do the syllabi frame gender as a rigid binary (e.g., presence of *s/he* and *him/her*) or in a more inclusive, gender-fluid manner (e.g., *they, their*)? Do the syllabi contain diversity statements or antidiscrimination policies? Do they acknowledge queerness anywhere? If so, where and how might the language be interpreted? If not, are there organic entry points for including gender and sexual orientation? Do course assignments highlight institutionalized oppression associated with sexual- and gender-based differences (i.e., assumptions about what does and does not constitute "normal" gender performances or "natural" sexual orientations) when addressing other forms of identity and social justice?

Urging faculty to explore website content is also worthwhile. As mentioned in Chapter 2, Horn et al. (2010) examined how teacher education programs address (or often do not address) queer lives and issues from the position of a prospective student with access to the Internet. The researchers asked the following questions (pp. 70–71), an exercise that can be easily replicated by faculty at any institution.

- Do teacher education programs include sexual orientation (SO) and gender identity (GI) in their definitions of diversity and/or conceptual frameworks?
- Do the colleges and universities where these programs reside include SO or GI in their antidiscrimination language?
- Do these colleges and universities have a campus-wide positive LGBTQ presence via queer clubs or offices dedicated to LGBTQ concerns?
- Conversely, do these campuses provide teacher preparation programs that ignore LGBTQ-specific content or stigmatize LGBTQ people by requiring pledges or oaths from students, faculty, and staff that they will not condone or engage in homosexual behavior?

Subsequent to the application and admissions processes, teacher educators often turn their attention to new student orientation. Analyzing orientation materials and procedures provides another opportunity for faculty to assess current practices. It is helpful to consider this event from the perspective of a queer student: Are the materials inclusive of diverse sexual orientations and gender identifications or presentations? Is there a queer presence visible on campus, within the department? Is there someone I can contact for questions related to my unique (queer) experience?

Finally, teacher educators need practice locating potentially oppressive practices beyond what is recognized in print. Interrogating instructor language and behaviors allows teacher educators to heighten their awareness and redirect practices that might be perceived as hetero- and/or cissexist. Faculty can be encouraged and supported to this end through the organization of structured observations, time to debrief, and access to quality audiovisual equipment that allows them to record and review their practice. Sumara (2007) captured one phenomenon that might be realized through this opportunity. "Sadly, university-based teacher education often is developed around an insidious kind of 'secret' knowledge, which is often camouflaged by attention to discourses of 'bullying' rather than around specific knowledge about what constitutes experiences and expressions of heterosexism and homophobia" (p. 55). In other words, if given an opportunity to analyze and discuss a well-intentioned lesson centered on bullying, a teacher educator might discover that avoiding queer discourse was not only a missed opportunity, but it also, perhaps, preserved an oppressive construct.

Elicit Faculty Development Needs

The fourth method for evaluating current practices recognizes teacher educators as a vital source of knowledge. It is essential that department leaders and/or queer task force members consistently self-evaluate by putting a pulse on how others respond to queer faculty development and by taking inventory of professional development needs. Our CI LGBTQ Task Force (see Chapter 6) strove to obtain feedback from faculty members quarterly. Often as a supplement to a ten-minute presentation, task force members would distribute a one- to three-question survey for teacher educators to complete and return. In the beginning our questions were vague. We asked, "Should we commit to looking at this issue?" and "What education, support, experiences do you want/appreciate/need/hope for?" The latter question produced some of the following responses (the numbers denote the frequency of request):

- More case studies/real-life student stories (6)
- Creation of safe space for faculty conversation (5)
- No specific suggestion—observation about self (3)
- Theoretical literature (3)
- Curricular materials to use in courses (2)
- First clarify department intentions and goals (1)
- Develop policy position (1)
- Support for balancing personal perspective with professional stance (1).

As our collective efforts toward queer inclusion advanced and teacher educators began queering their knowledge, skills, and dispositions, the task force began relying more on faculty to share their knowledge and expertise. We asked teacher educators to respond to the following prompts 17 months into our work:

1. What entry points can you identify for LGBTQ issues within the department's current curriculum?

2. Describe any stories or experiences you have with queer issues (in education) that might help colleagues.
3. Brainstorm and list any specific teaching methods and/or materials that would be valuable resources to include in an LGBTQ resource binder for faculty.

These three prompts generated a wealth of information that the task force used to inform our next leadership initiative, compiling an online library of materials and resources.

Overall, connecting with faculty in a proactive way and being responsive to their needs served the task force, and the department, well. Several ways exist to engage and excite faculty about queer issues once initial conversation has commenced. While faculty explores sexual orientation and gender as they relate to education, it is important not to underestimate the power of simply asking, "What is going well and what can be improved?"

Activities for Ongoing Faculty Development

After activating initial conversations and evaluating current practices, faculty members are in a prime position to cultivate their work through ongoing faculty development. This section offers three ideas for advancing teacher educators' knowledge, skills, and dispositions toward queerness in education. Although activities listed in the next chapter may also be used to assist teacher educators, the learning experiences listed here (in conjunction with Chapter 5 content) are intended for faculty meetings and teacher educator professional development.

Engage in Lesson Study

The first idea for ongoing faculty development involves lesson study, a professional development approach that originated in Japan and has become increasingly popular within the United States over the past decade. Essentially, lesson study involves planning, teaching, observing, and critiquing lessons with a group of colleagues. Researchers from Japan (Lewis & Tsuchida, 1997, 1998) as well as the U.S. (Lewis, 2002; Perry, Lewis, & Akiba, 2002) identified seven successful components of lesson study that lead to instructional improvement: (a) increased knowledge of subject matter, (b) increased knowledge of instruction, (c) increased ability to observe students, (d) stronger collegial networks, (e) stronger connection of daily practice to long-term goals, (f) stronger motivation and sense of efficacy, and (g) improved quality of available lesson plans.

To illustrate how lesson study can be used as a powerful tool for merging teacher educators with queer content, here's an example. Teacher educators divide into elementary, midlevel, and secondary focus study groups. Each group reviews its existing curriculum (syllabi, activities, lesson plans) to determine concrete opportunities for introducing gender and/or sexual orientation in their practice. Then, members collaboratively create a detailed lesson plan that one member of the group intends to implement in a course for teacher educators. Group members not responsible for implementing the lesson attend the class session to observe. The group then comes together to discuss their experiences and observations of the lesson. Frequently the group revises the lesson and another teacher implements it in a second class, which is once again observed. The group reconvenes to discuss observational data from this second attempt. Finally, the teacher educators generate a report summarizing their learning experiences.

This cycle of praxis can guide faculty as a whole toward increased understanding of subject matter (i.e., queer issues in educational settings). For example, elementary teacher educators critiquing a lesson on gender stereotypes may realize they lack the ability to think about gender in complex ways. Co-creating a lesson that deconstructs gender based on biology/sex, identity, expression, and perception while acknowledging social, historical, and cultural influences can simultaneously prepare for teacher candidates' learning while contributing funds of knowledge to teacher educators. Likewise, teacher educators with a secondary focus who collaboratively integrate queer persons and history into their unit examples that they plan to present to teacher candidates may learn something new about the ways that queer activism influenced the civil rights movement.

Lesson study also increases knowledge of instruction. Teacher educators need opportunities to observe and contemplate how queer issues are incorporated into the classroom because the controversial topic has historically been off-limits. Additionally, lesson study increases participants' ability to observe students. It offers teacher educators an opportunity to discuss the ways teacher candidates receive and respond to queer curriculum. Insight gleamed from observation and discussion can inform faculty about current levels of student comfort and also build teacher educators' confidence in actively challenging hetero-sexist and cissexist ideologies in their practice.

Finally, lesson study improves the quality of available lesson plans. Over time teacher educators engaging in lesson study centered on queer pedagogy will accumulate an extensive library of activities and reflective reports that can be used by all faculty.

Explore Research Opportunities

Exploring research opportunities constitutes a second opportunity for faculty development. Individuals or teams of teacher educators can be encouraged to generate research questions focused on sexual orientation and gender in education, perhaps revolving around a problem of practice. The purpose of this professional learning is the simultaneous development and application of knowledge. Department leaders and/or queer task force members can guide and support this process by offering existing research ideas and designs, brainstorming lines of inquiry, and embedding time in faculty or departmental meetings.

One example of research that can be replicated, or at the very least inspire other paths of inquiry, comes from faculty at George Mason University in Fairfax, Virginia. Gorski, Davis, and Reiter (2013) were interested in examining a distressing paradox within teacher education: "Heterosexism and homophobia permeate U.S. educational institutions. However, research heretofore has shown that [LGBTQ] concerns remain largely invisible in teacher education contexts" (p. 224). The researchers framed two questions to guide their inquiry:

> To what extent are issues and concepts related to LGBTQ identities, oppressions, and resistances visible in multicultural teacher education (MTE) courses taught in U.S.-based teacher education programs? And when such issues and concepts are incorporated into MTE courses, how are they framed?
>
> *(p. 226)*

Data sources included survey results from 80 instructors who taught MTE courses as well as a sample of 41 syllabi from MTE courses taught in the U.S. The researchers found that roughly 40% of students in MTE courses had no opportunity to consider the implications of heterosexism. Moreover, those who did were likely to be subjected to shallow learning experiences that largely ignored queerness as an intersection of identity and failed to address the sociopolitical context of heteronormativity. In their own words, the researchers concluded:

> When it comes to the identities, oppressions, and resistances of LGBTQ people, this study supports a growing body of evidence that teacher education, and MTE more specically, tends to perpetuate, both by omission and relatively conservative or liberal framing, a sort of episto-power [or the power of hegemonic knowledge, Kincheloe, 2008], which complies with the very conditions it is meant, at least theoretically (Gorski, 2006, 2008; Nieto & Bode, 2011), to redress.
>
> *(p. 237)*

Gorski et al. (2013) conducted a research study that any faculty could scale back and undertake internally to uncover a telling audit of current practice.

Cullen and Sandy (2009) conducted an action research project that revealed further insight into faculty-generated queer inquiry. The researchers' goal was to develop teaching practices to support "sexualities equalities" (p. 141) in the primary classroom. They provided approximately 20 elementary school teachers with a set of 25 picture books featuring nonheterosexual and/or non-gender-conforming characters, and with assistance from the researchers, the teachers developed approaches and issues they wanted to take forward in their schools. The researchers reported:

> A wide range of approaches emerged. Some teacher-researchers focused on developing policy and schemes of work to challenge gender inequality and promote sexuality equalities. Other schools used arts and drama practitioners to work in conjunction with the project books to challenge homophobic discrimination, and attempted to challenge some of the heteronormative discourses in operation in their school settings.
>
> (p. 142)

The researchers also found that although the resource books were useful tools for exploring diverse family structures and nonnormative gender performances, there is a need for more inclusive texts comprehensible to children. These findings, in turn, launched new lines of questioning. With access to the field, teacher educators could easily collaborate with teacher candidates and/or cooperating teachers to duplicate a similar study.

Organize a Panel Discussion

Finally, in addition to assisting teacher educators to engage with lesson study and conduct action research, department leaders and/or queer task force members can support faculty in queering their practice by organizing a panel discussion. The panel can include current teacher candidates, in-service teachers, and/or youth so long as participants represent a wide variety of life experiences. It is also essential to search for a range in age, race, ethnicity, sexual orientation, gender identity and presentation, religion, class, and ability.

The panel moderator should maintain open communication with panel participants in advance. It is a good idea to explain the structure of the discussion and ensure panelists have a clear vision of what they are expected to do. The moderator should also work with teacher educators (i.e., the audience) beforehand to determine which topics they want to cover and to synthesize a list of questions they want to ask. This list of questions should then to be filtered through panel participants with the opportunity to add their own. Finally, it is important to encourage teacher educators to actively participate in the discussion. After panelists introduce themselves and present aspects of their stories, teacher educators should ask questions, offer additional insights, and articulate critical connections.

Conclusion

Teacher education programs have the opportunity to be at the forefront in challenging gender oppression and sexual orientation oppression. The current educational system in the U.S. ignores and oppresses queer students on a daily basis. By not challenging queer oppression, the educational system is doing all students a disservice because all students are in danger of incurring punishments for crossing gender lines and for acquiring narrow definitions of love and attraction. This chapter offers department leaders and/or queer task force members with tangible methods for beginning the work of challenging the hetero- and cisnormative structures inherent within the field of education. With solid leadership in place, teacher educators can learn how to transform their practice in queer-inclusive ways that challenge the system and give rise to a new generation of emancipatory educators.

Reflection Questions

1. What, if any, experiences do you have with engaging faculty in initial conversations centered on gender and sexual orientation?
2. Which of the strategies, or activities, presented in this chapter would you be most comfortable implementing and why? Which would you be least comfortable or otherwise reluctant to implement and why?
3. Which method for evaluating current practices would be most helpful for your institution, department, or school? What other methods for evaluating current practices come to mind?
4. What do you know or imagine being the biggest challenge in approaching your faculty/staff with professional development centered on queer issues? How will you overcome this obstacle?
5. How would you justify your stance to include queer issues in your curriculum with a reluctant teacher educator or faculty member?

Recommended Resources

Readings About Lesson Study

Fernández, M.L. (2005). Exploring "lesson study" in teacher preparation. In H.L. Chick & J.L. Vincent (Eds.), *Proceedings of the 29th Conference of the International Group for the Psychology of Mathematics Education, Vol. 2*. Melbourne, Australia: PME.

Lewis, C. (2002). *Lesson study: A handbook of teacher-led instructional change*. Philadelphia: Research for Better Schools.

Lewis, C., & Hurd, J. (2011). *Lesson study step by step: How teacher learning communities improve instruction*. Portsmouth, NH: Heinemann. [DVD included]

Lewis, C., & Tsuchida, I. (1997). Planned educational change in Japan: The shift to student-centered elementary science. *Journal of Education Policy, 12*(5), 313–331.

Murphy, C.U., & Lick, D.W. (2005). *Whole faculty study groups: Creating student-based professional development* (3rd ed.). Thousand Oaks, CA: Corwin Press.

Stepanek, J., Appel, G., Leong, M., Mangan, M.T., & Mitchell, M. (2007). *Leading lesson study: A practical guide for teachers and facilitators*. Thousand Oaks, CA: Corwin Press.

Research Projects That Queer Practice

Cullen, F., & Sandy, L. (2009). Lesbian Cinderella and other stories: Telling tales and researching sexualities equalities [sic] in primary school. *Sex Education, 9*(2), 141–154.

DePalma, R., & Atkinson, E. (Eds.). (2009). *Interrogating heteronormativity in primary schools: The No Outsiders Project.* Oakhill, VA: Trentham.

Gorski, P.C., Davis, S.N., & Reiter, A. (2013). An examination of the (in)visibility of sexual orientation, heterosexism, homophobia, and other LGBTQ concerns in U.S. multicultural teacher education coursework. *Journal of LGBT Youth, 10,* 224–248.

Kosciw, J.G., Greytak, E.A., Bartkiewicz, M.J., Boesen, M.J., & Palmer, N.A. (2012). *The 2011 National School Climate Survey: The experiences of lesbian, gay, bisexual and transgender youth in our nation's schools.* New York: GLSEN.

References

Bobo, L., & Licari, F. (1989). Education and political tolerance: Testing the effects of cognitive sophistication and target group affect. *Public Opinion Quarterly, 53*(3), 285–308.

Bower, L., & Klecka, C. (2009). (Re)considering normal: Queering social norms for parents and teachers. *Teaching Education, 20*(4), 357–373.

Clark, C.T. (2010). Preparing LGBTQ-allies and combating homophobia in a U.S. teacher education program. *Teaching and Teacher Education, 26,* 704–713.

Cullen, F., & Sandy, L. (2009). Lesbian Cinderella and other stories: Telling tales and researching sexualities equalities [sic] in primary school. *Sex Education, 9*(2), 141–154.

DeJean, W. (2010). Courageous conversations: Reflections on a queer life narrative model. *Teacher Educator, 45,* 233–243.

Derman-Sparks, L., & Edwards, J. (2010). *Anti-bias education for young children and ourselves.* Washington, DC: The National Association for the Education of Young Children.

Evans, N.J., & Broido, E.M. (2002). The experiences of lesbian and bisexual women in college residence halls: Implications for addressing homophobia and heterosexism. *Journal of Lesbian Studies, 6*(3), 29–42.

Gorski, P.C., Davis, S.N., & Reiter, A. (2013). An examination of the (in)visibility of sexual orientation, heterosexism, homophobia, and other LGBTQ concerns in U.S. multicultural teacher education coursework. *Journal of LGBT Youth, 10,* 224–248.

Herek, G.M., Widaman, K.F., & Capitanio, J.P. (2005). When sex equals AIDS: Symbolic stigma and heterosexual adults' inaccurate beliefs about sexual transmission of AIDS. *Social Problems, 52,* 15–37.

Hermann-Wilmarth, J.M., & Bills, P. (2010). Identity shifts: Queering teacher education research. *Teacher Educator, 45,* 257–272.

Horn, S.S., Konkol, P., McInerney, K., Meiners, E.R., North, C., Nuñez, I., ... Sullivan, S. (2010). Visibility matters: Policy work as activism in teacher education. *Issues in Teacher Education, 19*(2), 65–80.

Jennings, T. (2007). Addressing diversity in US teacher preparation programs: A survey of elementary and secondary programs' priorities and challenges from across the United States of America. *Teaching and Teacher Education, 23*(8), 1258–1271.

Kincheloe, J.L. (2008). Critical pedagogy and the knowledge wars of the twenty-?rst century. *International Journal of Critical Pedagogy, 1*(1), 1–22.

Lewis, C. (2002). *Lesson study: A handbook of teacher-led instructional change.* Philadelphia: Research for Better Schools.

Lewis, C., & Tsuchida, I. (1997). Planned educational change in Japan: The shift to student-centered elementary science. *Journal of Education Policy, 12*(5), 313–331.

Lewis, C., & Tsuchida, I. (1998, Winter). A lesson is like a swiftly flowing river: Research lessons and the improvement of Japanese education. *American Educator,* 14–17, 50–52.

Nixon, D., & Givens, N. (2007). An epitaph to Section 28? Telling tales out of school about changes and challenges to discourses of sexuality. *International Journal of Qualitative Studies in Education, 20*(4), 449–471.

O'Connor, A. (1998). *The cultural logic of gender in college: Heterosexism, homophobia, and sexism in campus peer groups.* Unpublished doctoral dissertation, University of Colorado, Boulder.

Perkins, B.K. (2007). *Where we teach: The CUBE survey of urban school climate.* Alexandria, VA: National School Boards Association.

Perry, R., Lewis, C., & Akiba, M. (2002). Lesson study in the San Mateo-Foster City School District. Paper presented at the 2002 Annual Meeting of the American Educational Research Association, New Orleans, LA.

Rands, K.E. (2009). Considering transgender people in education: A gender-complex approach. *Journal of Teacher Education, 60*(4), 419–431.

Sexual and Gender Minority Youth Resource Center. (2013). *Gender Gumby.* Retrieved from www.pdxqcenter.org/wp-content/uploads/2013/02/gumby%20pp.pdf

Sumara, D.J. (2007). Small differences matter: Interrupting certainty about identity in teacher education. *Journal of Gay and Lesbian Issues in Education, 4*(4), 39–58.

Szalacha, L.A. (2004). Educating teachers on LGBTQ issues: A review of research and program evaluations. *Journal of Gay and Lesbian Issues in Education, 1*(4), 67–79.

TransActive. (2011). *Societal discomfort zone.* Portland, OR: Jenn Burleton.

Valentine, G. (1993). Negotiating and managing multiple sexual identities: Lesbian time-space strategies. *Transactions of the Institute of British Geographers, 18,* 237–248.

van den Akker, H., van der Ploeg, R., & Scheepers, P. (2013). Disapproval of homosexuality: Comparative research on individual and national determinants of disapproval of homosexuality in 20 European countries. *International Journal of Public Opinion Research, 25*(1), 64–86.

Vavrus, M. (2009). Sexuality, schooling, and teacher identity formation: A critical pedagogy for teacher education. *Teaching and Teacher Education, 25,* 383–390.

Wright, S.L., & Canetto, S.S. (2009). Stereotypes of older lesbians and gay men. *Educational Gerontology, 35,* 424–452.

8
ACTIVITIES AND MATERIALS FOR TEACHER EDUCATORS

In This Chapter

- Multileveled curricular entry points for teacher educators to become more attentive to the complicated and wonderful intersections of sex, gender, sexual orientation, and knowledge.
- Lesson plans, exercise descriptions, and resources (see the Companion Website for reproducible handouts that accompany these) to support rich class discussions, critical assignments, and other vital learning opportunities around interrupting hetero- and cisnormativity.

Introduction

Evans (2002) noted, "Bringing together Teacher and Queer is a complicated endeavor. It is public and private, in an arena in which constructions of what is public and private continually shift and change" (p. 179). Indeed, historical discourses combine with contemporary hetero- and cissexism to assist teacher educators in avoiding queer content to wavering degrees in their coursework. When queer curriculum *is* introduced, it often takes the form of tolerance, diversity, or anti-bullying education. Although this can teach the importance of antidiscrimination, which is a good start, it falls short of covering the ground necessary to change our course of action. Thus, by and large, we see the prevalence of heteronormative structures that suppress diverse sexual orientations as well as gender variance. The political, cultural, and ideological influences that maintain hegemony over nonnormative sexualities and ways of identity construction are accounted for in the Queer Inclusion in Education Framework offered in Chapter 3. The framework communicates that recognition of these structures is not sufficient. Hetero- and cisnormativity are limiting, and interrupting them, then, becomes an important way to broaden perception, to elevate cognition, and to strengthen the imagination of learners. Interpretation of the framework prompts the question, "What can teacher educators do to equip teacher candidates with the knowledge, dispositions, and skills necessary to implement queer-inclusive practices?"

Establishing curricular connections, or entry points, to acknowledge and understand the continuum of sexual orientation and gender identity and expression is vital. As Coiser and Sanders (2007) observed, "To equitably serve all students, teachers must consider matters of social justice and human rights, including histories and representations of those who are queer" (p. 24). As asserted in Chapter 5, queerness exists and is present in K–12 education. Queer students, students perceived to be queer, and students with queer family members comprise increasing numbers of student populations across the nation. Curricula should recognize and honor these individuals as well as guide non-queer students toward understanding and accepting diverse identities and cultures. In addition to the presence of queer individuals, anti-queer curriculum and pedagogy run rampant in schools. As noted in Chapter 1, heterosexist and gender-specific ideologies surface in kindergarten when teachers, sometimes unintentionally, perpetuate narrow and stereotypical definitions of gender and family structures. As students graduate to middle and high school, they are greeted by the surveillance and policing of knowledge and sexuality, which are explicitly heterosexualized. Proms and other dances such as the Sadie Hawkins, segregated gender spaces and opportunities (e.g., bathrooms, locker rooms, extracurricular activities), and literature and texts that acknowledge ridged conceptualizations of gender and sexuality are but a few examples.

To become more comfortable and skilled in queering the curriculum, teacher candidates need educators to guide and support them. By infusing relevant queer content into lectures, class discussions, and reading materials, teacher educators contribute to normalizing queerness for an inclusive curriculum. My conversations with Portland State faculty and other teacher educators from across the country revealed that even when willing and desiring to infuse queer content/pedagogy in their teaching, many educators don't know where to begin. Granted, no two teacher preparation programs are identical. On the contrary, the nation has a wide range of multiplicity in program scope and sequence, course content, faculty dispositions and capabilities, and school culture and policy. Yet as a result of nationwide educational standardization, most programs share some universal concepts and experiences. What follows is a description of how some of these common courses and experiences can be expanded to interrogate hetero- and cisnormativity and to include queer discourse.

Curriculum Design

The first entry point is coursework surrounding *curriculum design*. All teacher candidates learn how to develop unit-level and lesson-level learning opportunities for groups of students. Often, this work includes explicit instruction around viewing students holistically, as individuals with unique academic, social, and emotional needs. Teacher educators can help prospective teachers by acknowledging the distinctive needs of students questioning their sexual orientation or declaring nonnormative orientations (e.g., homosexual, bisexual, pansexual, asexual) as well as students presenting as gender nonconforming and gender transitioning. Some materials used to support teacher educators in this endeavor include audio and digital media.

Using Audio and Digital Media

Several films give voice to the queer experience and can help straight and cisgender teachers understand their own privilege and recognize the unique needs of queer youth and families. Frameline, Welcoming Schools, and Groundspark are three organizations that offer powerful documentaries about queerness, many of which are tailored to educators. For example, *Gender Matters* (Frameline, 2008) features six short films that provide a broad overview of gender identity, gender expression, and transgender issues through interviews, first-person essays, and narrative fiction from a diverse range of backgrounds and experiences. It comes with a free downloadable curriculum and an action guide to help facilitate conversations in the classroom. It's possible, then, for a teacher educator to present this video in a course on curriculum design and then pose the following question to teacher candidates: What are some unique needs of gender-nonconforming and transgender students, and how will you meet these needs? After discussing the film, teacher candidates can be led through the supplemental curriculum guide using acquired curriculum theory and pedagogy. Potential guiding questions might include these: How does the curriculum support learning? What is the scope and sequence? What kinds of knowledge and skills are participants being asked to acquire and perform? This process could be used with most of the videos produced by these organizations. (For more information about these film creators and distributors, see the "Recommended Film/Audio and Corresponding Curriculum Guides" at the end of this chapter as well as the Companion Website for direct web links.)

Similar to film, podcasts (MP3 or video files downloaded and played on a computer or portable media device) can be an effective means for teacher educators to approach the topic of queer inclusion in curriculum design. National Public Radio (NPR)'s *This American Life* archives several podcasts related to queer youth and families, for example, "Tom Girls" (NPR, 2009). This 17-minute audio clip introduces listeners to Lilly and Thomasina, eight-year-old transgender females. The children's personal accounts, as well as testimony from their parents regarding how the respective elementary schools mishandled the girls' transitions, is revealing and educational. In addition, the New York Times (2007) website, which contains an abundance of podcasts, features a 44-minute interview with Dan Savage about LGBT bullying and the It Gets Better Project. Other forums, such as YouTube and iTunes, offer additional video/audio and can be good places to start a search.

Finally, it is important to remember that teacher educators must take responsibility for critically examining all media before presenting them to students to ensure that the content is authentic and does not unintentionally perpetuate stereotypes.

Confronting Personal Assumptions and Stereotypes

Working with teacher candidates to confront personal stereotypes and taken-for-granted assumptions can also help guide prospective teachers toward understanding the queer experience. Two short activities that entail deep self-reflection and community discourse include the *heterosexual* and *cis privilege questionnaires* and an activity called *four corners*. The Heterosexual Privilege Questionnaire (Rochlin, 1972) and Cis Privilege Questionnaire (2007), which can be found on the Companion Website and elsewhere on the web, are based on McIntosh's (1989) article on white privilege and feature examples of the privilege that heterosexual and cisgender people possess. Although queer individuals have a range of different experiences, they cannot count on a majority of the conditions listed in these documents. A teacher educator can supplement McIntosh's article on white privilege, which is frequently used in college coursework, with either or both questionnaires. Students read the lists of privileges independently or in small groups and then discuss which items stood out, which were most surprising, which they are still struggling to understand, and perhaps which they believe have recently evolved in society.

On one occasion, I cut the heterosexual and cis privilege questionnaires into strips and taped one statement underneath each teacher candidate's chair. When we began discussing the invisible benefits afforded to straight and cisgender individuals, I instructed students to reach beneath their chairs to retrieve the items. Taking turns, students read statements such as these: "When I talk about my heterosexuality (such as in a joke or talking about my relationships), I will not be accused of pushing my sexual orientation onto others" and "I expect that a visa and passport will be sufficient documentation for me to enter any country, however difficult these may be to obtain." Having each statement read aloud in isolation is a powerful exercise to experience in community.

Four corners also encourages teacher candidates to reflect on and discuss queerness in new and interesting ways. In my curriculum development courses, I ask teacher candidates to reflect on personal values while simultaneously empathizing with other points of view. Here are my procedures for facilitating this activity:

1. Create signs in large font that read *strongly disagree, disagree, agree,* and *strongly agree*; post one in each corner in the classroom.
2. Distribute a value statements questionnaire (see Appendix D) to students and instruct them to *anonymously* use a Likert scale to match the language on the signs mentioned in step 1 with the ten values-based statements. For example, teacher candidates denote whether they strongly agree, agree, disagree, or strongly disagree with statements such as "I believe that lesbian, gay, and

bisexual teachers should be free to be out at school if they choose to be," "As a teacher, I feel very comfortable discussing transgender issues at school," and "I believe that birth control methods, including condoms, should be made available within all middle and high schools."
3. When everyone has answered the questions (I usually provide three to five minutes), students crumple their papers and a "snowball fight" ensues.
4. After all papers have been tossed around, each student retrieves one.
5. Students then go to the quadrant of the room (i.e., strongly agree, agree, disagree, strongly disagree) indicated in response to the first statement (it may or may not reflect their personal belief).
6. Volunteers from each area state some reasons people might respond in that way (e.g., "I strongly agree that LGB teachers should be free to be out in school because . . .").
7. Students then voice questionnaire items for which they are interested in "polling the room," and everyone repeats step 5.
8. After several questionnaire items have been debated, the facilitator ends with teacher candidates' responses to the values statement questionnaire item "I believe that all children have a right to an education in a safe and supportive environment" before leading a whole-group debrief.

The debrief discussion can last from 5 to 30 minutes. Some questions include these: What did it feel like to pose an argument counter to your core beliefs? What polling results most surprised you? What did you learn as a result of participating in this activity?

If not surfaced by students, the teacher educator should acknowledge the following big ideas: We all have different values informed by our unique beliefs and life experiences. Everyone is entitled to their own opinion on a variety of sociopolitical issues, and yet we also need to create a safe classroom for *all* students. Students deserve to feel safe and included at school. This final claim is almost always demonstrated by 100% of participants corralled in the "strongly agree" corner in response to the statement "I believe all children have a right to an education in a safe and supportive environment" (see the aforementioned step 8).

I find the four corners activity most effective and beneficial after considerable community building has occurred. It requires certain levels of honesty, respect, and trust, which are not fostered overnight. However, when executed discerningly (and tweaked with a specific purpose and audience in mind), the activity can help people come together around a subject and engage in unconventional ways that have a transformative impact. It can be used to help teacher candidates confront their own attitudes and beliefs about gender and sexual orientation, which may assist them in understanding the particular needs of students questioning their sexual orientation or declaring nonnormative identities. (See the Companion Website for full activity directions and an adjustable values statement questionnaire template.)

Critically Analyzing Curriculum

In addition to developing teachers' ability to know their K–12 learners and honor the core qualities they bring to the classroom, curriculum design courses prepare teacher candidates to be mindful of content. Inviting pre-service teachers to think about how issues are framed, how content is presented in the classroom, can assist in revealing heteronormativity. In other words, learning how to critically evaluate curriculum for hidden, as well as overt, messages that transmit stereotypical gender roles and compulsory heterosexuality is important.

One learning opportunity to assist teacher candidates in acquiring this skill set is for teacher educators to provide copies of current K–12 literature (i.e., popular children's books and adolescent novels, district-adopted middle and high school textbooks) and encourage teacher candidates to analyze and discuss queer (in)visibility. I developed an instrument called *Curriculum Analysis: A Tool for Interrogating Messages About Sexual Orientation and Gender* (see Appendix E) to support analysis by offering probing questions related to specific focus areas (photos and illustrations, characters, settings, story lines, and language). Using this technique to take inventory of curricula and discuss differing interpretations of texts enables teacher candidates to dissect hetero- and cisnormative rhetoric *and* to realize the need to design and adapt curriculum in critical, responsible, and inclusive ways.

Teacher educators should also be mindful to infuse queer content when sharing examples of integrated curriculum units. Imagine a teacher educator modeling how to construct a series of comprehensive civil rights or poetry lessons. Now envision an explicit learning objective within this exemplar unit that recognizes queerness, such as contributions of queer individuals like Bayard Rustin and Langston Hughes, and current theories about traditional poets such as Emily Dickinson. This subtle approach requires no major rewriting of curriculum on the part of the teacher educator and yet goes a long way toward naturalizing the integration of queer content in pedagogy and practice.

Integrating Queer Content Into Curriculum

A final entry point for surfacing queer issues in a teacher preparation course on curriculum design includes teaching when, where, and how queer content can be addressed in developmentally appropriate ways at K–12 levels. As evidenced by the research captured in Chapters 5 and 6, current and prospective teachers desire to incorporate inclusive, queer content and pedagogy in their practice, but they often do not know how or where to begin. What follows are descriptions of three specific activities teacher educators can use to assist teacher candidates in queering the curriculum. The first (*timeline activity*) is an overarching lesson to help teacher candidates identify developmentally appropriate entry points for queer inclusion across grades K–12. The second (*family diversity*) is a module that teacher educators facilitate for teacher candidates to model queer conversation starters in the elementary classroom. The third (*queer representations in contemporary media*) is an activity that prospective middle and secondary teacher candidates can place in their toolboxes for later use. (See the Companion Website for all three lesson plans and accompanying reproducible materials.)

The timeline activity is my favorite for working both with teacher educators and teacher candidates. The power of this activity lies in the fact that it authenticates the voices of youth and adolescents and provides teachers with curricular entry points for teaching about gender and sexual orientation in K–12 education. The materials for the activity include timeline labels, personal stories, and teaching points. Activity preparation includes designating a large space on the wall to display the timeline labels, posting "elementary," "middle school," and "high school" from left to right high on the wall. The teacher educator then distributes one or two "personal stories" to each teacher candidate. These first-person narratives are printed individually on standard sheets of paper and depict actual experiences from youth and families. For example:

> I've always known I was a boy. My parents gave me a girl name, and want me to wear dresses, and play with dolls. But it's not who I am. I had short hair and so the other kids thought I was a boy. Until the teacher called me Katie. I begged her to call me Josh, but she refused.
>
> One of my friends just got pregnant. She's a lesbian, but she had this fake boyfriend so people wouldn't harass her. I don't think she expected to have sex, so she didn't think about birth control or anything.
>
> I read on the Internet that transgender kids can get hormone blockers. If they take them before they get too far in puberty, their bodies won't change. My mom is considering letting me do it, but she hasn't said yes for sure.

After quietly reading the statement distributed to them, teacher candidates take turns vocalizing one personal story at a time and place it onto the timeline at the age they think the experience might have happened/might happen. When all the stories are read and mounted onto the timeline, participants take time to reflect and discuss. Sample probing questions include these: Do the stories seem realistic? Are there any questions about the language/terms or any of the issues brought up? What related stories, or life experiences, do you know or imagine to be true that are not listed here? When discussion stalls, the teacher educator initiates the next phase of the activity by distributing the teaching points to teacher candidates. Examples of teaching points include:

> Someone who feels as if their body is a sex other than the one they were assigned at birth might call themselves "transgender." Approximately 1 in 100 children identify as transgender. This is different from being bisexual,

gay, or lesbian. Most gay, lesbian, and bisexual people don't think they are or don't want to be the other sex.

You can't tell if people are bisexual, gay, or lesbian by how they look or act. Only some people fit the stereotypes; that's what makes them stereotypes. Some people who *aren't* gay also fit stereotypes about gay people. It's okay to be a bisexual, gay, or lesbian who fits those stereotypes, but many people don't. If you hear somebody put down gay people—or *any* people—you can tell them you think it's mean (unfair, unkind), and you can ask them to stop using "gay" as a put-down. If you hear students use terms like "That's so gay!" you can say: "It's not okay to say, 'That's so gay!' to mean that you don't like something. It shows prejudice and it hurts people."

Some lesbian, gay, bisexual, transgender, queer, and questioning (LGBTQ) people have made incredible contributions to this world. They have been scientists, diplomats, athletes, artists, soldiers, and human rights activists. Some of the people in your history books were LGBTQ, but you never learned that about them either because of the prejudices of the people who wrote those books or because the person lived at a time when people didn't understand or talk about sexual and gender diversity.

Sometimes to shorten the activity and leave more room for discussion, I bypass asking teacher candidates to read aloud the teaching points. Rather, I ask them to privately read and then place their one or two items on the timeline according to when (elementary through high school) they think the curriculum is relevant and developmentally appropriate. Following this, I invite everyone to engage with the completed timeline in a silent "gallery walk." What one typically observes, using a prior example, is the personal story of "Katie" always knowing he was a boy overlapping with teaching points such as the one that begins, "Someone who feels as if their body is a sex other than the one they were assigned at birth might call themselves *transgender.*" This, multiplied by 15–20 stories and teaching points, provides a visual landscape with a powerful message: Children are impacted by queer issues, which can be collected through authentic (both painful and joyful) stories, *and* there are organic and multiple entry points for including queer content in the K–12 curriculum. After allotting teacher candidates time to read the teaching points and digest the timeline in its entirety, the activity is concluded with a discussion, which can be ignited by the following questions:

- What stood out to you about the personal stories and/or the teaching points?
- Do you agree with what is presented at what age? Why or why not?
- Which teaching points seem more difficult to implement? Why? How could these challenges be resolved?
- Does anyone have overall reflections on this activity?

It is important for teacher educators to highlight the following points if these points are not raised in the concluding discussion.

- Sexuality and gender are relevant topics across the lifespan.
- Whether we like it or not, young people hear messages about these topics, and teachers can help ensure the young people have accurate information.
- Inclusive education benefits all students, and teachers can model inclusion and respect for people of all identities/experiences.
- People's perceptions of sex education are often very narrow. Most people don't actually disagree with content, but they may not know what sex education in elementary school could really look like.
- Our own comfort/discomfort is conveyed by how we approach these topics. The idea that "they're not ready" may be more a reflection of we're not ready to talk about these topics. Practice can make it easier.

A second way for instructors to surface queer issues in a teacher preparation course on curriculum design is to model and deconstruct an inclusive lesson on family and gender diversity. Welcoming Schools offers an abundance of online resources and lesson plans for K–12 teachers on embracing family diversity, preventing gender stereotyping, and combating name-calling. Their website (welcomingschools.org) contains a fully developed lesson called "What is a family?" The goal of this lesson is for students "to see that the common bond that holds all kinds of healthy families together is love and caring." In addition to an overarching goal, the lesson plans offered by Welcoming Schools include measurable learning objectives. With regard to "What is a family?" students will be able to define what makes a family and describe a variety of families, identify common characteristics within all families, and learn that families have some similarities and some differences.

When I demonstrate this lesson for my teacher candidates, I require their active participation. In addition to exposing them to queer content, I explicitly model the pedagogical and instructional strategies covered in a curriculum design course. For example, I begin the lesson by referring to the learning targets, or objectives, and our agenda of activities. The lesson plan provided by Welcoming Schools features an engaging introduction that I use to model an effective "hook." We engage in inquiry and discourse when I pose the essential and follow-up questions: "What do we know about families?" followed by "Who is in a family? What do family members give or share with each other? What responsibilities do family members have?" Here I try to model good instructor listening skills, varied questioning techniques, differentiation, metacognition, and other best practices. I also work to greet student inquiry, particularly as it relates to addressing queerness, with openness and authenticity so teacher candidates can observe how to navigate difficult, and historically silenced, discourse.

When I complete the demonstration—I try not to exceed 20 minutes—I provide teacher candidates with a printed copy of the lesson plan (most Welcoming Schools lesson plans include grade level, length of time, goal, objectives, standards, materials, literacy integration, activity procedures, extensions, assessment and evaluation) and we dissect it. Thus, teacher candidates exit this 40-minute learning experience with a vision, and at least one tangible tool, for queering their practice. As the course instructor, I have also ensured, as a result of this exercise, that teacher candidates have grappled with curriculum and observed and critiqued effective instructional strategies.

As the name suggests, the queer representations in contemporary media activity enables teacher candidates to critically examine the ways sexual orientation and gender are currently represented in television, film, radio, advertising, and so forth. Looking at contemporary media has a place in a queered curriculum design course because it allows a focus on a range of curricula and integrated methods, and, when modeled by a teacher educator, it can also serve as a potential lesson teacher candidates can use with their current and future middle and high school students.

Certainly exploring media culture is not a new pedagogical practice, but given the current LGBTQ social movement, it is especially timely for understanding and making sense of society's evolving views on queer identity. "Educating the Simpsons: Teaching Queer Representations in Contemporary Visual Media" by Padva (2008) examines how the episode "Homer's Phobia" from Matt Groening's animation series *The Simpsons* can be used to "deconstruct queer and straight codes of behavior, socialization, articulation, representation, and visibility" (p. 57). I facilitated an activity in my curriculum design course wherein middle and high school teacher candidates viewed and discussed this particular episode. I strongly recommend reading Padva's article, which includes a synopsis of the episode complete with illuminating commentary that interrogates meaning. In essence, the episode "Homer's Phobia" (Hauge & Anderson, 1997) tells the story of how the Simpsons befriend John, a flamboyantly gay kitsch trader. Homer fears John's potential "recruitment" of Bart, and after a series of outrageous attempts to transform Bart into a "real man," Homer assures his son that he loves him whether he is straight or gay. Homer's initial homophobia stems from ignorance and evolves over the course of the episode in a beautiful way. He is not demonized, and Padva observed:

> From this perspective, not only gays but also straight Homer are victims of the same oppressive "natural" sexual order that stigmatizes and discriminates against sexual minorities and imposes restricting hetero-masculine codes of visibility, behavior and sexual expression on men.
>
> *(p. 66)*

After watching the episode, my teacher candidates engaged in a lively conversation. They noted homophobia on an overt/covert continuum by referencing exact phrases and behaviors from the episode. Some voiced perspectives of a changing landscape, noting that until the 1990s, LGBT people were largely absent in films and TV programs unless portrayed in stereotyped and derogatory roles. Operating under the assumption that many school-age youth watch *The Simpsons* (as well as other media), the group discussed implications for teachers. One student raised the question, "Are teachers responsible for supporting or debunking popular messages conveyed through media?" Finally, as a group we processed the means by which we discussed queer issues on a meta level and came to the conclusion that the use of modern media enriched our understanding of contemporary queerness and overall learning experience. As our discussion drew to a close, I brought us back to a focus on curriculum design by distributing Padva's (2008) article, which contains a plan for discussing *The Simpsons* episode with adolescents. Padva based the curriculum on his analysis of the episode and focused on ten major subjects organized chronologically according to the development of the plot (stereotypes, effeminacy, homophobia, naming the *Other*, etc.). The following excerpts represent two of the ten subject-based teaching points.

> *Effeminacy.* The class can analyze the politics of effeminacy in regard to John's portrayal as a stylish, sissy drama queen (Bristow, 2000; Letts, 2005). The main question is whether this sort of articulation reconfirms the immediate association of homosexuality and effeminacy, or rather whether it celebrates effeminacy as a legitimate variation of contemporary masculinity, particularly in gay camp subculture (Padva, 2000).
>
> *(Padva, 2008, p. 69)*

> *Different Readings, Different Perspectives.* Finally, the teacher can relate to the polysémie [sic] character of this episode that enables different audiences to enjoy it from their varying perspectives. The students can suggest some possible alternative interpretations of different groups: straight adolescents, queer adolescents, parents of straight children, parents of queer children, open queers, closeted queers, and Afro Americans (who are conspicuously ignored in this episode).
>
> *(Padva, 2008, p. 70)*

Padva's (2008) curriculum plan thus contextualizes queer oppression and liberation. By making sense of the episode, students discuss and understand complex constructs in community. Of the learning experience itself, Padva noted the following:

> Through analysis of queer representations in contemporary visual media, the teacher can relate to the position and contribution of the queer subjectivity

to the narrative framework, from the exposition through the climax and resolution; to the visibility of the queer protagonist (physique, clothing, makeup, hairstyle, accessories, etc.); to the (non)conventional and (un)acceptable acts of the queer character; and, of course, to the sexual language in the dialogue.

(pp. 57–58)

Addressing queer issues in K–12 classrooms takes comfort, confidence, knowledge, and skills. When teacher educators provide curricular entry points and exemplar lessons/activities, and when they are willing to model the facilitation of queer inclusion, it seems possible for teacher candidates to confront homophobia and transphobia in a similar way.

Classroom Management

The second entry point for queering practice rests in classroom management. I have taught courses on classroom management for years that tend to discourse and activities focused on the organization and logistics of classroom procedures, communication and classroom routines, procedures for prevention and resolution of challenging events or behaviors, problem solving and decision making, culturally responsive practice, and communication issues involving staff, administrators, and families.

During the course, teacher candidates examine classroom management based upon principles of community building and cultural pluralism and explore approaches like culturally responsive classroom management (see Weinstein, Tomlinson-Clarke, & Curran, 2004) and restorative justice (see Ashley & Burke, 2009; Mirsky, 2003). As such, queer content has a logical and relevant place in the course curriculum. What follows are strategies teacher educators can employ to help teacher candidates recognize queer issues as they relate to responsibilities around classroom management, specifically bullying and name-calling and communicating with queer parents and family members.

Interrupting Bullying and Name-Calling

As cited earlier, nearly 82% of LGBT students across the nation are verbally tormented and 38% are physically harassed in K–12 education (Kosciw, Greytak, Bartkiewicz, Boesen, & Palmer, 2012). Although no child is immune from becoming the target of name-calling and bullying, it is clear that, on average, queer students (and students perceived to be queer or "different") are targeted more than their straight, cisgender, and "passing" classmates. Theoretical research on antigay bullying suggests that the use of homophobic insults can be motivated by multiple factors, including peer group dynamics, sexual prejudice, traditional gender role beliefs, and situational factors such as exposure to gender role violations (Collier, Bos, & Sandfort, 2013). In a study on homophobia, "Inside the Mind of People Who Hate Gays," Franklin (2000) identified four overarching motivations for most antigay assaults:

- *Peer dynamics:* Committing an act to prove masculinity or heterosexuality;
- *Antigay ideology:* Accomplishing some ideological motive or agenda;
- *Thrill seeking:* Trying to have a good time at someone else's expense, often done by young people who feel socially alienated;
- *Perceived self-defense:* Because gay people are stereotypically portrayed as sexual predators and purely sexual beings, innocent acts such as a glance or gender-nonconforming self-expression can be interpreted as threatening.

Addressing name-calling and bullying is important because experiencing high levels of in-school victimization can lead to lower academic achievement, increased truancy and dropout rates, lower levels of self-esteem, and higher levels of depression (Kosciw et al., 2012).

The topics of name-calling and bullying often surface in classroom management courses because prospective teachers need to be prepared to recognize, stop, educate, and support students involved. Without substantial acknowledgment of queerness and other aspects of identity, teacher educators fail to address the issue in an authentic way. One place to start is for teacher educators to understand and then explain the epistemology of bullying. Sumara (2007) suggested that schools sort students within "tiny" and inflexible categories of possibility. He contended:

> This is one of the reasons that bullying in schools continues to be such a problem, and why it is so difficult to interrupt. When narratives of identity are so tightly structured, the minor differences that separate the acceptable from the not acceptable are dramatically foregrounded. Many of us have experienced the effects of being associated with these minor differences when we were public school students: those of us who were considered fat, or physically unattractive, or poor, or effeminate.
>
> *(p. 51)*

It is also important to research basic statistics to share with teacher candidates. In addition to noting the frequency and types of harassment queer students face, it is important to know which subgroups are at higher risk. For instance, the social cost of gender nonconformity is especially high for adolescent boys (Diamond & Savin-Williams, 2003). Knowing this information can be helpful for teachers who work with male students who defy stereotypical gender expectations. Also, studies of homophobic name-calling among adolescents have found that males perpetrate and are targeted in this manner more frequently than females (Burn, 2000; Gruber & Fineran, 2008; Poteat & Espelage, 2005, 2007).

Beyond keeping up with research, teacher educators can implement a didactic experience called *interrupting hateful language*. For this activity I provide teacher candidates with a handout describing seven strategies for stopping homo- and transphobic language (although they can be generalized to address any type of prejudicial language). The handout includes the following strategies.

The stall technique: If you are unable to think of what to say, or are too angry or triggered to respond, call for a "time-out." Say something like, "I am really uncomfortable with what just happened. I need to think about it and we will come back to it later." Then, call for a class meeting or individual conversation after you've had time to think more clearly about how to respond.

Make it personal: Tell how it made you feel when you heard the comment. Use the relationship you have with the student(s) to build empathy and understanding. Say something like "I felt . . . when you said . . ." or "I am offended when you say . . . because . . ."

Call it what it is: That is, use the terms *homophobic/transphobic*. If you haven't already introduced these terms in class, take the time to explain what they mean and describe their impact.

Use education: Use accurate statistics, language, and history to respond with corrective information the students lack. For example, explain the etymology of the offensive word(s) used. Say something like, "Actually the word *faggot* means 'bundle of sticks' and comes from the Middle Ages. Gay men were rounded up, tied together, and set on fire" (definition from Ausburn, 2005, p. 104). Take adequate time to unpack this; perhaps offer a series of lessons on the persecution of gays in Nazi Germany before and during World War II.

Reference norms or policy: Most schools have basic building-wide rules such as "be respectful, be kind," and these can be stated to remind students they are breaking these rules by using queer epithets. Increased numbers of schools now have specific anti-bullying policies in place, and when referring to that, you can say, "When you say . . . , it makes our community unsafe and those words are not acceptable in our community/class/school because we respect all people . . ."

Assume the best: Although some students knowingly say offensive things with intention, others say the same words without fully understanding their meaning, power, or the extent to which they inflict pain. In assuming the best, you can say, "I imagine you did not mean to be hurtful, but . . ." or "You might not have meant to be offensive and yet . . ."

Ask a question: Before intervening, you may require more information to determine a student's intention and the context. Asking something like "What did you mean by that?" or "What do you mean when you say that shirt is gay? Do you know what gay means?" You can follow up with the "use education" strategy and a whole-group lesson to break down stereotypes, clarify language, and naturalize diverse sexual orientations and/or gender variations.

After providing a few minutes for teacher candidates to review all interruption strategies, I ask, "Which strategies are you naturally drawn to? What strategy are you least likely to use? Have you observed or experienced any of these strategies in the classroom? Can you describe a strategy you use or know about that's not listed?" Prior to applying the strategies in class, teacher candidates discuss the varied school contexts and factors in which they will need to interrupt hateful language. They are asked to reflect on how a response may be influenced by space (public vs. private), time (ample vs. restricted), and setting (structured vs. unstructured).

Next, I arrange teacher candidates in small groups of three to five. Each group receives a different scenario they must read, discuss, and, most importantly, apply what they now know about interrupting hateful language/behaviors. Here's an example of a scenario for early childhood/elementary teacher candidates: "One of your students comes to you complaining that another student is lying. When you ask what they were lying about, the student says 'Janie said Rowena's mom is really a dude.'" Or midlevel and secondary teacher candidates may be asked to respond to this scenario:

> It is school spirit week and a group of students are working together to assemble a booth. One boy starts to fall off the chair he's standing on, and another boy reaches out to steady him. While regaining his balance, the boy on the chair calls out "Oh, no, homo now."

See the Companion Website for the interrupting hateful language handout and a listing of scenarios that can be altered for individual use. From here teacher educators can require groups of candidates to perform skits illustrating their scenario and effective teacher responses. To conclude the learning experience, teacher educators should lead a short discussion about the contextual factors involved and how those influenced the candidates' decision making.

Communicating With Queer Parents and Family Members

In addition to name-calling and bullying, a classroom management course offers an ideal opportunity to explore constructive ways to communicate with queer parents and family members. One way to approach this is through *problem-posing*, a method that delves deeply into any issue or problem, demonstrating the extent of its social and personal connections. Coined by Freire (1970), problem-posing "focuses on power relations in the classroom, in the institution, in the formation of standard canons of knowledge, and in society at large" (Shor, 1992, p. 31). As a classroom technique, it is dynamic, participatory, and empowering, and it requires high levels of critical thinking.

Auerbach (1990) simplified problem-posing to five important steps. These steps and supplemental probing questions are listed here.

STEP 1: Describe the Content

What did you see/What is the dialogue about?
What is happening?

STEP 2: Define the Problem

What is the problem?
What is the cause of the problem?
Why is this a problem?

STEP 3: Personalize the Problem

How does this problem affect our community?
How does this problem relate to our own lives and cultures?

STEP 4: Discuss the Problem

What are the social reasons for this problem?

STEP 5: Discuss Alternatives to the Problem

How can we work together to resolve the problem?
What are the consequences of various courses of action?

Problem-posing can be framed, or launched, in various ways. A teacher educator can begin by asking questions such as "What potential problems occur between teachers and parents/family members?" and "What unique problems can occur between teachers and queer parents/family members?" Responses to these prompts can be recorded on chart paper as the teacher educator leads the class through the five steps of problem-posing. Alternatively, the teacher educator can present a skit, case study, personal narrative, or selection of published readings to illuminate a problem and then call upon candidates to work through the five steps. Regardless of how problems are presented, they must originate from the students' concerns and experiences, which makes them relevant to their daily lives. Thus, one way of eliciting skit or case study content is for teacher educators to distribute and collect a brief written personal reflection during a class session leading up to the activity. Possible questions can include these:

- Describe a time in school when you experienced/witnessed intolerance toward an LGBTQ student, staff, or parent.
- What strategies have you witnessed or used to promote a safe and respectful environment for LGBTQ students and parents?
- What questions do you have about the role you can play in supporting and including your LGBTQ students and families?

In a recent course on classroom management, I used participants' responses to these questions to arrive at the three case studies that follow, which I used to frame potential problems surrounding queerness that teachers face when communicating with family members.

"Choice" time: A kindergarten teacher is monitoring choice time one afternoon when she notices a child sadly hovering over the dress-up box. The teacher approaches Eric and says, "Oh, are you considering what to be today... maybe a nurse or a chef?" Eric turns to his teacher and replies, "My daddy told me I can't play dress up because it will turn me gay."

Exclusive language in correspondence: A fourth-grade teacher greets students outside the classroom door in the morning when he spots an angry parent coming his way. Ralph, one of Josh's dads, is waving a copy of the most recent classroom newsletter that reads in large bold letters at the top, "Dear Mom and Dad..." This generalized language that assumes every child has a mom and a dad and denies the existence of same-sex parents really upsets Ralph and was apparently noticed by Josh as well. Ralph is particularly frustrated because this is not the first time the school has alienated Josh's family through the use of exclusive language in home-school correspondence.

Parent chaperone: A ninth-grade teacher is elated to have a parent chaperone join her on a field trip. As students arrive on the bus, the teacher overhears some comments they make about the parent, who presents herself in a stereotypical masculine manner (e.g., short hair, no makeup, androgynous clothing). The teacher ignores the comments as not to call attention to, or embarrass, the parent. That evening the teacher receives an e-mail from the parent chaperone, who was upset at the teacher's unwillingness to intervene.

After I presented the case studies, teacher candidates worked through the five-step method for problem-posing to achieve the following outcomes:

- Name potential conflicts around queerness and heteronormativity and identify unique attributes to working with queer families.
- Articulate the tension around such conflicts.
- Explore the impact of these problems for the classroom community and personal livelihood.
- Discuss social and historical roots to the problems.
- Brainstorm ways teachers can be more inclusive, understanding, and supportive of queer families.

It was a fruitful activity to encourage teacher candidates to think about queer inclusion "globally," by taking into account social, historical, and cultural contexts, and also "locally" by grounding problems of practice in case studies that they experienced or considered.

Addressing queer content in classroom management courses, which tend to be rooted in problem solving and community building, is worthwhile and important.

Teacher educators can begin to queer their curriculum by using the interrupting hateful language activity and problem-posing methods to articulate obstacles teachers are sure to encounter and to brainstorm solutions.

Subject-Based Methods Courses

A third point of entry for creating inclusive, queer-affirming teacher education curricula is subject-based methods courses. By this I mean content-specific courses that prepare K–12 educators to teach specific subject areas. Various methods courses, such as math, science, literacy, social studies, and art and movement, can be enriched through queer infusion. This section offers ideas for exposing teacher candidates to curricula capable of cultivating system-level change in K–12 education.

Math

Using the free, 135-page National School Climate Survey report published every two years by GLSEN is a great tool for teaching math concepts. Teacher educators can demonstrate (or acknowledge the possibility of) using this mathematical oasis in the classroom. The report syndicates current research and relevant social issues with a wealth of mathematical concepts addressed in K–12 standards, such as percentages, algorithms, graphing, statistics, probability, mean, median, and mode.

Science

Today, queer people make contributions in every branch of the physical, social, natural, engineering, and computer sciences. In fact, queer scientists (e.g., Sir Francis Bacon, Sara Josephine Baker, Margaret Mead) have existed as long as heterosexual and cisgender scientists despite their unacknowledged queer identities in modern classroom textbooks. Teacher candidates enrolled in a science methods course might be invigorated to learn ways of incorporating the scientific contributions of gay, lesbian, bisexual, and transgender people into their curriculum. Rather than requiring teacher candidates to construct a "gay and transgender scientist unit," I am suggesting teacher educators model acknowledging aspects of scientists' identities, in particular, queerness, as a way to demonstrate how subtle yet powerful naturalizing such discourse can be. Similar to the way that many current K–12 teachers intentionally highlight the accomplishments of women and racial minorities in the areas of math and science, queerness specifically should also be recognized and affirmed.

Literacy

Literacy methods courses offer numerous entry points for queering curriculum and several established resources for teacher educators to share with teacher candidates. Welcoming Schools offers annotated bibliographies for children's literature relating to highlighting all kinds of families, inclusive of gay family members and characters; looking at gender; and hurtful teasing, name-calling, and bullying. This substantial book list (available online) is a valuable resource for teachers building their classroom libraries. Teacher candidates working with older students (middle, high school, or postsecondary) can be encouraged to browse the GLBT genre of Goodreads (www.goodreads.com).

A teacher educator can zoom in on one piece of literature to demonstrate sound methodological techniques (e.g., conducting literacy circles or writers' workshops; lessons about elements of fiction and nonfiction) *and* explicitly model how queer content can be included in the K–12 curriculum. In "Interrupting Heteronormativity," Sumara and Davis (1999) discussed a two-month project they facilitated with a teacher and her grade 5/6 class. The authors developed a teaching unit around readings and responses to Lowry's book *The Giver* (1993). The book takes place in a futuristic society where all historical memory is lost to the general population and is retained by one person, the "receiver of memories," who is responsible to use this knowledge as necessary to advise political leaders. *The Giver* relates to themes of sexuality and gender because attraction, or "stirrings," are forbidden among adolescents in this fictional work and quickly extinguished with daily doses of medication. The exception, however, is that the "receiver of memories" (the story's protagonist, 12-year-old Jonah) has been advised to refuse the medication that controls his desires and must "learn to understand the complex way in which desire and knowledge intertwine with experiences of identity" (p. 198).

Prior to reading the novel with the children, Sumara and Davis (1999) participated in two reading group discussions—one with teachers from the school and one with teachers from the school and a number of parents who also had read the book. The authors of the project explained, "The shared reading of this novel with teachers and parents of school-aged children created an opportunity for us to consider, with them, important issues related to the surveillance and regulation of knowledge and sexuality" (p. 198). To their surprise, parents and students were willing and able (even excited) in focus group discussions to talk about the way in which particular knowledge generated complex changes in one's experienced and expressed identity and one's perceptions and interpretations of others' identities. They were open to talking about sexuality—and diverse "stirring" orientations, at that.

What does this research study have to do with teacher educators? I believe they can learn from this research and build from it in a way that helps teacher candidates (and their future K–12 students) read and interpret texts that aid in better understanding how heteronormativity in educational settings might be interrupted. I imagine a teacher educator using excerpts of *The Giver*, for example, to replicate literacy circles (student-led discussions that revolve around a book) while simultaneously modeling effective ways of engaging in courageous conversations with students about sexuality, identity, and difference.

Social Studies, Civics, Art, and Movement

The last content area is an integration of social studies, civics, art, and movement. Teacher educators of these methods courses can rely on queer history (oppression and social movements), politics (historic and contemporary LGBTQ laws and policies), and culture (queer art, music, dance, and theater) as segues for disrupting hetero- and cisnormative practice. Teaching Tolerance has a series of history lesson plans available to teachers, which teacher educators can pass along to candidates. "The Role of Gay Men and Lesbians in the Civil Rights Movement" (available free for download from www.tolerance.org), for example, offers four comprehensive lesson plans about queer individuals of African descent with whom students might not be familiar yet who were vital to the civil rights movement. Another library of queer history resources comes in film. Frameline (mentioned earlier) has produced a number of documentaries (and accompanying curriculum guidelines) recounting the lives of LGBTQ civil rights activists. *Brother Outsider: The Life of Bayard Rustin* (2002) and *Visionaries and Victories: Early Leaders in the LGBT Movement* (2008) are two examples. Frameline also promotes a film and teaching guide called *Arts in Action* (2010) that showcases five artists and their diverse approaches to creatively processing questions of gender, sexual orientation, race, and ethnicity through art forms. This film is particularly salient for demonstrating the complex ways identity markers such as race and sexuality are always intersecting.

Civics is another natural area to surface queer content. I have discovered that teacher candidates find solace in knowing what they can and cannot say and do in the K–12 classroom with regard to the topics of gender and sexual orientation. When asked what is allowable, I tell my students the answer is largely influenced by school culture and set by building administration. Still, this is not enough. Teacher candidates need to learn about local/district, state, and national laws in place to protect queer teachers and students. As stated in Chapter 6, during the *LGBTQ Advocacy in K–12 Classrooms* course, I shared three Oregon state laws that affect LGBTQ advocacy in schools. Briefly discussing these laws and providing resources for future reference was viewed as highly relevant and appreciated by teacher candidates. Covering antidiscrimination laws and policies is particularly important for queer candidates who likely fear a hostile or closeted work environment. Teacher educators can consult local school websites, contact district offices, and review their state department of education website to identify current laws and policies related to queerness. In addition, the Human Rights Campaign updates their online maps of state laws and policies, and both the American Civil Liberties Union (ACLU) and GLSEN have extensive resources on LGBT youth rights.

Finally, aspects of culture, such as visual and performing arts, are often integrated into one methods course for teacher candidates. Such a class can include queerness as a means for learning about the *Other*, making sense of the *Other* as a sociohistorical construct, and acquiring skills for replicating a queered practice. One technique that effectively achieves this is introducing teacher candidates to *tableaux*. A tableau is a still image. Using their bodies, teacher candidates as individuals, pairs, small groups, or the whole class create an image that communicates an idea or a single moment of action from a story or event. "When done well, a tableau consists of bodies frozen in the midst of strong action suggesting what the characters are doing, how they are interacting with other characters, and how they are reacting to the situation" (Kelin, 2005, p. 9). It is widely held that tableaux contain four essential elements, including a frozen "frame," (animated) facial expressions, varying heights, and a focal point.

Using this technique, a teacher educator could, for instance, divide candidates into groups and ask that they prepare separate tableaux on specific historical (or contemporary) queer events (e.g., civil rights struggles or accomplishments, bullying and teen suicide, gay marriage). Alternatively, teacher candidates could be asked to perform a tableau representing a piece of a poem or literary work written by a queer individual capturing the queer experience. Or candidates could perform still images representing their individual journey and self-discovery related to gender and sexual identity. Regardless of the prompt, ample time needs to be given to candidates to think about and conceptualize their image.

When an individual or group performs a tableau, it is important to engage other course participants by asking questions: "What do you see in the tableau? Who is involved? What actions are being performed? Where does the scene take place? What do you notice about facial expression and what can you infer from this?" When everyone is finished performing, teacher candidates can process the activity in two ways: Content (What did it feel like to present the material?) and process (What did it feel like to create and perform your image?). (See the Companion Website for more resources on facilitating this activity.)

Tableau is an effective strategy to develop comprehension. In the process of creating tableaux, teacher candidates evoke their senses, build and activate prior knowledge, ask questions, make inferences, and synthesize new material that is presented (or reconstruct current knowledge depending on how the tableau is framed). It also gives teacher candidates an expressive and fun way to explore queerness through the arts.

Multicultural Education, Social Justice, and Equity

Fourth, courses centered on principles of culture, diversity, and justice can seamlessly integrate explicit queer coverage. This should not translate to a "gay day" or "a rainbow pride celebration" as the "flavor of the week" approach has been shown to trivialize multicultural education (see "Curriculum and Instruction" in Chapter 2). Rather, queerness, like every aspect of identity and diversity, can be embedded within all classes.

Evans (2002) shared an example of a straight teacher educator using a small but profound moment in class to make heteronormativity visible for her students.

> After telling a story in which she mentions her male spouse, a professor could then ask her education students how they feel about the fact that she just "came out" to them as heterosexual. She could then generate a discussion about why, and to what effects, teachers share their "personal" lives with their students and colleagues. This could point to how all teachers are positioned socioculturally. She could ask how this experience made the students feel, which could highlight the sociohistorical components of feelings.
>
> (p. 180)

In addition to class discussion, course assignments offer an opportunity for teacher candidates to wrestle with queerness as it relates to diversity, inclusiveness, and political and sociological influences in the U.S. education system. Here are two assignments that challenge teacher candidates to view sexuality and gender in more complex ways (*autobiographical writing*) and to develop as an effective queer ally for K–12 students (*sociodrama*).

Autobiographical Writing

The autobiographical writing assignment (Letts, 2002) offers an example of queer curriculum integration modeled by teacher educators for prospective middle and high school teachers. This exercise, assigned to teacher candidates, can "defamiliarize or 'queer' the identity categories we inhabit and the versions of the self we enact" (p. 127). Teacher candidates are asked to write a short autobiographical piece about some period from their schooling that was challenging for them. As they explore the aspects that troubled them, students can write in ways that transfer "autobiography in education from its modernist emphasis on producing predictable, stable, and normative identities and curricula to a consideration of 'selves' and curricula as sites of 'permanent openness and resignifiability'" (Miller, 1998, p. 367 as cited in Letts, 2002, p. 127).

Letts (2002) noted, "Using autobiography in this way can allow teacher candidates to strategically evoke difference, something not possible through modernist autobiographical tales that reinscribe normative silences and reiterate stable, coherent selves" (p. 127). By interrupting assumed identity categories, candidates write oppositional truths about their lives and their relation to others. Autobiography in this context enables teacher candidates to explore the constant negotiation of multiple and often-conflicting identity constructions, some of which are denounced in certain schools. Autobiography is logically housed in a multicultural course because in addition to examining a range of sexualities, teacher candidates can analyze intersections of class, race, ethnicity, gender, language, and ability. "This explicit, though undervalued, stance can allow students to engage in more generative modes of thinking about the ways that difference matters" (Letts, 2002, p. 128).

Sociodrama

Simply put, a sociodrama is a social skit. It is derived from popular education (in Spanish, *educación popular*), which is a mode of teaching and learning that seeks to bring about more just and equitable social, political, and economic relations (Wiggins, 2011). Popular education emerged in Central and South America in the early twentieth century as political and military leaders promoted socialist education and universal literacy (Gómez & Puiggrós, 1986). Freire, who is considered the foremost influence in popular education, began using it in adult literacy in northeastern Brazil in the 1950s. Unlike traditional education, where the teacher is considered to be the expert, in popular education students are regarded as having their own expertise. Popular education also asserts that people should be active participants rather than passive recipients in their own learning process.

Sociodrama involves participants acting out a situation using words, movement, and props. It often entails the re-creation of a real-life event or experience followed by an analysis to study and remedy problems of difference or injustice. I use it as a technique in every class I teach that pertains to culture and social justice. These social skits help teacher candidates achieve a number of learning outcomes and enable teacher educators to:

- Identify how much teacher candidates already know about a theme;
- Facilitate a process whereby teacher candidates look in detail at some aspect of a theme;
- See what conclusions teacher candidates have drawn from the study of the theme.

The sociodrama assignment I delegate to my teacher candidates toward the end of the term serves as an example of this final learning outcome. We spend weeks leading up to this task, exploring *Others* and *Self* around issues of identity, culture, sexual orientation, gender, race, ethnicity, social class, ability, and other forms of diversity. We also consider the importance of understanding and valuing individuals' similarities and differences within classrooms and schools. For the sociodrama, teacher candidates are divided into groups of three to five and are charged with brainstorming, writing, and performing a skit that simulates a realistic situation focused on one or more of the course topics listed earlier (e.g., identity, culture, sexual orientation)—thus, situations that classroom teachers may experience on a regular basis. Collaboratively, teacher candidates grapple with complex issues such as how aspects of identity are benefited or burdened in schools, the content and delivery of education services, school structure and politics, and teaching pedagogy. It is hoped that teacher candidates achieve deeper levels of understanding around course objectives through the construction and observation of sociodrama presentations, which spark important follow-up dialogue.

A detailed description of this assignment, accompanied with scenarios to inspire queer-themed sociodramas, and a grading rubric can be found on the Companion Website, but for the purposes of transparency, the specific steps that I lay out for my teacher candidates include the following.

1. Form a self-selected group of three to five.
2. Read and think about the brief case study/context you have been assigned.
   a. Your group should feel free to infer and provide missing context.
   b. If your group amicably agrees to trade with another group, who also shares consensus among their respective group (to trade), then by all means trade.
3. Discuss the issue or problem presented in the case study in depth. *How does this show up in your work? How does it affect others, the school, and the community? What are the social or political reasons for the issue/problem? How can the issue/problem be resolved? What are the consequences of various courses of action?*
4. Brainstorm a sociodrama that illuminates the issue/problem and reflects reality (given what you experience, read, research, and/or imagine).
5. Collaboratively write a script that includes all participants engaging in an active role.
6. Construct and/or gather props.
7. Consider facilitation points and questions for the discussion that will follow your skit.
8. Conduct research on your topic and construct a one- or two-sided handout of information and resources for your colleagues.
9. Practice your 20-minute presentation (this time limit includes performance and facilitated discussion) and come to class ready to present.

I generally provide brief case studies/context for teacher candidates rather than requiring them to brainstorm the focus content to ensure we cover a wide range of issues and to reduce duplication of themes. I purposefully provide vague language within the cases to challenge teacher candidates to "build their own situations." For example, a group preparing to teach elementary students might receive the following case study and guiding questions.

Providing student supports. You are a second-year first-grade teacher with increased responsibility this year. Last year your district decided to cut back a number of positions, including that of an early intervention specialist. So now, on top of everything else, you are solely responsible for implementing Response to Intervention (RTI) in your classroom to be compliant with new district policy. The cutbacks come at a horrible time because you have concerns about quite a number of students in your class. One student in particular, Johnny, seems to be struggling academically, and you wonder if this has to do with him questioning his gender identity. Additionally, you are unsure about his home support. The Student Support Team (SST) is meeting in a couple of weeks, and you plan on attending the meeting to discuss some of your students, especially Johnny, and get much needed guidance and support.

- How will you prepare for this meeting? What information will you consider including in your report to the SST?
- What kinds of supports will you advocate for?
- What will be your next steps?

Similarly, teacher candidates preparing to teach middle and high school students may engage with the following case study and guiding questions to prepare their sociodrama.

Confronting tragedy. You are a ninth-grade teacher working in an urban public school. Earlier this year a tenth grader committed suicide. In a note he cited his reasons: daily torment and teasing from classmates for being gay. The administration responded initially with compassion and outreach, but as the weeks trudged on, the incident seemed to be forgotten. Initial plans to start a Gay-Straight Alliance (GSA) have since dissipated, for example.

- What is the problem?
- What, if anything, can you do to address the problem?
- What information do you need to gather from staff, parents, and students to move forward?
- What obstacles might you face, and how will you overcome these?

Like the technique of problem-posing, sociodrama requires individuals to apply critical thinking in order to resolve challenges. One of the major advantages of using sociodrama is the identification of problems, or aspects of problems, that do not emerge in discussion but are communicated nonverbally within the presentations. For instance, in the second case study, assume teacher candidates create a sociodrama illustrating the problems that resulted when the principal failed to adequately address the tragic suicide and to help students/staff recover from the incident. In acting out this problem, other problems emerged. The ways in which staff neglected to hold administration accountable, did not take ownership for forming committees, and failed to engage in courageous conversations with their students made it clear that the teacher candidates felt the entire staff was at fault. The teacher candidates realized, through the sociodrama experience, that the school faculty as a whole was insensitive to the problems of the student and of the larger community; perhaps this issue would not have surfaced in a discussion but could only be articulated through the sociodrama.

Field-Based Practicum and Student Teaching

Finally, practicum, or student teaching, offers integral opportunities for field-based observation and reflection. Here I describe three experiences teacher educators can present to teacher candidates during student teaching to aid in their ability to make sense of gender identity and sexual orientation in an educational context: *field observation and report*, *critical incident journaling*, and *critical conversations*.

Field Observation and Report

As noted in Chapter 5, Lingley and I created an assignment for our *LGBTQ Advocacy in K–12 Classrooms* course called field observation and report. This assignment addresses InTASC Standard 3n, "The teacher is committed to working with learners, colleagues, families, and communities to establish positive and supportive learning environments" (Council of Chief State School Officers, 2011, p. 12) and our course objective, which read, "Participants will develop a personal framework for encountering and making sense of gender and sexual identity as they manifest in schools."

For the assignment, each teacher candidate conducted one observation of an event or activity related to education. Examples of settings to observe included classrooms, staff meetings, PTA meetings, site council meetings, school cafeteria/library/playground at lunchtime, sports/arts events, school board meetings, and so forth. Teacher candidates were asked to take field notes during the observation and were encouraged, if possible, to videotape/audiotape the experience for later analysis. Afterward, these notes were analyzed for implications for gender identity and/or sexual orientation issues (e.g., legal, psychological, pedagogical). Each person then wrote a two- to three-page summary report that described the setting/participants for the observation, explored interpretations of what was observed, and suggested implications for personal work as an educator and LGBTQ advocate.

Lingley and I were overwhelmed by the quality of student submissions. One student observed a Spanish-immersion preschool classroom in a building that housed gender-neutral bathrooms. She noted:

> Our bathrooms have been a topic of conversation and interest for many reasons among the teachers and children. It's a place where the children spend a lot of their time, washing hands, changing, going to the bathroom, and

cleaning up after studio activities as the studio is without a sink or washing station. At this age children are very curious about gender and specifically are more aware of sexual organs. This has been prevalent among this group this year. I wonder if having gender-specific bathrooms would change that dynamic at all?

Another student observed two separate high school staff meetings and recounted:

The meetings stood against a backdrop of heteronormativity. For example, the small talk that occurred among the meetings' attendees frequently concerned their children, opposite sex spouses, or upcoming activities. I usually sit quietly while contributing nothing to the conversation, but now I saw this differently: Speaking meant revealing something hidden, so I remained silent and unheard. This may be due to the room's perceived demographics or it may be due to the self-editing that often accompanies being queer. Overall, the meetings' conversations focused on our students as a vague, unsubstantiated whole without addressing or specifying gender identity or sexual orientation. One side of the story is omnipresent while the other is absent; such silence appears marginalizing of those who are different. What surprised me most about this observation experience were the bubbles of anger and resentment I felt upon reflection. Something inside me has awakened and ended its extended hibernation, even if I remain uncertain about what woke up or how to harness and guide its restlessness. Indeed, how do I convert such volatile energy into productive action? Many possibilities come to mind. First, I need to take more risks at school, reasonable risks that may cause discomfort for me, for others, or both. For example, why silently accept omission? I have a spouse, a life, and weekend plans just like everyone else. My story is worthy of being told and heard too, by students and teachers alike! If some stories fail to find voice in school, how can we expect our queer students to find either their voice or a receptive audience? What message do students, all students, hear when we remain silent? Whatever message they hear, it is not one that leads to health, wholeness, happiness, truth, or liberation.

Critical Incident Journaling

Another assignment appropriate for field-based coursework is critical incident journaling. Here, teacher candidates work to deconstruct notions of difference and how they play out in educational settings, specifically looking at gender norms and heteronormative assumptions. The intention of this assignment is to help teacher candidates move beyond an uncritical reporting of their experiences to an examination of those experiences with an eye toward deconstructing them to uncover assumptions and biases that are at the heart of how we make sense of things. To that end, teacher candidates are asked to keep a journal of what they notice with regard to gender and sexuality in their field experience setting. The teacher educator provides ongoing prompts (such as those provided in the following) to stimulate candidates' thinking and to challenge their perceptions.

- Take inventory of the classroom curriculum.
  - What books are available to students? How are gender and sexuality typified in the literature?
  - Browse your classroom's adopted textbooks and record words, phrases, concepts, lessons, and visuals (photos and illustrations) that you notice. Is the language inclusive or exclusive? What, if any, assumptions are being made about the audience/readers?
- Observe students' choice in tasks, classroom roles/jobs, materials selection, recess or downtime behaviors, clothing, mannerisms, and so forth. What decisions do you see being influenced by gender expectations and/or heteronormativity?
- Observe your cooperating teacher instructing a lesson looking specifically for intentional or unintentional lessons about gender or sexuality.
- How is the content or presentation of the lesson queer inclusive or exclusive?
  - How do the students react to the lesson?
  - Do learning routines and/or procedures separate girls from boys, and if so, how is this dichotomy communicated? How do students react to this segregation?
  - Are there heteronormative assumptions about family structures, interactions/relationships, and individual identities?
- Take a walk through the school hallways. What do you notice about student work on display? What about school posters—what kinds of pictures and language are showcased?

Journaling is a powerful tool to promote critical reflection and allow teacher candidates to express personal feelings about their educational experiences. This assignment can be taken in any number of directions depending on the journaling method a teacher educator chooses to implement (e.g., personal, interactive with educator and/or classmates) and the required frequency (e.g., daily, weekly entries).

Critical Conversations

The third field-based assignment, critical conversations, consists of teacher candidates conducting interviews with school personnel about sexual orientation and/or gender identity and presentation. Teacher candidates are encouraged to independently interview one to three individuals at their field site. Interviewees may include the school administrator, teachers, support staff (e.g., instructional assistants, specialists, psychologists, counselors), students, and parents/family members. Engaging in critical, courageous conversations that bring queer issues into focus facilitates teacher candidates' learning and also surfaces the often invisible nature of hetero- and cisnormativity to seasoned school personnel.

Teacher educators can structure this field-based assignment in several ways. Teacher candidates can be encouraged to brainstorm their own interview questions after spending some time learning about queer issues in education. Alternatively, teacher educators can supply questions (such as the ones that follow) as a base structure for conversation.

- Have you personally worked with a student or family member who you knew or perceived to be lesbian, gay, bisexual, and/or transgender? Describe the relationship and how this aspect of the person's identity was embraced or rejected at school by staff, students, and the larger community.
- Does the school take a visible stance to adequately support students and staff who reside outside stereotypical gender norms (e.g., females who prefer blocks over Barbies, who enroll in woodworking or automotive classes, or try out for the football team; males who excel in dance, drama, or volleyball)? Explain.
- Does the school take a visible stance to adequately support students and staff who identify as lesbian, gay, or bisexual? Explain.
- What messages do students receive (e.g., through curricula, rituals or routines, interactions, school policies) about gender and sexual orientation?
- Can you identify areas of your practice where heterosexuality is assumed? How about the assumption that everybody is cisgender (i.e., when an individual's self-perception of their identity corresponds with their assigned sex at birth)?
- What conversations or situations have you experienced at school regarding LGBT people, history, culture? How, if at all, have these conversations influenced your practice?
- Have you ever received any formal faculty training or professional development on LGBT issues in education? If so, what were your reactions to this experience? If not, would you be open to receiving such training? Why or why not?

Following the actual field interviews, teacher candidates should gather to debrief as a whole class or in small groups. Engaging in collective discourse as a way of processing a myriad of contexts and perspectives can illuminate current pools of knowledge, skills, and dispositions toward queerness. If class time is limited, teacher candidates can be asked to process their interviews and reflections on such discourse in a personal essay. On a final note, it should be acknowledged that among certain homophobic/transphobic school cultures, this assignment might put teacher candidates at risk or unfairly jeopardize their relationships with others in the field. In such cases, alternative questions or assignments should be provided.

Conclusion

Indeed, as Evans noted (2002), "Bringing together Teacher and Queer is a complicated endeavor" (p. 179). Yet, hopefully, after reading this chapter, it seems a little more possible to you. Teacher educators are in a critical position to prompt transformative change in education, change that interrupts heteronormativity, bridges the gender divide, and illuminates a queer perspective. Teacher candidates need, and want, educators to guide and support them in this undertaking. By incorporating relevant queer content into lecture and class discussions, as well as reading materials, teacher educators contribute to a growing number of LGBTQ advocates in K–12 education.

Reflection Questions

1. This chapter begins and ends with a quotation from Evans (2002), "Bringing together Teacher and Queer is a complicated endeavor. It is public and private, in an arena in which constructions of what is public and private continually shift and change" (p. 179). In what ways are Teacher and Queer complicated in your current position? How do you negotiate your gender and sexual orientation within the public sector?
2. Which curricular entry points presented in this chapter seem most realistic for the context you work in? What activities and resources are you most likely to use? Why? Which activities are inappropriate or irrelevant for you to use? Why?
3. How would you justify your stance to include queer issues in your curriculum with a reluctant teacher candidate?

Recommended Resources

Further Reading

Letts, W.J. (2002). Revisioning multiculturalism in teacher education: Isn't it queer? In R.M. Kissen (Ed.), *Getting ready for Benjamin: Preparing teachers for sexual diversity in the classroom* (pp. 119–131). Lanham, MD: Rowman & Littlefield.
Mirsky, L. (2003). SaferSanerSchools: Transforming school culture with restorative practices. Retrieved from www.restorativepractices.org
Padva, G. (2008). Educating the Simpsons: Teaching queer representations in contemporary visual media. *Journal of LGBT Youth, 5*(3), 57–73.
Sumara, D., & Davis, B. (1999). Interrupting heteronormativity: Toward a queer curriculum theory. *Curriculum Inquiry, (29)*2, 191–208.

Recommended Film/Audio and Corresponding Curriculum Guides

Frameline. www.frameline.org/distribution/k12
Groundspark. www.groundspark.org
National Public Radio. (Producer). (2009, February 13). *Tom Girls* [Audio podcast]. Retrieved from www.thisamericanlife.org/radio-archives/episode/374/somewhere-out-there
New York Times. (Producer). (2007, July 5). *Talking about the It Gets Better Project* [Audio podcast]. Retrieved from http://well.blogs.nytimes.com/2011/07/05/talking-about-the-it-gets-better-project/
Welcoming Schools. www.welcomingschools.org

References

Ashley, J., & Burke, K. (2009). *Implementing restorative justice: A guide for schools*. Chicago: Illinois Criminal Justice Information Authority.
Auerbach, E. (1990). *Making meaning, making change: A guide to participatory curriculum development for adult ESL and family literacy*. Boston: University of Massachusetts.
Ausburn, T. (2005). Two years in the life of a queer teacher. In K. Jennings (Ed.), *One teacher in 10* (2nd ed., pp. 100–116). New York: Alyson Books.
Bristow, J. (2000). Effeminacy. In G.E. Haggerty (Ed.), *Gay histories and cultures: An encyclopedia* (pp. 268–270). New York: Garland.
Burn, S.M. (2000). Heterosexuals' use of "fag" and "queer" to deride one another: A contributor to heterosexism and stigma. *Journal of Homosexuality, 40*(2), 1–11.
Cis privilege questionnaire. (2007). Retrieved from http://takesupspace.wordpress.com/cis-privilege-checklist
Coiser, K., & Sanders, J.H., III. (2007). Queering art education. *Journal of Art Design Education, 26*(1), 21–30.
Collier, K.L., Bos, H.M., & Sandfort, T.G. (2013). Homophobic name-calling among secondary school students and its implications for mental health. *Journal of Youth Adolescence, 42,* 363–375.
Council of Chief State School Officers. (2011, April). *Interstate Teacher Assessment and Support Consortium (InTASC) model core teaching standards: A resource for state dialogue*. Washington, DC: Author.
Diamond, L.M., & Savin-Williams, R.C. (2003). Gender and sexual identity. In R.M. Lerner, F. Jacobs, & D. Westlieb (Eds.), *Handbook of applied developmental science, Vol. 1: Applying developmental science for youth and families, historical and theoretical foundations*. Thousand Oaks, CA: Sage.
Evans, K. (2002). *Negotiating the self: Identity, sexuality, and emotion in learning to teach*. New York: Routledge.
Frameline. (Producer). Kates, N., & Singer, B. (Directors). (2002). *Brother Outsider: The life of Bayard Rustin* [DVD]. San Francisco, CA.
Frameline. (Producer). (2008). *Gender matters* [DVD]. San Francisco, CA.
Frameline. (Producer). Slade, E., & Biren, J.E. (Directors). (2008). *Visionaries and victories: Early leaders in the LGBT Movement* [DVD]. San Francisco, CA.
Frameline. (Producer). (2010). *Arts in action* [DVD]. San Francisco, CA.
Franklin, K. (2000). *Inside the mind of people who hate gays*. Retrieved from www.pbs.org/wgbh/pages/frontline/shows/assault/roots/franklin.html
Freire, P. (1970). *Pedagogy of the oppressed*. New York: Continuum.

Gómez, M., & Puiggrós, A. (1986). *La educación popular en América Latina 1* (Popular education in Latin America 1). Mexico City, Mexico: Secretaria de Educación Pública.

Gruber, J.E., & Fineran, S. (2008). Comparing the impact of bullying and sexual harassment victimization on the mental and physical health of adolescents. *Sex Roles, 59*(1–2), 1–13.

Hauge, R. (Writer), & Anderson, M.B. (Director). (1997). Homer's phobia [Television series episode]. In M. Groening, & J.L. Brooks (Executive producers), *The Simpsons*. Los Angeles, CA: Twentieth Century Fox Film.

Kelin, D.A., II. (2005). *Telling stories: Drama strategies for ESL students*. Retrieved from www.prel.org/eslstrategies/pdfs/dramastrategies.pdf

Kosciw, J.G., Greytak, E.A., Bartkiewicz, M.J., Boesen, M.J., & Palmer, N.A. (2012). *The 2011 National School Climate Survey: The experiences of lesbian, gay, bisexual and transgender youth in our nation's schools*. New York: GLSEN.

Letts, W.J. (2002). Revisioning multiculturalism in teacher education: Isn't it queer? In R.M. Kissen (Ed.), *Getting ready for Benjamin: Preparing teachers for sexual diversity in the classroom* (pp. 119–131). Lanham, MD: Rowman & Littlefield.

Letts, W. (2005). Sissy boy. In J. Sears (Ed.), *Youth, education, and sexualities: An international encyclopedia, Vol. 2* (pp. 795–799). Westport, CT: Greenwood Press.

Lowry, L. (1993). *The giver*. New York: Random House.

McIntosh, P. (1989). White privilege: Unpacking the invisible knapsack. *Peace and Freedom*, 9–10.

Mirsky, L. (2003). SaferSanerSchools: Transforming school culture with restorative practices. Retrieved from www.restorativepractices.org

National Public Radio (NPR). (Producer). (2009, February 13). *Tom Girls* [Audio podcast]. Retrieved from www.thisamericanlife.org/radio-archives/episode/374/somewhere-out-there

New York Times. (Producer). (2007, July 5). *Talking about the It Gets Better Project* [Audio podcast]. Retrieved from http://well.blogs.nytimes.com/2011/07/05/talking-about-the-it-gets-better-project/

Padva, G. (2008). Educating the Simpsons: Teaching queer representations in contemporary visual media. *Journal of LGBT Youth, 5*(3), 57–73.

Poteat, V.P., & Espelage, D.L. (2005). Exploring the relation between bullying and homophobic verbal content: The Homophobic Content Agent Target (HCAT) Scale. *Violence and Victims, 20*(5), 513–528.

Poteat, V.P., & Espelage, D.L. (2007). Predicting psychosocial consequences of homophobic victimization in middle school students. *Journal of Early Adolescence, 27*(2), 175–191.

Rochlin, M. (1972). *Heterosexual privilege questionnaire*. Retrieved from http://sap.mit.edu/content/pdf/heterosexual_privilege.pdf

Shor, I. (1992). *Empowering education: Critical teaching for social change*. Chicago: University of Chicago Press.

Sumara, D.J. (2007). Small differences matter: Interrupting certainty about identity in teacher education. *Journal of Gay and Lesbian Issues in Education, 4*(4), 39–58.

Sumara, D., & Davis, B. (1999). Interrupting heteronormativity: Toward a queer curriculum theory. *Curriculum Inquiry, 29*(2), 191–208.

Weinstein, C., Tomlinson-Clarke, S., & Curran, M. (2004). Toward a conception of culturally responsive classroom management. *Journal of Teacher Education, 55*(1), 25–38.

Wiggins, N. (2011). Critical pedagogy and popular education: Towards a unity of theory and practice. *Studies in the Education of Adults, 43*(1), 34–49.

9
A CALL TO ACTION

In This Chapter
- A summary of ideas.
- One teacher candidate's transformational story.
- Optimistic conclusions.

Summary of Ideas

More than four million K–12 queer students are receiving an education in the United States. Far greater numbers of additional children and adolescents question their sexual orientation and present their gender in creative, fluid, and nonnormative ways. Moreover, millions of cisgender and heterosexual youth live with queer parents and family members. In light of these realities, it is tragic and damaging that most K–12 schools not only go on ignoring these truths but also allocate curricula saturated in assumptions that people are, or should be, heterosexual and cisgender. Such messages are often invisible to the teachers who perpetuate them, but they present quite visibly to the people they invalidate.

In this book I have sought to uncover the devastating "here and now" experience whereby teacher education follows the standard set by K–12 institutions, to present ideas that interrupt the cycle of queer ignorance and oppression present in schools with a focus on teacher education. By offering background, supporting literature and theory, current research, and useful materials for teachers to queer their practice, my goal is to elevate a conversation that positions teacher educators at the forefront of this process. If teachers entering the profession develop competencies and acquire tools around sexual and gender diversity, then perhaps the system will undergo a much-needed transformation by which people self-identified or perceived as heterosexual and/or cisgender work alongside queer individuals to create safe and supportive learning environments imbued with social justice.

This book highlights perspectives from scholars, researchers, and queer activists. It includes voices from K–12 learners, teacher candidates, and teacher educators. These contributions, I hope, help readers look beyond my own examinations and arguments to form independent thoughts and beliefs about queer issues in education. Personal experience largely informs my work in this arena, but often more illuminating are the stories I encounter from others. For instance, I met Poppy last year when she enrolled in my classroom management course. She had simultaneously begun her first stint in student teaching, which she described as overwhelming and breathtaking.

> To say that I underestimated the multitude of levels of physical, mental, and emotional preparedness that would be required of me would be inaccurate. I actually thought about this experience a lot, before it ever began, from many different angles. Even still, there is nothing comparable to the level of engagement that kicks in once you are actually there, standing in front of 30 living, breathing personalities, attempting to jump into the driver's seat and navigate completely uncharted territory.

As weeks passed, Poppy and I got to know each other, and she discovered my passion for "troubling" gender and sexuality in public schools. Perhaps this is why she confided in me about one of her students, whom she called K. In essence, Poppy was in the driver's seat navigating uncharted territory, and she asked me to get in the car. She took the wheel and ended up teaching me many things about understanding, empathy, and the capacity for human connection. What follows is her personal account of processing this extraordinary ride.

Poppy's Story

The most profound learning experience that I encountered was carried in on the shoulders of a 14-year-old, freshman student in my Spanish I class. I believe this student, K, self-identifies as transgender or is in the process of exploring an identification other than the gender at birth: female. My experience with K was a gradual evolution. At first, I saw a quiet, unassuming, friendly adolescent boy. He was a face in a crowd of many with whom I was trying to build quicker recognition. As I began to assume more classroom duties (during my observation period) and started taking attendance, I was puzzled searching the faces for a female student whose name I did not recognize. By process of elimination, my eyes finally rested once again on K, and I pondered this student's appearance and affect differently for the first time. That day I realized this would actually be my first time having a student of "my own" who outwardly expressed a nontraditional gender identity. I do not even know if that is the right way to conceptualize or state it, but that is the thought process I engaged in. At the time, my first thought was that I was glad I was aware, but beyond that I did not foresee how knowing this would have a far-reaching impact on my instruction.

As it turns out, I was wrong. Although the dialogue and the interpersonal exchanges that unfolded would not be visible to anyone else, they were crucial to my role as a teacher and to building a relationship with this student. First, I think it is important to recognize one impact this initial knowledge had on my own internal thought process. Where I had previously always thought of K as a male student, the simple act of having seen the student's full name and recorded gender caused a switch in my brain that I struggled with. Without intending to or realizing it, I started thinking of this student as female. I had a hard time not saying "she" when I referred to K. I felt uncomfortable not knowing if the student preferred to be referred to as "she," "he," or neither, but I also did not know if it was appropriate to ask. And if I determined it was appropriate to ask, when and how would I do so?

As I considered this, I suddenly had a realization about my impending instructional unit that I had not anticipated. I was preparing to teach a unit about noun and adjective agreement in Spanish, the concept of which is inherently tied to gender in this language. I was amazed to realize that I had never considered how limiting and archaic it could be to have nearly every single description one makes about oneself reflect one's gender. I guess I do not know the exact percentage of adjectives in Spanish that have an alternating masculine/feminine ending, but I believe they are the majority. I wondered how native Spanish speakers approach this issue, and if it is an issue. I assume it might be approached as with changes in names and pronouns . . . a gradual getting used to saying "I am tall (female)" versus "I am tall (male)." However, I wonder if there is any sort of movement to reject these gender-specific word endings, a movement toward more gender neutrality? If there is, I did not find the answer. I did some brief research to see if I could find any information about how this issue is addressed and found nothing. It warrants a more in-depth search. In the midst of my student teaching, however, I had to rely on my own resources. I knew I was going to be calling on students in class, "putting them on the spot" to make statements that accurately reflect noun/adjective agreement, and asking them to write about themselves with grammatically (gender) appropriate language. So what would this mean for K?

I decided to call a friend and ask, in confidence, for some guidance. What I really needed was a push to overcome my fear that I would offend K or seem as though I was invading K's privacy. My friend simplified the situation for me and gave me the confidence to approach my student. "Simply ask," my friend suggested, "Do you have a preferred pronoun?" Just like that, I thought. I worried that my student would not know what in the world I was talking about. Teenagers can seem so unforgiving when they think you have asked a "dumb" question. I was worried that I was not "hip" enough to know that just because K dressed like a "boy" and spoke in lower tones, that it might have nothing to do with identifying as anyone other than a female. Yet, what ultimately gave me the confidence to have this conversation—even more than the implications in my instructional unit—was the fact that I wanted to talk to this student. I wanted to know this student, and I certainly did not want to avoid K in direct or indirect conversation because I didn't know which pronoun to use.

Additionally, I respect K, and I also respect what an unbelievably trying time it is to be a teenager. At the time, I had no idea where K was on a hypothetical continuum of gender exploration, transition, questions of identity, questions of sexuality . . . but I knew that these experiences, compounded with that of being a teenager, most likely made K an extremely vulnerable young student. I did not want to put K on the spot. I did not want to draw attention to anything that K did not wish to receive additional attention for. On the other hand, I didn't want to confuse privacy with secrecy or, heaven forbid, shame. I did not want my student to think that the exploration of gender, using different pronouns or adjective endings, whatever that might mean, was not a welcome part of the fabric of the class. I only wanted to invite K to participate in whichever ways would be comfortable and safe.

I will never forget my feeling of surprise and gratitude when, the very next morning after speaking with my friend, K unexpectedly walked into my classroom before the start of the school day. "Hi, I am just wondering if I have any missing work . . . " K stated. Puzzled, I replied, "Well, no, you don't! You have been very consistent with turning in your work." K lingered for a moment as if there was something else to say, and without hesitating I took the opportunity. I explained the topic that we were about to cover in class and mentioned that I wanted to know how K would like to approach the semantics of gender in Spanish and in turn how I should approach K. "Do you have a preferred pronoun?" I heard myself ask.

I cannot overstate how surprised, impressed, and inspired I was by K's candor in replying. I am self-conscious making that statement because I think it indicates a fear/unfamiliarity with the topic of gender identity that I wish I might have grown beyond by this point in my life. Instead, a 14-year-old taught me how simple and un-"loaded" these aspects of our existence can be if we only treat them that way. K informed me that she uses female pronouns "right now" because her mom "freaked out" when she found out K was doing otherwise. However, she also informed me that she uses male pronouns in Spanish. "Oh!" I said, with surprise and almost delight. It was as if K was finding a way to express something about himself in a safe and exploratory manner, free from the scrutiny of parents who were perhaps not ready to accept such a change. I felt like we had an agreement, solidarity.

After that day, K's and my relationship as student and teacher only grew. On one of the last days of school, well after my teaching unit had concluded, I was there to help prepare for finals when K approached me with a smile to say, "You are my favorite teacher!"

When I think about this experience in its entirety, it brings tears to my eyes. The emotion of it all is ever present for me. I am honored to think that I had any sort of positive impact on this individual's experience, however brief, but I feel I benefitted at least as much as my student. I feel better about myself as a future teacher knowing that I continue to learn how important it is to take steps to know our students. I am learning that it is "easy" to overcome feelings of uncertainty or fear when coming from a place of respect and care for the student, and that students will know your intent when it is such. I feel so grateful that K was in my classroom to teach me.

Optimistic Conclusions

In many ways Poppy's experience and honest reflection represents both the thesis and antithesis of this book; it highlights the problem and illuminates the solution to queering education. The fact that Poppy's cooperating teacher was unable to guide or support her with regard to K during her spring student teaching experience indicates that K's Spanish teacher had failed to inquire about, and affirm, K's identity all year. Poppy also had to turn to someone outside her teacher preparation program for advice. Although she talked with me about it briefly, Poppy did not feel comfortable going to her cohort leader, and none of her coursework up to that point had prepared her for encountering a student like K. In other words, the teacher preparation program disappointed Poppy just as K–12 schools were failing K. Luckily, though, the two found each other. Poppy's hunger for investigating queer issues in education to improve her practice and to develop skills as an ally aligns with research that suggests teacher candidates desire queer coverage in the preparation phase of their careers (Athanases & Larrabee, 2003; Larrabee & Morehead, 2010; Payne & Smith, 2010, 2011, 2012). Poppy's willingness to recognize, learn, reflect, and act, in concert with her desire to understand and empathize with K, forged a connection between the two that changed their lives forever. As Poppy indicated, the experience influenced her practice and her approach to students. It affirmed her as a teacher who is capable of interrogating curriculum, initiating courageous conversations with students, and supporting student agency in her classroom. The process, it seems, also validated K in unexpected and invigorating ways.

Poppy demonstrated how teacher interventions in response to hetero- and cisnormativity improve conditions—including feelings of self-worth—for queer youth (Robinson & Ferfolja, 2008; Russell, Seif, & Truong, 2001). Because of the benefits of such interference, many scholars have argued that teachers must be trained to recognize and disrupt hetero- and cissexism in their classrooms (Cosier & Sanders, 2007; Rofes, 2005). This book argues that teacher education serves as the logical and necessary space to provide such preparation. The Queer Inclusion in Education Framework (see Appendix B), which serves as both a road map for this book as well as a conceptual tool to guide practice, is one concrete place to start. Learning about queer theory and critical pedagogy as they relate to sexual orientation and gender, and engaging teachers in discourse to develop knowledge, skills, and dispositions around queerness, can break the culture of queer silence that persists in schools. As a matter of social justice, it is vital we consider how homophobia and transphobia, as well as hetero- and cisnormative practices, benefit some people in society while causing others pain and suffering.

People featured in this book give me hope that this is the path we are headed down, a path toward empowering and preparing our educators to meet the needs of *all* learners and to help them leave this world a better place. My source of optimism comes from the second grader who thinks that Rhonda and Megan are "good matches" and from Jack, who refuses to give up on his dream of teaching with integrity as an out transgender elementary school educator. And from leaders like Christine Chaillé who decide that issues of social justice and human dignity come before budget meetings and workload schedules. My confidence comes from individuals like Moses, who confront their own homophobic beliefs to ensure that every student in their classroom is affirmed, and from Poppy, who navigated uncharted territory with an open mind and a willing heart. Ultimately, my hope lies in what you, the reader, decide to do in response to engaging with this text.

References

Athanases, S.Z., & Larrabee, T.G. (2003). Toward a consistent stance in teaching for equity: Learning to advocate for lesbian- and gay-identified youth. *Teaching and Teacher Education*, *19*, 237–261.

Cosier, K., & Sanders, J.H., III (2007). Queering art teacher education. In N. Stanley (Ed.), *International journal of art and design education*. National [UK] Society for Education in Art & Design. Corsham, Wiltshire, UK: Blackwell.

Larrabee, T.G., & Morehead, P. (2010). Broadening views of social justice and teacher leadership: Addressing LGB issues in teacher education. *Issues in Teacher Education*, *19*(2), 37–53.

Payne, E., & Smith, M. (2010). Reduction of stigma in schools: An evaluation of the first three years. *Issues in Teacher Education*, *19*(2), 11–36.

Payne, E., & Smith, M. (2011). The reduction of stigma in schools: A new professional development model for empowering educators to support LGBTQ students. *Journal of LGBTQ Youth*, *8*(2), 174–200.

Payne, E.C., & Smith, M.J. (2012): Safety, celebration, and risk: Educator responses to LGBTQ professional development. *Teaching Education*, *23*(3), 265–285.

Robinson, K.H., & Ferfolja, T. (2008). Playing it up, playing it down, playing it safe: Queering teacher education. *Teaching and Teacher Education, 24*, 846–858.

Rofes, E. (2005). *A radical rethinking of sexuality and schooling: Status quo or status queer?* Lanham, MD: Rowman & Littlefield.

Russell, S.T., Seif, H., & Truong, N.L. (2001). School outcomes of sexual minority youth in the United States: Evidence from a national study. *Journal of Adolescence, 24*, 111–127.

APPENDIX A

Gender and Sexual Orientation Diversity Continuum

A visual to guide the understanding of sex, gender identity, gender expression, and sexual orientation as fluid, diverse constructs located on a continuum.

Gender Diversity

Assigned sex at birth: Biology

⟵——————————————————————⟶

Male   Intersex   Female

Gender identity: How you feel inside

⟵——————————————————————⟶

Man or masculine   Androgynous   Woman or feminine

Gender expression: Outer appearance and behavior

⟵——————————————————————⟶

Stereotypically masculine   Androgynous   Stereotypically feminine

Perceived gender expression: How others read your gender expression

⟵——————————————————————⟶

Stereotypically masculine   Androgynous   Stereotypically feminine

Sexual Diversity

Sexual orientation: Gender identity of partner

⟵——————————————————————⟶

Man or butch-identified   Genderqueer   Woman or femme-identified

Sexual orientation: Gender expression of partner

⟵——————————————————————⟶

Stereotypically masculine   Androgynous   Stereotypically feminine

APPENDIX B

Queer Inclusion in Education Framework

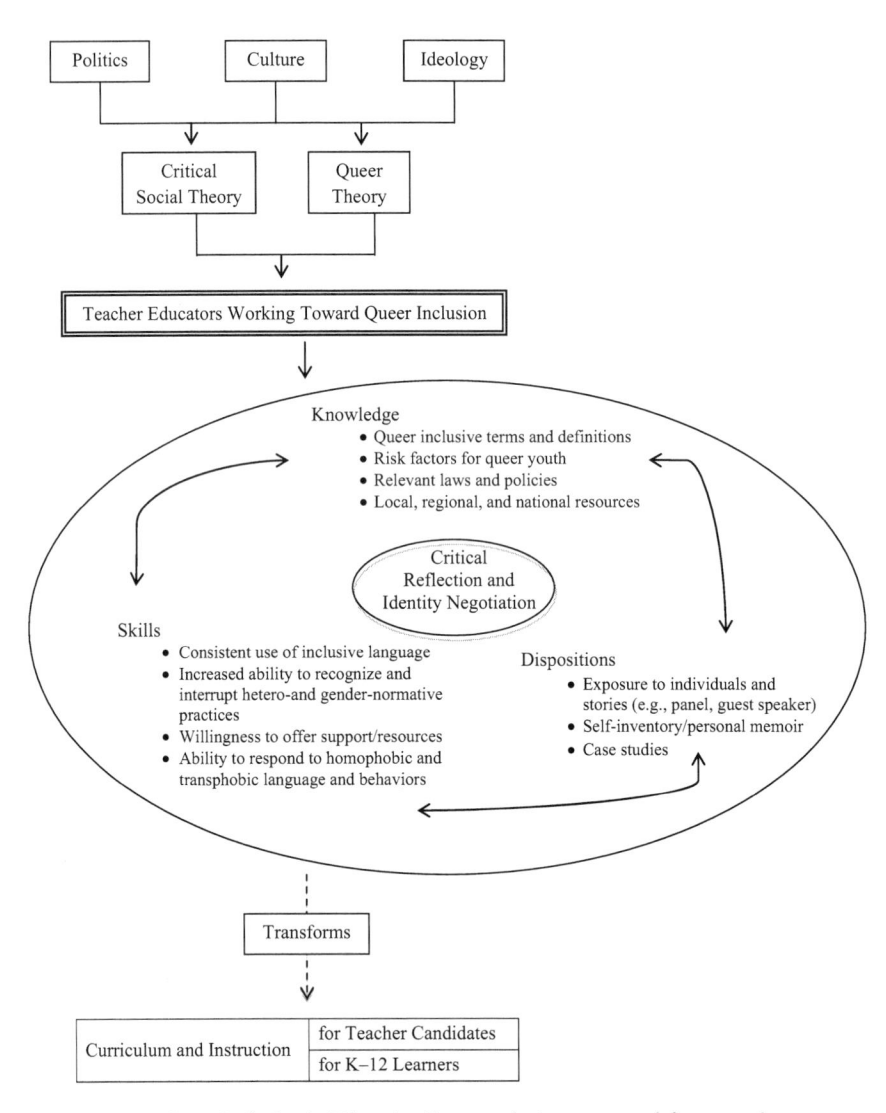

```
                    Politics      Culture      Ideology
                       │             │             │
                       ▼             ▼             ▼
                    Critical                    Queer
                  Social Theory                 Theory
                       │                           │
                       └─────────────┬─────────────┘
                                     ▼
                ┌──────────────────────────────────────────┐
                │ Teacher Educators Working Toward Queer Inclusion │
                └──────────────────────────────────────────┘
                                     ▼
                              Knowledge
                                • Queer inclusive terms and definitions
                                • Risk factors for queer youth
                                • Relevant laws and policies
                                • Local, regional, and national resources

                                    Critical
                                  Reflection and
                                Identity Negotiation

             Skills
               • Consistent use of inclusive language
               • Increased ability to recognize and     Dispositions
                 interrupt hetero-and gender-normative    • Exposure to individuals and
                 practices                                  stories (e.g., panel, guest speaker)
               • Willingness to offer support/resources  • Self-inventory/personal memoir
               • Ability to respond to homophobic and    • Case studies
                 transphobic language and behaviors

                                  Transforms
                                      ▼
                ┌──────────────────────┬───────────────────────┐
                │                      │ for Teacher Candidates│
                │ Curriculum and       ├───────────────────────┤
                │ Instruction          │ for K–12 Learners     │
                └──────────────────────┴───────────────────────┘
```

APPENDIX B. *Queer Inclusion in Education Framework.* A conceptual framework proposing an intentional and explicit presence of queer content and pedagogy in education by equipping teachers with the knowledge, skills, and dispositions necessary for implementing inclusive practices that interrupt hetero- and cisnormative discourse.

APPENDIX C
LGBTQ Advocacy in K–12 Classrooms Outline and Schedule

Scope and sequence for the one-credit class including course topics, objectives, activities, and readings/assignments for each session.

APPENDIX C: *LGBTQ Advocacy in K–12 Classrooms Outline and Schedule.* Scope and sequence for the course *LGBTQ Advocacy in K–12 Classrooms,* a one-credit elective offered through Portland State University.

Session	Class Topics	Objectives	Activities	Standards	Assignments and Reading
1: *What's happened before?*	• Introduction and syllabus • Reflect on knowledge and experiences with LGBTQ content in school settings • Situate new lens	1. Reflect on personal biases to deepen own understanding of gender and sexual orientation, which are culturally and socially constructed	• Personal writing/storytelling • Community agreements • Intuitive art • Constructing meaning of heteronormativity and cisgender dominance	InTASC: 9e GSE:1.1, 3.1	
2: *What can I now know?*	• National, regional, and local laws and policies that protect and support LGBTQ students • Privilege • Instructional and curricular resources for infusing queer content into their curricula • Theory and practice	2. Investigate legal responsibilities for addressing gender and sexual orientation in K–12 schools 3. Identify instructional and curricular resources for addressing gender and sexual orientation in K–12 schools	• Video/audio presentations • laws and role-play • Timeline activity	InTASC: 2n GSE:3.3	**Reading** Course Packet Pages: 371–376; 423–429; 376–385; 393–399; 441–444; and 451–452 **Assignment** Memoir/Self-Inventory

| 3: *What happens next?* | • LGBTQ advocacy
• Finding/creating allies | 4. Develop a personal framework for encountering and making sense of gender and sexual identity as they manifest in schools | • Debrief/present field observations
• Personal writing/storytelling
• Course self-assessment | InTASC: 3n
GSE: 1.2, 3.1 | **Reading**
Course Packet Pages: 413–421 and 455–456

Assignments
Field Observation Report

Written Analysis (Graduates Only) |

APPENDIX D

Values Statement Questionnaire

Directions: Please **DO NOT** put your name on this. Circle the letter(s) on the left that best reflect your feelings and/or beliefs on the adjacent statement.

Key: SA = Strongly Agree
 A = Agree
 D = Disagree
 SD = Strongly Disagree

SA-A-D-SD 1. I believe that marijuana should be legalized.
SA-A-D-SD 2. I believe that it is never okay to hit or spank one's child.
SA-A-D-SD 3. I believe that birth control methods, including condoms, should be made available within all middle and high schools.
SA-A-D-SD 4. I believe that pregnant girls under age 15 need to abort their pregnancies.
SA-A-D-SD 5. I believe that lesbian, gay, and bisexual teachers should be free to be out at school if they choose to be.
SA-A-D-SD 6. As a teacher, I feel very comfortable discussing transgender issues at school.
SA-A-D-SD 7. I believe that all teenage mothers should continue to receive public education with day care provided.
SA-A-D-SD 8. I believe it is best, healthiest, and safest for school-aged people not to have intercourse.
SA-A-D-SD 9. I believe that all children have a right to an education in a safe and supportive environment.
SA-A-D-SD 10. I believe that every student should have National Rifle Association (NRA) gun safety training in the schools.

APPENDIX E

Curriculum Analysis: A Tool for Interrogating Messages About Sexual Orientation and Gender

APPENDIX E: *Curriculum Analysis: A Tool for Interrogating Messages About Sexual Orientation and Gender.* An instrument to critically analyze messages about sexual orientation and gender in literature.

Text Title:
Author(s):
Copyright Date:

Focus Area	Description Sexual Orientation Gender	Observations	Inferences	1–5 Rating (1 = low)
Photos and Illustrations	• Is gay, lesbian, and bisexual identity/culture represented in photos and illustrations (e.g., same-sex parents, photos with captions that acknowledge queer identities or political/social movements)? • If present, are gay, lesbian, and bisexual orientations depicted as caricatures or in authentic contexts? • Are photos/illustrations of gay, lesbian, and bisexual people more or less sexualized than those depicting heterosexual individuals and relationships? • Do photos and illustrations perpetuate narrow and stereotypical views of gender (e.g., girls in pink and boys in blue; women taking care of children and men tending to construction sites and management positions)? • Are androgynous or gender-nonconforming individuals visually represented, and if so, how are they portrayed?			
Fiction and Nonfiction Characters	• Are all characters assumed to be heterosexual? • Can diverse sexual orientations be identified? • Do some characters represent simplified generalizations or "tokens" of gay, lesbian, and bisexual people (e.g., effeminate males with floppy wrists wearing capri pants or masculine women with buzz cuts and Birkenstocks)? • If queer people are represented, what are they doing (are they protagonists or in leadership positions), and what are their interactions with other characters like? • Are all characters assumed to be cisgender?			

- Do most characters perform traditional gender roles?
- Are androgynous or gender-nonconforming characters represented in simplified generalizations or as "tokens" (e.g., cross-dressing men with stubble wearing pantyhose and red lipstick)?
- If transgender and genderqueer people are represented, what are they doing (are they protagonists or in leadership positions), and what are their interactions with other characters like?

Settings
- Are gay, lesbian, and bisexual characters shown only to reside in closets, gay bars, art shows, and political rallies?
- Within text settings are queer individuals separated from heterosexuals in a way that depicts them as isolated or alienated?
- Are transgender people solely located at pride parades and drag queen shows?
- Are references to bathrooms, sport activities, and professions segregated by gender?
- Within text settings are transgender and gender-nonconforming people separated from cisgender individuals in a manner that deems the former inferior?

Story Lines
- Is asexuality acknowledged, or is it assumed that everyone experiences sexual attraction?
- Does it take a straight person to accept or help a gay, lesbian, or bisexual character?
- Does "making it" translate to fitting into a heterosexist society?
- Is homosexuality presented as a problem that needs to be resolved?
- Does the author oversimplify homosexual culture or present it in an authentic way?
- Do queer characters have to exhibit certain qualities (e.g., financial stability, successful career, currently in a long-term relationship, etc.) to compensate for their sexual orientation?
- Does it take an understanding cisgender person to accept or help a transgender or genderqueer character?
- Does "making it" translate to "passing" as either male or female?
- Is gender variance presented as a problem that needs to be resolved?
- Does the author oversimplify gender dysphoria or present it in an authentic way?
- Do transgender and genderqueer characters have to exhibit certain qualities (e.g., financial stability, successful career, long-term relationship status, etc.) to compensate for their gender identity and corresponding presentation?

(Continued)

APPENDIX E: *(Continued)*

Focus Area	Description Sexual Orientation Gender	Observations	Inferences	1–5 Rating (1 = low)
Language	• Is there homophobic language that excludes or demeans queer individuals? • Are there loaded words or figurative language with offensive overtones (e.g., characterizing gay, lesbian, and bisexual people as "confused" or "sinful"; phrases like "that's so gay")? • Is there transphobic language that excludes or demeans transgender and genderqueer individuals? • Are there loaded words or figurative language with offensive overtones (e.g., characterizing transgender people as "deceptive" or "fooling" other people; use of words like *she-male*, *he-she*, *it*, and *trannie*; phrases like "throws like a girl" or "strong as a man")?			

"See the Companion Website to download a user-friendly version?"

INDEX

Page numbers in italics indicate figures.

acceptance 117
acculturation 123
ACLU (American Civil Liberties Union) 193
action research 110
ACT UP 112
Adams, E. 11
Adams, M.: *Readings for Diversity and Social Justice* 140
admissions *132*
advertising 86
advocacy 100–5, 134–50
AIDS activism 112
allies 132–4, 137, 141
Allman, P. 44
Althusser, L. 44
American Academy of Pediatrics 6–7
American Civil Liberties Union (ACLU) 193
American Educational Research Association 26
American Psychological Association 88–9
And Tango Makes Three (Richardson and Parnell) 124
Anti-Bias Education (Derman-Sparks and Edwards) 159
anti-bullying discourses 14
antidiscrimination legislation 3, 103, 193

antigay ideology 186
art courses 193–4
Arts in Action (Frameline) 193
asexual 69
assault 9–10
assigned sex 7, 81, 213
assumptions 31, 177–8
Athanases, S.Z. 28–9
Atkinson, E. 13; *Interrogating Heteronormativity in Primary Schools* 14; *No Outsiders Project* 14
attachment theory 8
Attitudes Toward Lesbians and Gay Men (ATLG) scale 33–4
audio 176–7
Auerbach, E. 188–9
autobiographical writing 195–6

Bacon, F. 191
Baker, S.J. 191
Baldwin, E.S. 24–5
banking model 45
Banks, J. 23–4
banned books 124
Barry, N.H. 22
"Becoming an Ally: A New Examination" (Evans and Washington) 141
Bennett, C.I. 22

Berndt, T.J. 6
Bickmore, K. 12–13
Bieber, J. 87
binary gender system 70
bisexual 69
Blumenfeld, W.J.: *Readings for Diversity and Social Justice* 140
Bochenek, M. 9–10
both–and construct 97
Bright, A. 112–13
"Broadening Views of Social Justice and Teacher Leadership: Addressing LGB Issues in Teacher Education" (Larrabee and Morehead) 28–9
Brookfield, S. 30–1
Brother Outsider: The Life of Bayard Rustin (Frameline) 193
Brown, E.L. 22
Buckel, D. 11
bullying 3–4, 8, 124; discourses of 14, 166; interrupting 185–8
Bully Project, The 129
Bush, G.W. 4
Butler, J. 34; *Gender Trouble* 48, 69–70

Cahill, B. 11
Cahill, S. 9–10
Campos, D. 9
case studies 157–60
Castañeda, C.: *Readings for Diversity and Social Justice* 140
censorship 99
Chaillé, C. 110–13, 129–31, 211
Child Development and Family Service department (Portland State University) 119
childhood 13, 85–6
children's literature 12, 59–60, 124, 192
CI (Curriculum and Instruction LGBTQ Task Force; Portland State University) 60, 63–4; LGBTQ Task Force Visibility Campaign and *128*; resolution statement of 117–32, *118*; themes of and faculty responses to *115*
cisgender biases 3, 86–9
cisgender dominance 7, 112
cisnormativity 6, 11–12, 210–11
Cis Privilege Questionnaire 177–8
cissexist language 166
civics courses 193–4
civil rights movement 14, 21–2, 123
classism 88

classroom management 124, 185–91
closeted classrooms 89, 92–3, 98
Cochran-Smith, M. 23
co-creating 168
Coiser, K. 175
Colleary, K. 27
collective agency 73
coming out 6, 159
Comprehensive Sexuality Education act (2009) 140
"Considering Transgender People in Education: A Gender-Complex Approach" (Rands) 27, 163
content analysis 14–15
content integration 23–6
contextual awareness 31
Continuing Education department (Portland State University) 119
"Core Values and the Identity-Supportive Classroom: Setting LGBTQ Issues Within Wider Frameworks for Preservice Teachers" (Sadowski) 34–5
Counseling Department (Portland State University) 119–20
Courage to Teach, The (Palmer) 61
critical discourses 44, 201–3
critical incident journaling 200–1
critical reflection 29–31
critical social theory 43–6
"Critical Social Theory and Transformative Knowledge" (Leonardo) 45
critical theory 103
Critical Theory and Educational Research (McLaren and Giarell) 44
criticism 44–5
cross-dressing 75–6
cross-gender play 11
Cullen, F. 169–70
cultural capital 124
Cultural Diversity and Education courses 28
current practices 119–21, 163–7
curriculum 11–15, 21–9, 116, 124, 138; critically analyzing 179; design of 175–85; evaluation of 165; hidden 14–15, 157; language in 88–9; transgender teacher candidates and *132*
Curriculum Analysis: A Tool for Interrogating Messages About Sexual Orientation and Gender 179, *224–6*
Curriculum and Instruction (CI) LGBTQ Task Force (Portland State University) 60, 63–4; *LGBTQ Task Force Visibility*

Campaign and *128*; resolution statement of 117–32, *118*; themes of and faculty responses to *115*
cycle of praxis 73, 161, 168

D'Augelli, A.R. 8–9
Davies, B. 30
Davis, B. 58; "Interrupting Heteronormativity" 192
Davis, S.N. 169
Delamont, S. 11
DePalma, R. 13; *Interrogating Heteronormativity in Primary Schools* 14; *No Outsiders Project* 14
Derman-Sparks, L.: *Anti-Bias Education* 159
desired practices 121
Developmental Perspectives in Adult Education (course) 120
Dewey, J. 29, 44
dialogue 12, 44–6, 101, 104, 119, 137
Diaz, E.M. 27
Diaz, R. 8–9
Dickinson, E. 179
digital media 176–7
discourses: of bullying 14, 166; critical 44, 201–3; gender hegemonic 21; heteronormative 75–6, 86–9, 155–6; normalizing 78; of protection 12–13; queer-as-danger-to-children/queer-as-deviant 62
discussion questions 157
Disney 86
diversity 13, 21, 24
diversity statements 164
divided selves 62–3
don't ask, don't tell 14
Doty, A. 46–7

educación popular (popular education) 196
"Educating the Simpsons: Teaching Queer Representations in Contemporary Visual Media" (Padva) 183–5
Educational Leadership and Policy department (ELP; Portland State University) 119–21
Edwards, J.: *Anti-Bias Education* 159
effeminacy 184
either–or construct 97
encounters 69
English language development (ELD) 59
Epistemology of the Closet (Sedgwick) 48

equal rights legislation 3
equity courses 194–9
equity pedagogy 23–4
Erickson, G.L. 30
Evans, K. 75, 174, 195, 203; *Negotiating the Self* 61–2
Evans, N.J.: "Becoming an Ally: A New Examination" 141
exclusion 124
expression 75

faculty 118, 130–4, 155–71
faggot 187
Fairclough, N.: *Language and Power* 78
families 8–9, 13, 59–60, 188–91
family diversity activity 179–83
Fanon, F. 44
fear 84, 93, 98–100
Federal Bureau of Investigation (FBI) 4
federal hate crime legislation 4
Feldman, A. 45–6
femininity 73–6, 81
Ferfolja, T. 30
field-based practicum 199–203
field placements 104–5, 131–4, *132*
Fierstein, H.: *The Sissy Duckling* 82
film 176–7
four corners activity 177–8
Frameline: *Arts in Action* 193; *Brother Outsider: The Life of Bayard Rustin* 193; *Gender Matters* 176; *Visionaries and Victories: Early Leaders in the LGBT Movement* 193
Franklin, K.: "Inside the Mind of People Who Hate Gays" 186
Freire, P. 44–5, 188, 196
Fricke, A.: *Reflections of a Rock Lobster: A Story About Growing up Gay* 12
Fromm, E. 44

gay baiting 8
"gaydar" 75–6
Gay, G. 22
Gay, Lesbian and Straight Education Network (GLSEN) 7–8, 124, 160, 191, 193
"gayness" 62–3
gender: binaries 44, 69, 76, *80*, 87, 141–2; category oppression 162–3; conformity 8, 76; defined 75; dichotomies 69, 76–83, *79*; diversity 6, 12, 69, 135, 213–14; expectations 156; expression

69, 78, 213; hegemonic discourses of 21; identity 6–7, 69, 141–2, 165, 213; norms 11–14, 76, 97; presentation 75; segregation 81; sexuality and 69–70; as social construct 80–1; in Spanish language 92–3, 208; stereotypical preferences 73–6; stereotyping of 94–8; variance 5
gender-based violence 141–2
Gender-Based Violence/Gender Binary Awareness (Scheepstra) 141–2
gender-complex approach 27
Gender Gumby (Sexual and Gender Minority Youth Resource Center) 161
Gender Matters (Frameline) 176
gender-specific language 134
gender transgression oppression 162–3
Gender Trouble (Butler) 48, 69–70
George Mason University 169–70
"Get Low" (song) 86
Getting to Know You Survey 136
Giarelli, J.M.: *Critical Theory and Educational Research* 44
girls 12, 98
Giver, The (Lowry) 192–3
global, the 61–2, 90
GLSEN (Gay, Lesbian and Straight Education Network) 7–8, 124, 160, 191, 193
Goodreads 192
Gorski, P.C. 169
Graduate School of Education (GSE; Portland State University) 110, 119, 124, 128
Graduate Teacher Education Program (GTEP; Portland State University) 70–1, 91–2, 103–5, 110, 125–7, 130–4, *132*
Gramsci, A. 44
Grant, C.A. 23–4
Grimmett, P.P. 30
Groening, M.: *The Simpsons* 183–4
Grossman, A.H. 8–10
Groundspark 15, 176
group dialogue 101, 104
group identity development 94
GSE (Graduate School of Education; Portland State University) 110, 119, 124, *128*
GTEP (Graduate Teacher Education Program; Portland State University) 70–1, 91–2, 103–5, 110, 125–7, 130–4, *132*

Hackman, H.W.: *Readings for Diversity and Social Justice* 140
Hansen, D.T. 61
harassment 7–10, 185–8
Hasbro 86
hate crimes 4–5
hateful language 187–8, 191
Hatred in the Hallways (Human Rights Watch) 10–11
hegemonic discourses 21
heteronormative culture 68
heteronormative discourses 75–6, 86–9, 155–6
heteronormative language 124
heteronormativity 6, 11–14, 112, 210–11
heterosexism 61; as acquired 13; higher education and 25; ideologies of 11, 156; language of 88–9, 166
heterosexual 69
heterosexual privilege 62, 94
Heterosexual Privilege Questionnaire, The 177–8
heterosocialization 13
hidden curriculum 14–15, 157
higher education 21, 24–5, 155–6
high school 14–15
Holmes, S.E. 9–10
"Homer's Phobia" (episode of *The Simpsons*; Groening) 183–4
homophobia 6, 44, 83, 99, 140; as acquired 13; gender role beliefs and 11; higher education and 25; institutionalized 62–3; visible opposition to 117
homophobic language 14, 87, 159
homosexual 69
(homo)sexualities 13, 70
homosexuality 5–7, 34, 82–3
Horn, S.S. 165; "Visibility Matters: Policy Work as Activism in Teacher Education" 26, 114
Howard, J. 22
H.R. 1913 4
Huebner, D. 8–9
Hughes, L. 14, 179
human relations approach 23
Human Rights Campaign 193
Human Rights Watch: *Hatred in the Hallways* 10–11

identity 21–2, 61–4, 75
IHP (Internalized Homophobia) scale 33–4

Index **231**

imaginative speculation 31
inclusion/exclusion 26, 117, 124
information 137–41
innocence 12–13
"Inside the Mind of People Who Hate Gays" (Franklin) 186
instruction 21–9, *132*
InTASC (Interstate Teacher Assessment and Support Consortium) 22, 199
InTASC Standard 2 22
Integrated Methods I: Reading, Language Arts 124
integrity 61–3
intentionally proactive practices 117, *118*
Internalized Homophobia (IHP) scale 33–4
interpretivism 70
Interrogating Heteronormativity in Primary Schools (DePalma and Atkinson) 14
"Interrupting Heteronormativity" (Sumara and Davis) 192
"interruption run amok" 84
Interstate Teacher Assessment and Support Consortium (InTASC) 22, 199
Intrator, S.M.: *Stories of the Courage to Teach* 124
(in)visibility 114, 179
"Invisible Minority: Preparing Teachers to Meet the Needs of Gay and Lesbian Youth" (Mathison) 29
It Gets Better Project (Savage) 5, 124, 176
It's Elementary (film) 28
iTunes 176

Jennings, T. 25
journaling 200–1

K–12 environments 5–7, 21, 73–6; gender dichotomies and 76–83; LGBTQ advocacy and 134–50; literature for 179
Kennedy, S. 4–5
Kimmel, M.S. 8
kindergarten 11, 59–60
King, L. 4–5
King, M.L. 14
Kluth, P. 27
knowledge 45, 137–8
knowledge construction process 23–4
Kosciw, J.G. 27
Kronenberg, A. 14
Kumashiro, K.: *Troubling Education* 48–9

Lambda Legal Defense and Education Fund 11
language 160–1; cissexist and heterosexist 88–9, 166; destabilization of heteronormative 124; gender in Spanish 92–3, 208; gender-specific 134; hateful 187–8, 191; homophobic 14, 87, 159; instructor 165–6; Northern Sotho 59; power of 83–9; transphobic 88–9
Language and Power (Fairclough) 78
Larrabee, T.G. 114; "Broadening Views of Social Justice and Teacher Leadership: Addressing LGB Issues in Teacher Education" 28–9
Lechner, J.V. 22
Leonardo, Z. 44–5; "Critical Social Theory and Transformative Knowledge" 45
Lesbians in Academia: Degrees of Freedom (Mintz and Rothblum) 64
lesson plans 103
lesson study 167–8
Letts, W.J. 195–6
LGBTQ: advocacy 134–50; children's books 124; higher education and 155–6; (in)visibility 114; resolution statement 124; teacher education and 113–14, 169; youth 3–11
LGBTQ Advocacy in Education web site 125–7, *126*
LGBTQ Advocacy in K–12 Classrooms (course) 108, 134–50, 193, 199–200; Outline and Schedule for *217–19*
LGBTQ-identified teacher candidates 110
LGBTQ Task Force Visibility Campaign 128, 128–9
Lingley, A. 111–14, 119, 123, 134–50, 199–200
Lipkin, A. 25–6, 27
Liston, D.P.: *Reflective Teaching: An Introduction* 29
literacy methods courses 124, 191–3
local, the 61–2, 90
Lowry, L.: *The Giver* 192–3

Mackinnon, A.M. 30
Mahler, M. 8
masculinity 73–6, 81
Massachusetts 2005 Youth Risk Behavior Survey (Massachusetts Department of Education) 7–8
math courses 191

Mathison, C.: "The Invisible Minority: Preparing Teachers to Meet the Needs of Gay and Lesbian Youth" 29
Matipa (gay people) 59
McInerney, B. 4–5
McIntosh, P. 177
McLaren, P.L.: *Critical Theory and Educational Research* 44
Mead, M. 191
media 86, 176–7, 180, 183–5
melting pot theories 21
Memmi, A. 44
Memoir/Self-Inventory assignment 138–40
memoir writing 139
men 141–2
Mezirow, J. 30
micro-teaching 103
middle school curricula 14–15
Milk, H. 14
mini-grants 128–9
minority students 22
Mintz, B.: *Lesbians in Academia: Degrees of Freedom* 64
misogyny 88
Morehead, P. 114; "Broadening Views of Social Justice and Teacher Leadership: Addressing LGB Issues in Teacher Education" 28–9
Moss, G. 31
movement courses 193–4
MTE (multicultural teacher education) courses 169
Multicultural and Urban Education 124, 134
multiculturalism 5, 21–4, 29–31
multicultural teacher education (MTE) courses 169
multiple-case study design 70–1
multiple-definition words 85
multiple group identities 123
music 86
Mutwatwasi, Limpopo province, South Africa 58–9
My Little Pony 86

Nackerud, R. 113
name-calling 83–4, 185–8
National Coalition for the Homeless, The 9
National Coalition of Anti-Violence Programs (NCAVP) 4
National Council for Accreditation of Teacher Education (NCATE) 22, 32–3

National Council for Teachers of English 26
National Public Radio (NPR): *This American Life* podcasts 176
National School Climate Survey 7–12, 84, 160, 191
NCATE (National Council for Accreditation of Teacher Education) 22, 32–3
NCAVP (National Coalition of Anti-Violence Programs) 4
Negotiating the Self (Evans) 61–2
Nespor, J. 32
New Leadership Charter School, The 4
New York Times 176
Nieto, S. 22–3
No Outsiders Project (DePalma and Atkinson) 14
normalizing discourses 78
Northern Sotho language 59
NPR (National Public Radio): *This American Life* podcasts 176

Obama, B. 4
Oberlin College 112
oppositional gender system 70
Oregon Equality Act (2007) 140
Oregon Safe Schools Act (2009) 140
Orenstein, A. 9
orientation *132*
other/othering 48–9, 90–2, 112, 123–4, 140, 194
oversights 159

Padva, G.: "Educating the Simpsons: Teaching Queer Representations in Contemporary Visual Media" 183–5
Palmer, P.J. 62–3; *The Courage to Teach* 61
panel discussions 170
Pang, V.O. 22
pansexual 69
Parnell, P.: *And Tango Makes Three* 124
participatory action research 110
Payne, E. 35; Reduction of Stigma in Schools (RSIS) program 28–9
Peace Corps 58–9, 112
pedagogy 11–14, 23–6
peer dynamics 81, 186
personal assessments and stories 56–65, 122–4, 142–50
personal/home life 62
personal, the 23

Peters, M.L.: *Readings for Diversity and Social Justice* 140
Petrovic, J.E. 27, 32–4, 76, 84
physical harassment and abuse 7–9
Pinar, W.F. 47
Plummer, K. 46–7
podcasts 176–7
policy statements 164
popular education (*educación popular*) 196
Portland State University (PSU) 60–3, 70–1, 104, 110, 119, 130, 175, *217–19*
poster contest 128–9
power 44, 124
practices: current 119–21, 163–7; desired 121; heterosexist 61; intentionally proactive 117–18, *118*; queer-inclusive 117; queering of 108–50; reflective 29–30; transforming 51
praxis 46, 73, 102, 161, 168
prejudice reduction 23–4
pre-writing activities 139
principals 10
privilege 44, 140
problem-posing 158, 188–91
professional preparedness 116
program clarity and commitment 116
pronouns 133
protection, discourses of 12–13
PSU (Portland State University) 60–3, 70–1, 104, 110, 119, 130, 175, *217–19*
public/private polarity 60, 90
public/work life 62

queer 46–8
queerinclusion.com 113
Queer Inclusion in Education Framework 35–6, 43, 50–2, 109–10, 156, 174–5, 211, *216*
queerness: discourses of 62; higher education and 156–71; inclusion and 6, 108, 117; invisibility of 111; K–12 education and 5–7, 73–6; marginalization of 21; multiculturalism and 5, 24; perceptions of 73; as "the new black" 123
queer representations in contemporary media activity 180, 183–5
Queer Resource Center 119, 130
queer scientists 191
queer/straight alliances 134
queer theory 43, 46–50
queer youth 3–11

questions 121–2
Rainbow Fairies, The 78
Rands, K.E. 162–3; "Considering Transgender People in Education: A Gender-Complex Approach" 27, 163
Readings for Diversity and Social Justice (Adams, Blumenfeld, Castañeda, Hackman, Peters, Zúñiga) 140
"real" women and "real" men 141–2
"Reclaiming Identity" (Tonningsen) 124
reconstructionist education 23
Reduction of Stigma in Schools (RSIS) program (Payne and Smith) 28–9
reflection 29–31, 73, 102, 110
reflection-on-action and *reflection-in-action* 29
Reflections of a Rock Lobster: A Story About Growing up Gay (Fricke) 12
reflective skepticism 31
Reflective Teaching: An Introduction (Zeichner and Liston) 29
reflective writing 110
Reis, B. 10
Reiter, A. 169
research: assertions of 73–105; context and methods of 70–1; cyclic process of 110; goals and paradigm for 69–70; opportunities for 168–70; participants 72
restorative justice 185
Richardson, J.: *And Tango Makes Three* 124
Riecken, T.J. 30
Robinson, K. 30
Rodemeyer, J. 5
"Role of Gay Men and Lesbians in the Civil Rights Movement, The" *(Teaching Tolerance)* 193
romantic love 12
Rosenbloom, S.R. 32–3
Rosiek, J. 27, 32–4, 76, 84
Rothblum, E.D.: *Lesbians in Academia: Degrees of Freedom* 64
RSIS (Reduction of Stigma in Schools) program (Payne and Smith) 28–9
Rummell, C. 47–8
Russell, S.T. 8–10
Rustin, B. 179, 193
Ryan, C. 8–9

Sadowski, M. 114; "Core Values and the Identity-Supportive Classroom: Setting LGBTQ Issues Within Wider Frameworks for Preservice Teachers" 34–5

safety 43–4
Sanchez, J. 8–9
Sanders, J.H. 175
Sandy, L. 169–70
Sapon-Shevin, M. 27
Savage, D.: *It Gets Better Project* 5, 124, 176
Savin-Williams, R.C. 6
Scheepstra, T.: *Gender-Based Violence/Gender Binary Awareness* 141–2
Schmidt, S.: *Unexpected Stereotypes and How to Combat Them* 87
Schön, D. 29
school climate 7–9, 15, 25, 108, 163–4
School House Rock: Three Is a Magic Number (video) 88–9
school policies 164, 187
school staff 9–10, 14, 110–50
school violence 8
science courses 191
Sears, J. 13–14, 33–4
Sedgwick, E.K.: *Epistemology of the Closet* 48
Seif, H. 10
self-defense, perceived 186
self-identity 89–100, 123
semantics 122
sexist language 88–9
Sexual and Gender Minority Youth Resource Center: *Gender Gumby* 161
sexual attraction 75
sexual classifications 69
sexual diversity 6, 12, 69, 135
sexual equalities 169–70
sexual identity 6, 13
sexuality 69–70, 75
sexual minorities 159–60
sexual orientation 5–7, 12–14, 75, 165, 214
shame 93
Shepard, M. 4–5
Sherwin, G. 25
Silin, J. 11–12
Simpsons, The (Groening) 183–4
single group studies approach 23
Sissy Duckling, The (Fierstein) 82
Sleeter, C.E. 22–4
Smith, M. 35; Reduction of Stigma in Schools (RSIS) program 28–9
socialization 11, 157
social justice 6, 23–4, 104, 194–9
social status 124
social studies courses 193–4
Societal Discomfort Zone (TransActive) 161
sociodrama 196–9
Socratic method 158
South Africa 58–9, 112
Special Education department (Portland State University) 119–20
Spectrum of Visibility 113, 118
stall technique 187
Stambach, A. 49
Stambaugh, S. 111–12, 122
Standard 4 22
Starks, M.T. 8–9
stereotypes 141–2; confronting personal 177–8; debunking of 161–3; of femininity and masculinity 81; gender preferences and 73–6
Stonewall Riots 14
S.T.O.P. (Students Together Opposing Prejudice) 57
Stories of the Courage to Teach (Intrator) 124
strategic responsiveness 117, *118*
Straut, D. 27
student orientation 165
student queer task force 132–4
Students Together Opposing Prejudice (S.T.O.P.) 57
student supports 165–6
student teaching 199–203
subject-based methods courses 191–4
Sullivan, N. 48
Sumara, D. 6, 58, 157, 166, 186; "Interrupting Heteronormativity" 192
Swartz, P.C. 28
syllabi 165

tableaux technique 194
Taylor, C. 99
"teachable moments" 103
teacher candidates 24; LGBTQ-identified 110; queer phenomena and 34, 67–106; queer/straight alliance for 134; as research participants 71, *72*; self-identity and 89–100; transgender and gender-nonconforming 130–4, *132*; in transition 158–9
teacher education 21–9; literature of LGBTQ issues in 113–14; programs 24–1, 155–71; teacher dispositions and 32–5; transforming hetero- and cisnormative practices in 51
teacher educators 108–50, 174–203
teachers 5–7, 9–14, 22–3; deconstruction of gender binaries and *80*; dispositions of 32–5, 97–9; interventions by 210–11

"teacher voice" 95–6
Teaching Tolerance 87; "The Role of Gay Men and Lesbians in the Civil Rights Movement" 193
Temple, J.R. 14–15
terminology 160–1
Tharinger, D. 8
theory 43–52
This American Life podcasts (National Public Radio [NPR]) 176
Three Is a Magic Number (*School House Rock* video) 88–9
thrill seeking 186
timeline activity 141, 179–81
tolerance 14–15, 62, 84, 117
tolerance.com 193
"Tom Girls" (*This American Life* podcast) 176
Tonningsen, K.: "Reclaiming Identity" 124
TransActive: *Societal Discomfort Zone* 161
transformative action 44–6, 141
Transgender Focus Group Discussion Guide 132
transgender identity 5–9
transgender teacher candidates 130–4, *132*
transition 158–9
transnational teacher educators 123
transphobia 6, 88–9, 140
triad models 95
Troubling Education (Kumashiro) 48–9
Truong, N.L. 10

Unexpected Stereotypes and How to Combat Them (Schmidt) 87

Valentine's Day Math Challenge 67, *68*
Valli, L. 31

Values Statement Questionnaire *221*
verbal harassment and abuse 7–9
video games 86
videos 176–7
visibility 63–4, 128–9
"Visibility Matters: Policy Work as Activism in Teacher Education" (Horn) 26, 114
Visionaries and Victories: Early Leaders in the LGBT Movement (Frameline) 193
vocation 61–3

Walkerdine, V. 12
Walker-Hoover, C. 3–5
Walker, S. 4
Washington, J.: "Becoming an Ally: A New Examination" 141
Washington State Safe Schools Coalition 10
Way, N. 32–3
Welcoming Schools 15, 176, 182–3, 192; *What Do You Know? Six-to Twelve-Year-Olds Talk about Gays and Lesbians* 129
welcomingschools.org 182
Wells, G. 8
What Do You Know? Six-to Twelve-Year-Olds Talk about Gays and Lesbians (Welcoming Schools) 129
white privilege 59, 177
women 96–7, 141–2

YouTube 176

Zeichner, K.M. 22; *Reflective Teaching: An Introduction* 29
Zúñiga, X.: *Readings for Diversity and Social Justice* 140